RAIN GARDENS FOR THE PACIFIC NORTHWEST

This excellent book is a call-to-arms for Northwest gardeners about our ever-changing environment, and explains what concerned citizens can do to benefit their homes and communities alike. A wealth of photos, charts, and illustrations accompany this very practical approach, condensed from the personal experiences of the authors.
— Walt Bubelis, Professor Emeritus, Horticulture,
Edmonds Community College

After reading this informative book, I guarantee you'll want to include a rain garden in your landscape. Not only to protect our waterways and the environment, but to add spectacular beauty to your home—all who visit your garden will exclaim, "Oh, la, la!"
— Ciscoe Morris, gardening advice columnist,
radio/TV host, and author

DESIGN &
BUILD YOUR
OWN

RAIN GARDENS FOR THE PACIFIC NORTHWEST

ZSOFIA PASZTOR
KERI DETORE

ILLUSTRATIONS BY
JILL NUNEMAKER

SKIPSTONE

Copyright © 2017 by Zsofia Pasztor and Keri DeTore
Illustrations © 2017 by Jill Nunemaker
Published by Skipstone, an imprint of Mountaineers Books
Printed in China
20 19 18 17   1 2 3 4 5

Copy editor: Barry Foy
Design: Jane Jeszeck, www.jigsawseattle.com
Layout: Jennifer Shontz, www.redshoedesign.com
Front Cover (clockwise from top left): *Cotinus coggigria* (Holli Margell); *Rudbekia fulgia* (Vicki Demetre);
    Rain garden (Zsofia Pasztor); Dry swale (Zsofia Pasztor); Plant roots (Sindea Kirk); *Camassia* (Roseann
    Barnhill). Spine: Pesticide-free sign (Keri DeTore). Back cover (top to bottom): Rain garden detail (Keri
    DeTore); Rain chain (Hanson Family); *Mahonia* (Vicki Demetre).
All illustrations by Jill Nunemaker.
Photographs by the authors unless otherwise noted.

Library of Congress Cataloging-in-Publication Data on file

ISBN (paperback): 978-1-68051-041-6
ISBN (ebook): 978-1-68051-042-3

Skipstone books may be purchased for corporate, educational, or other promotional sales, and our authors
are available for a wide range of events. For information on special discounts or booking an author, contact
our customer service at 800-553-4453 or mbooks@mountaineersbooks.org.

Skipstone
1001 SW Klickitat Way
Suite 201
Seattle, Washington 98134
206.223.6303
www.skipstonebooks.org
www.mountaineersbooks.org

LIVE LIFE. MAKE RIPPLES.

In memory of Karen Hartung Pastori,
for her love and willingness to give me the job
of answering calls and orders so that I could learn
to speak, read, and write English.
Thank you, my friend.
— *Zsofia Pasztor*

CONTENTS

Why Does the Northwest Need Rain Gardens?

Here in the Pacific Northwest, we all love looking at the mountains and ocean, lakes and creeks, our huge evergreen trees and silvery sagebrush, and the vast fields and endless horizons stretching out both east and west of the mountains. That is why we live here, why we call the Northwest region home.

Out here, we crave contact with the natural environment, a desire that is sometimes at odds with the growth of our cities and with the expansion of suburbs into areas where wildlife habitat once thrived. Trees, shrubs, meadows, and forests are reduced to small pockets, while new developments often lack even backyards and parking strips. From birds and insects to frogs and newts, we seem to have less nature to connect with every day, even at the most basic levels. It is not only healthy soil that is missing from cities: Our unique Northwest ecosystems are disappearing under hard, concrete shells.

These unnatural, sometimes even devastated conditions lead to many challenges. Water provides a good example: Rain hitting our roofs makes its way onto the hard surfaces that blanket our neighborhoods. There, instead of soaking naturally into the ground, this stormwater sweeps into local waterways through our sewer systems, carrying pollutants from streets, sidewalks, and

FROG SONGS

An ecosystem is a complex set of processes and living and non-living factors and each part affects each of the other parts, from air, soil, and water quality to the happiness of the residents. As wildlife declines, so do our air and water quality, and vice versa. Frogs function like the proverbial canary in the coal mine: They sing if they have suitable habitat. If you hear frogs all the time, chances are the ecosystem is good enough to provide what the frogs need. But when no frogs sing, the environment is overdeveloped and too toxic for them. The few frogs that survive usually end up with terrible developmental and genetic problems. A healthy frog literally symbolizes a healthy ecosystem.

A healthy frog symbolizes a healthy ecosystem.

and acidic. This decimates the creatures that live in them, from shellfish to salmon to orcas.

It's hard to know what we can do in the face of such challenges, but we believe that our yards are a place to start. Creating something even as small-scale as a rain garden can help our local ecosystem return to better shape and even head toward recovery.

A rain garden is what is called a *Low Impact Development* (LID) technique. Think of LID as a box of tools to help reduce and repair damage to the environment caused by conventional development. While LID techniques don't return a habitat to its predevelopment state (such as old-growth forest supporting a wide variety of wildlife), they can restore a site's basic functions for managing stormwater. And that's a great place to start.

Rain gardens are a beautiful and relatively simple way to remove pollution from stormwater runoff and allow it to slowly, naturally infiltrate into the ground. They do this work within the laboratory of their soil and roots, slowing, cooling, and decontaminating stormwater while also replacing groundwater stores for the dry season. This is nature's original stormwater mitigation plan!

In short, rain gardens have it all. Because they can be built to suit most yard sizes and conditions, they're perfect for most urban sites. They also offer lots of non-stormwater benefits, such as habitat for birds, insects, frogs, and newts, as well as appealing landscaping that increases property value. Rain gardens create a unique and special sense of place; you can fill them with plants that reflect the particular geology and climate of your specific area of the Pacific Northwest.

The three of us—Zsofia, Keri, and Jill—have years of experience in professional gardening, landscape design, and LID practices. Many of the

lawns: garden fertilizers, motor oil, chemicals, even pet waste from the sidewalks.

Eventually, everything added to the water here ends up in the creek at the local park, and from there it rushes into Puget Sound, the Columbia River, and other crucial bodies of water. And what are the consequences? The increasing pollution is making the rivers and oceans too warm, stressed, topics and issues described in this book reflect questions Zsofia gets during the classes and workshops she leads. Informed by our hands-on experience, this book aims to show you how to plan and implement the right rain garden solution for your home, as well as make use of other compatible LID tools. You will learn to assess your site, design a rain garden, and build it, either by yourself or with professional help. You'll also find resources such as plant lists and planting plan ideas, as well as detailed explanations of some of the most important, yet least talked-about, components of a rain garden: soils and soil mixes.

We also offer long-term maintenance guidance. Not just a fashionable accessory to do away with in a few years, a rain garden is a living system that often improves over time as plants get established and microorganisms spread in the soil. As you design and build your rain garden, you'll want to think about how it will fit into your yard for a long time to come.

Rain gardens will not bring back the Pacific Northwest's majestic woods or original ecosystem. LID techniques aren't going to dig up the parking lots that sprawl for acres and acres around shopping centers, or the roads that connect them. What a rain garden can do is change how water moves through an individual site and change the condition it leaves in. Improving the water that then flows into the creek at that local park and eventually the ocean gives the natural systems within and around urban areas a big, hopeful chance of functioning as they did before development.

Improving the water that flows within a city creates a ripple effect (pun intended!) on the rest of the ecosystem. Cleaner waters mean more life in and around natural water bodies, which can mean more mini–wildlife habitat pockets in developed areas, and even renewed health for natural

There are lots of creative options for integrating a rain garden into your yard's design.

areas that haven't been developed. As ecologically sound systems expand and spread one yard at a time, the result is a healthier habitat for all creatures—including people. Our goal in this book is to empower you to be the solution, right in your own yard.

JILL NUNEMAKER

Hydrology:
The Movement of Water Around Us

Understanding how rain gardens work begins with understanding the hydrologic cycle, or the constant movement of water, and specifically how it happens in the Northwest.

THE NATURAL HYDROLOGIC CYCLE

Long before strip malls and parking lots, nature mediated the movement of water and its effect on forests, streams, and oceans by a series of barriers, filters, and catchment systems. These included layers of vegetation, from giant towering trees to shrubs to tiny mosses on the ground, that cushioned rain's impact on the soil, allowing the water to gently percolate beneath the soil's surface layer. From there the rainfall could gradually migrate into streams and underground aquifers, providing a steady supply of water as needed during dry seasons. In an ever-repeating cycle, surface water and water brought back up to the surface returned to the atmosphere through evaporation and plant transpiration.

Vegetation

In the regions of coastal Oregon, Washington, and southern British Columbia, evergreen conifer forests are the natural vegetation. If you've ever stood under a large Douglas-fir (*Pseudotsuga menziesii*) during a rainfall, you know that even in a hard rain you barely get wet.

The canopy over your head (the leaves and branches of the tree, also called the crown) captures most of the precipitation; conifer needles make up a large surface that not only intercepts

A Douglas-fir (*Pseudotsuga menziesii*) wears its evergreen crown.

THE SCIENCE OF EVAPOTRANSPIRATION

Water doesn't only move *down* in the hydrologic cycle. It also rises into the air from surfaces where it collects, including leaves and branches. This process is called *evaporation*. In another process, transpiration, water travels through a plant and evaporates from surface pores on leaves, stems, and flowers. *Transpiration* is a vital function that allows plants to control their temperature, dispose of unnecessary minerals or even toxins, and maintain their nutrient uptake.

The combined effect of transpiration and evaporation is called *evapotranspiration*. Water entering the air as vapor through evapotranspiration will have certain observable, predictable, and measurable effects, all of which combine to create the climate we live in. It will rise and become clouds, which will turn into precipitation and repeat the cycle, falling to the ground as rain or snow again.

most of the rain but also transpires it back into the atmosphere. What rain does sneak through descends slowly onto obstacles such as lower understory trees and large shrubs before finally reaching the perennials and groundcovers at the bottom.

Vegetation is a key rainfall buffer, mitigating and preventing potential damage from heavy rainfall or stormwater surges. Furthermore, pollutants stick to leaves, roots, and eventually to soil particles, where many compound molecules are broken down and altered chemically so that they become nontoxic or immobile and no longer threaten the environment.

The duff layer covers and enriches the soil of the forest floor.

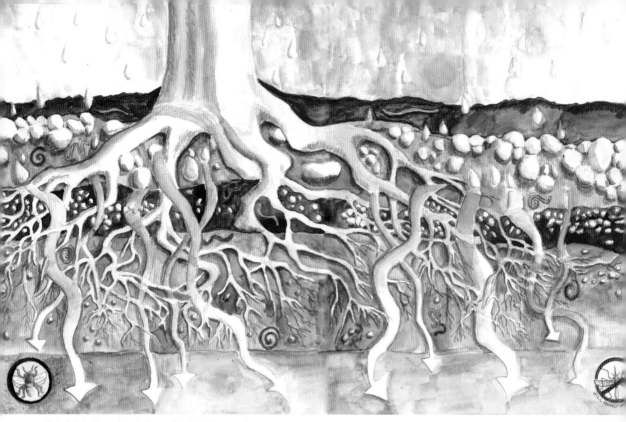

Rainfall is slowed and cleaned as it infiltrates through the root systems of trees and other vegetation to the water table.

Soil Layers

In the forest, by the time any rain contacts soil, even during big storms, it has slowed to a gentle flow that slowly seeps into the soil and causes no erosion. The duff layer is the first soil it hits. Duff is what makes forest soil spongy. It consists of chunky and recognizable organic material that is in the process of composting (decomposing): twigs, crumbling rotted wood, leaves, mosses, lichens. Duff smells like the forest, holds lots of water, and becomes humus as it breaks down. *Humus* means soil in Latin, and in soil science it refers to decomposed organic matter that has reached a stable state and will not break down any further—if conditions do not change severely, it will remain the same for millennia. The combined duff and humus layers soak up water and hold on to it, keeping plant roots moist long after the rains are gone. Humus and other organically rich soils harbor millions of microorganisms, and if you lift up the leaves and duff layer in a forest on a hot, dry summer day, the soil below will be moist and teeming with life.

Infiltration

During the rainy season in the Pacific Northwest, especially in the winter and when rains are heavy and the soil is already very wet, rain seeps downward into the soil's deeper, drier layers through crevices in a process called infiltration; in cold weather, the water in the crevices freezes and expands, opening up new crevices. The water will eventually find its way into aquifers, cleansed and purified by the soil layers.

Aquifers

An aquifer is a reservoir of water in a layer of soil and/or rock. It is filled to capacity with water but still allows water to flow through it, because the soil or rock layer is made of permeable, often porous materials such as sand and sandstone, or glacial outwash-type mixes, gravels, fractured rocks, limestone, granite, or basalt. Permeable layers in volcanic soils called rubble zones make wonderful aquifers. Granite layers are not the best

TAPPING AQUIFERS

A well is a hole drilled into an aquifer that allows water to reach the surface through pumping. As water is removed, groundwater will flow in to replace it, but if water is removed faster than it refills, the well will run dry.

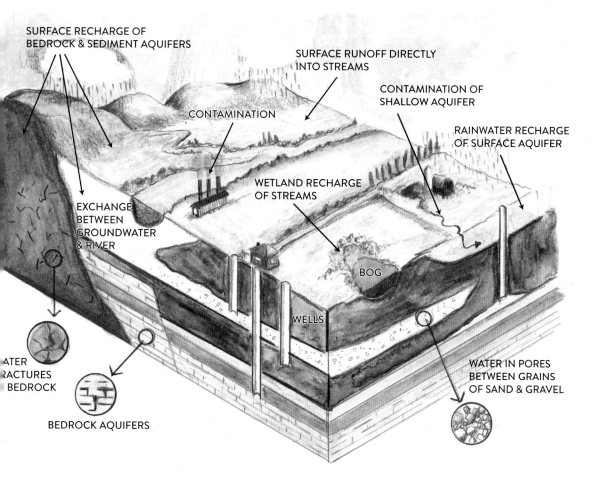

SURFACE RECHARGE OF
BEDROCK & SEDIMENT AQUIFERS

SURFACE RUNOFF DIRECTLY
INTO STREAMS

CONTAMINATION

CONTAMINATION OF
SHALLOW AQUIFER

RAINWATER RECHARGE
OF SURFACE AQUIFER

EXCHANGE
BETWEEN
GROUNDWATER
& RIVER

WETLAND RECHARGE
OF STREAMS

BOG

WELLS

ATER
RACTURES
BEDROCK

BEDROCK AQUIFERS

WATER IN PORES
BETWEEN GRAINS
OF SAND & GRAVEL

Representation of a groundwater system showing the interaction of key elements aquifers as they are usually not porous, but they can hold water as long as the granite is not one single slab (which can actually block the access to soil below). The best aquifer is one with lots of crevices, but most water-holding barrier layers will do at least some of the job. What matters is that the water is held in place underground.

An aquifer is refilled, or recharged, through infiltration. How fast that happens depends on many factors, including the season. If the duff layer is fairly dry (such as during the summer

This development's overflow design dumps stormwater and all its pollutants directly into Longfellow Creek in Seattle.

months) or precipitation is low, plant roots may absorb the infiltrating water before it can reach the aquifer.

The Hydrologic Cycle, Modified

A funny thing happened during the Pacific Northwest's evolution that drastically altered its hydrologic processes: people. People who needed solid surfaces to live under and travel on, who created industries, who needed to move their waste products from their living areas to "out-of-sight" places.

When the first US cities were planned and built, their sewer systems were designed to collect both raw sewage from buildings and stormwater from the streets. The idea was to direct it all into sewage treatment facilities to be filtered and cleaned before safely releasing it into waterways or even recycling it into the city's water system. What no one anticipated was how fast urban

This is the critical habitat that toxic stormwater drains directly into: where kids play and animals make their homes.

FISH ARE IN HOT WATER

Warm water holds much less oxygen than cold water, because warm water allows for larger spaces between water molecules where oxygen can readily escape. As the water in a lake or stream warms, oxygen levels drop and fish and other aquatic animals can begin to suffocate. Runoff from hot asphalt and rooftops in summer can compound the problem.

areas and their populations would grow—or how greatly impervious surfaces such as driveways, streets, sidewalks, and building surfaces would expand, resulting in larger volumes of stormwater runoff and waste pouring into treatment systems. So what, exactly, is happening with all that rainy runoff these days, and why should we care?

Let Us Illustrate

A few years ago, at Olivia Park Elementary School in Everett, Washington, a daylong heavy rain dumped 0.35 inch (9mm) of rainfall in a twenty-four-hour period. This large volume of rain fell on compacted lawn areas, asphalt parking lots, and metal roofs, then rushed along the ground, picking up recently applied fertilizer from lawns, heavy metal residue from car brakes, and leaked automotive fluids including coolant and oil. Dust and fecal matter deposited on rooftops by wind and birds floated into the gutters and joined the toxic brew as it accumulated bits of trash and rushed into the nearest storm drain. At the end of the storm drain's pipeline, the water poured into Upper North Creek, creating a sudden rise in water level that caused extreme surges and erosion on both banks.

"Well," you might think, "if stormwater like that goes into a sewage treatment facility, it will

Bank erosion caused by heavy rainfall and rushing water undermines vegetation, causing it to topple and dam the flow.

Calm waters and various sizes of rock and gravel create healthy aquatic ecosystems.

The Devastation of CSOs

You may be surprised to know that CSOs are not only legal, but in many older urban areas they are downright necessary to prevent flood damage to nearby neighborhoods. And yet they can do significant harm: In addition to its polluting effects, an unexpectedly large influx of water can cause significant destruction. Don't underestimate the muscle of moving water: It is one of the most powerful forces in nature and has helped shaped mountains, plains, valleys, and canyons for eons. The speeding runoff can wash away banks and shorelines. Soil eroding from tree and shrub roots causes them to topple, and as vegetation is undermined and falls in large quantities, woody debris can accumulate and dam the water's flow. This can result in urban flooding, as well as depriving streams of a protective overhead canopy that keeps them sufficiently cool in the summer and insulated in the winter.

The damage isn't limited to plants. We have all seen creeks flowing with coffee-colored water. The color comes from eroded fine soil particles that settle into small crevices along the shores. Aquatic life needs a variety of loose gravel and natural debris, rounded rocks, and woody material in slowly flowing, gentle streams to rest in, lay eggs in, and raise young. But this sediment can cover fish eggs and tiny creatures, causing these vulnerable waterway inhabitants to drown in the mud in their own homes.

High water flows also wash away bacteria that feed on nitrites. Nitrification is a natural process that is part of the breakdown of organic matter in soil. Ironically, our love of farmed and landscaped areas contributes to high levels of nitrogen and phosphorus in water bodies: All fertilizers, not only manufactured and chemical ones but even excess organic solutions such as compost and manure, generate higher nutrient levels if washed

be cleaned." But that didn't happen at Olivia Park Elementary, and it is true only to a degree. Sudden, heavy rainfalls, especially in summer, when the soil is hard and packed, or in winter when it's saturated, can send so much water into the drains that it maxes out the sewage treatment system, triggering what are called Combined Sewer Overflow (CSO) events. As the amount of water entering the system becomes unmanageable, the facility overflows, allowing the release of untreated sewage mixed with stormwater into the nearest natural water body in order to avoid a facility failure.

into a stream or lake and promote the growth of algae. As algae proliferates, oxygen levels drop, further jeopardizing native waterway inhabitants. Nitrite-feeding bacteria can multiply to consume the increased feed source, but they require calm waters and lots of loose gravel to cling to.

As our climate changes and rainfall comes more sporadically but in larger volumes, the negative effects of our traditional stormwater management practices are becoming increasingly obvious. Streams often dry out between rainfalls, and then, once the rain comes, the water gushes in at flash flood levels, warm and filthy, suffocating and washing away everything in its path. No matter how we look at it, the way we built our communities is proving to be destructive. We must do better—and we know how.

GENERAL PURPOSE FERTILIZER 20-10-20	
Guaranteed Analysis:	
Total nitrogen (N)	20%
Available phosphate (P_2O_3)	10%
Soluble potash (K_2O)	20%
Magnesium (Mg)	0.05%
Boron (B)	0.0068%
Copper (Cu)	0.0036%
Iron (Fe)	0.05%
Manganese (Mn)	0.025%
Molybdenum (Mo)	0.0009%
Zinc (Zn)	0.0025%

Typical ingredients in a home-use fertilizer that contribute to nitrification

Allowing fallen leaves to break down naturally composts the soil, eliminating the need to fertilize. (Photo by Holli Margell)

THE RAIN GARDEN AS HYDROLOGIC CYCLE

The cycle of rainfall in our cities is a far cry from what it was before development, when a combination of vegetation and healthy soil filtered and held rainwater in a natural form of bioretention— an engineering term referring to stormwater management. A bioretention system (or cell) is a Low Impact Development method based on the concept of natural infiltration but in a limited space. Rain is collected in a specifically designed area, held for a certain period of time, infiltrated into the ground at a calculated speed, and treated by soil and vegetation. All bioretention systems are essentially stormwater management facilities, and they are often regulated under governmental drainage and stormwater management agencies.

Rain gardens (also called storm gardens in many parts of the Northwest) are small

Even canine neighbors appreciate the value of healthy bioretention cells.

bioretention cells, but you don't need to be an engineer or a professional to design one. When finished and planted, these shallow depressions in the ground collect and absorb rainwater. Their soil is well-draining and spongy, plants drink the runoff, and both the plants and the healthy soil filter it before it moves deeper into the ground toward subsurface waterways and aquifers. These small pockets of infiltration mimic nature by allowing rain to be absorbed and transpired as close as possible to where it fell. Just like nature, an established rain garden needs very little or no irrigation and, if well designed, it is generally a low-maintenance site.

The most efficient arrangement of rain gardens in cities utilizes lots of smaller rain gardens rather than a few large ones. This is why cities encourage homeowners to have their own individual rain gardens rather than building one large neighborhood-sized rain garden. A rain garden in a yard can collect the runoff from a roof, a driveway, and/or a lawn (usually less than 10,000 square feet, 929m^2). It will contribute to balanced flow in nearby natural waterways, provide habitat for birds and insects, and look good!

By providing water, vegetation, and compost-based organic matter, rain gardens help improve soil health, allowing life to return to the abused ground. And any water moving through the rain garden comes out cleaner than it was when it flowed in.

Snohomish County in Washington State funded a project to create multiple rain gardens, many in neighboring yards, in the Sierra neighborhood of Edmonds, Washington. (Bottom photo by Cynthia LaBlue)

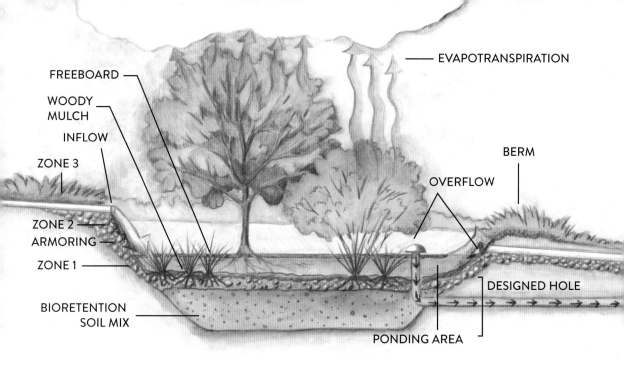

EVAPOTRANSPIRATION

FREEBOARD

WOODY MULCH

INFLOW

ZONE 3

BERM

OVERFLOW

ZONE 2

ARMORING

ZONE 1

DESIGNED HOLE

BIORETENTION SOIL MIX

PONDING AREA

Anatomy of a rain garden

The Anatomy of a Rain Garden

Rain gardens are built with very specific elements that comprise their "anatomy":

Contributing area: the surfaces from which the runoff collects; usually lawns, roofs, driveways, parking areas, and walkways.

Ponding area: the bottom section of the rain garden where the runoff water collects and, during heavy rain events, may "pond," meaning it stays for a brief period, making the rain garden look like a pond temporarily.

Freeboard: an optional gap between the overflow and the top of the rain garden, that acts as a backup area for runoff collection. In cases of very heavy rain events, if the overflow is already at full capacity, this space prevents accidental spills or overflows.

Berm: the side and edge of the rain garden, a designed mound of soil that holds the ponding water in place on sloped terrain.

The rise of the freeboard area helps prevent overflow.

Inflow: the way the collected runoff moves into the rain garden.

Overflow: the way water can leave the rain garden during heavy storm events when the rain garden receives more runoff than what it can immediately absorb.

Armoring: a layer of protection, usually rocks, placed on the ground in the inflow and overflow areas to protect the soil from erosion and washout.

Designed hole: the basin of the rain garden, into which soil and plants are placed based on zones and design calculations.

Bioretention soil mix: the designed and carefully measured rain garden soil mix.

Woody mulch: carefully measured, covers the soil as a duff layer.

Rain gardens can combine manmade and natural materials.

Using correct soil mixes and mulches is critical to a thriving, functioning rain garden.

CHAPTER 2

Weather and Soil: A Little Meteorology and Geology for the Pacific Northwest

What we call the Pacific Northwest is in fact a large geographical area that extends north from central Oregon to southern British Columbia. Since it encompasses coasts, mountains, plains, and slopes, each portion of the region has different climatic and geologic characteristics that affect the way a rain garden must be designed and planted in order to perform as it should—as a system with the right soil and plants to filter the right amount of runoff. To get the most out of this book, you must understand your region. Familiarize yourself with your area's weather conditions, major soil types, and geography, and you'll be able to create the rain garden that is most responsive to its environment.

RAIN FOREST TO DESERT: THE NORTHWEST'S VARIED SUBCLIMATES

We usually use the term *climate* to describe the combination of weather patterns that occur repeatedly in an area, over a period of time. The word can be applied to a large geographical region or to an area the size of a single garden bed (usually referred

to as a *microclimate*). Variations in geography and topography within our major climate regions create subclimates as well, spanning the spectrum from the mild temperatures, rain, and clouds that the Pacific Ocean provides west of the Cascades, to the drier skies and more extreme temperatures

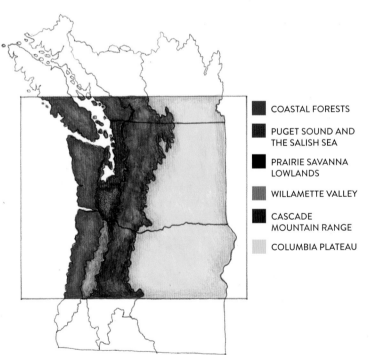

COASTAL FORESTS

PUGET SOUND AND THE SALISH SEA

PRAIRIE SAVANNA LOWLANDS

WILLAMETTE VALLEY

CASCADE MOUNTAIN RANGE

COLUMBIA PLATEAU

The six subclimates of the Pacific Northwest

CHARACTERISTICS OF MAJOR SUBCLIMATES (OR ECOREGIONS)

Use the chart and map to identify your geographic region and its climate, precipitation, and vegetation.

REGION	GEOGRAPHICAL AREA	CLIMATE (SIMPLIFIED)	ANNUAL PRECIPITATION	VEGETATION
Coastal Forests	Olympic Mountains; Vancouver Island, Pacific Ocean coast	Wet to very wet mild fall/winter/spring to dry cool summer; marine west coast; cooler summers, warmer winters	200 inches / 500 cm	Temperate conifer rainforests: Sitka spruce, western red cedar. Douglas-fir and bigleaf maple
Prairie Savanna Lowlands	Dry lowlands in southern WA and northern OR; near the coast typically in the rain shadow of the mountain ranges	Moderately dry mild fall/winter/spring to very dry and warm summer	10 inches / 25 cm	Pacific madrona and garry oak forests, wildflower meadows
Puget Sound and the Salish Sea	Immediate area around Puget Sound (the Salish coastline by Vancouver, BC, and OR are similar)	Wet mild fall/winter/spring to very dry summer; maritime mediterranean; cooler summers, warmer winters	35-55 inches / 90-140 cm	Conifer forests: Sitka spruce, western red cedar, Pacific yew. Douglas-fir, Pacific madrona, and bigleaf maple
Willamette Valley	The valley along the Willamette River in OR	Moderately wet mild fall/winter/spring to very dry and warm summer	35-55 inches / 90-140 cm	Pacific madrona and garry oak forests, wildflower meadows
Cascade Mountain Range	Cascade Mountains from southern BC to northern OR; eastern slopes include the Okanogan–Wenatchee National Forest	Wet and cold fall/winter/spring to cooler, relatively dry summer alpine maritime on the western slopes; moderately wet cold fall/winter/spring and very dry warm summer on the eastern slopes	120 inches / 300 cm or more rain on the west side 15 inches / 38 cm on the eastern slopes	Conifer forests: Douglas-fir, western hemlock, silver fir, grand fir, subalpine fir, on the western slopes and Douglas-fir, mountain hemlock, and ponderosa pine on the eastern slopes
Columbia Plateau	Eastern region of most of WA and OR, ending by the Rocky Mountains on the east and by the Cascade Mountains on the west, includes the Palouse in WA and the Blue Mountains in OR	Continental patterns with very cold, moderately dry fall/winter/spring followed by very hot and dry summer	7 inches / 17.5 cm	Shrub steppe vegetation, aromatic drought loving vegetation, sagebrush, grasses, some ponderosa pine, and Douglas-fir, willows, shrubby dogwoods, sedges, and rushes next to water

The northern Oregon coastline is misty, with lush evergreen forests.

Puget Sound, Willamette Valley, Cascade Mountain Range, and Columbia Plateau. Differences and microclimates do exist within these ecoregions and these local patterns should be observed for each site you are designing for.

Coastal Forests: Typically the coastal areas are the wettest. Before intense development, the coasts of Washington, Oregon, and British Columbia were covered with dense and lush temperate rain forests. These majestic woods evapotranspired the water back into the air, resulting in constant mist and light to moderate rainfall for nine to ten months of the year. The summers lasted two to three months, and were warm and very dry. These periods allowed the ground to dry out a little, readying it to receive the rainfall of the next wet period. During the winter months the precipitation often fell as snow because of the cold, but the temperature did turn mild during the spring and autumn seasons. This area remains cloudy during the late fall, winter, and spring periods and receives a high volume of rainfall. The subclimate region includes the Olympic Mountains and Washington's Pacific coast, the Oregon Coast, and Vancouver Island. Its larger cities and towns include western-facing areas around Victoria, Port Angeles, Forks, Ozette, Ocean Shores, Westport, Aberdeen down to Long Beach, Astoria, Rockaway Beach, Tillamook, and Pacific City.

found to the east. There are many ways to categorize the Pacific Northwest's climate and myriad microclimates. Scientists have divided the region into six large areas known as subclimates or ecoregions: Coastal Forests, Prairie Savanna Lowlands,

Puget Sound experiences wet falls, winters, and springs, with dry summers.

Puget Sound and the Salish Sea: Further inland, the Salish Sea—the binational body of water that includes Puget Sound, the Strait of Juan de Fuca, and the Strait of Georgia—has a maritime climate marked by gray skies, cloudy days, rain, and wind from late fall through late spring. This subclimate contains the major cities of Vancouver, BC, Bellingham, Seattle, and Tacoma; all the smaller cities in between them (Mount Vernon, Marysville, Everett, Lynnwood, Mill Creek, Woodinville, Kirkland, Bellevue, Renton, Seatac, Federal Way, and Fife); and parts of the San Juan and Gulf Islands. Despite its damp reputation, Seattle actually receives less rain than many other places, but also less light. Several studies show that people from these parts of the Northwest are more likely than

Central Washington's low, rolling hills are covered with vegetation that tolerates extreme temperatures and low rainfall.

people living in sunny areas to wear muted, grayish colors and paint their homes gray. It's either the cloudy season and we're dressing for the rain (not carrying umbrellas), or it's summer, and we've forgotten where we've put our sunglasses.

Prairie Savanna Lowlands: A Prairie Savanna subclimate features moderately dry but mild weather three seasons of the year—fall, winter, spring—and then very dry and hot summers. Because of our unique topography, you'll find dry lowlands often near the coast but also in the rain shadow of mountains, such as in southern Washington and northern Oregon, starting roughly around inland south Tacoma, Olympia, and Fort Lewis, stretching through DuPont, Tillicum, Chehalis, and Centralia, and reaching to Clark

EL NIÑO AND LA NIÑA

When the equatorial Pacific Ocean experiences warmer-than-average surface water temperatures, the result is high air pressure over the western Pacific and lower air pressure over the eastern Pacific. This in turn generates warmer-than-average temperatures and lower-than-average precipitation for the Americas. Because this pattern was noticed by Central American fishermen around Christmas, it was named "El Niño," referring to the baby Jesus.

La Niña (the female child) is just the opposite. Below-average surface water temperatures in the tropical central Pacific lead to lower air pressure over the western Pacific and higher air pressure over the eastern Pacific. Stronger, colder weather patterns form over the Pacific coasts of the Americas, bringing precipitation that is much higher than average.

THE SCABLANDS

Over long periods of time, ice dams and gushing flood waters carved deep scabs into this region's landscape. These raging rivers flowing out of the ancient lakes forced their way through weak basalt layers, creating giant waterfalls and leaving the land as fast as they arrived. The large channels that formed in the basalt are dry today, but you can see that water was flowing in them some time ago. Dry Falls in Washington State, for example, is today a dry, steep, rock formation. When it wasn't dry, the waterfall was a mile and a half (2.4km) across and more than 400 feet (122m) tall. By comparison, Niagara Falls is (only!) a mile (1.6km) wide and 165 feet (50.3m) tall.

County and across the Columbia River. Some areas around Victoria, BC, and parts of the San Juan Islands that are in the rain shadow are also Prairie Savanna subclimates, just smaller. These are often protected and rare ecological sites.

Willamette Valley: This subclimate's area matches its name, following the course of Oregon's Willamette River Valley, from the city of Portland south through Salem, Corvallis, and Albany to Eugene. This is also some of region's finest wine country—moderately wet and mild through most of the year, but with dry, hot summers that are perfect for ripening grape harvests. The area sees more precipitation than the Prairie Savanna region, but less than the Coastal Forests or the Cascades. It is also sunny and relatively dry during the spring through summer and fall seasons. The valley rarely sees extreme weather, as temperatures are mild during the winters and very warm, but not scorching hot, during the summer. The climate resembles a Mediterranean pattern.

Cascade Mountain Range: The Cascade Mountain Range extends south from British Columbia through Oregon and differs in climate depending on whether you're on the western or eastern slope. The western side of the mountains has an alpine maritime climate strongly affected by the Pacific Ocean, while the eastern side is semi-arid to arid. Average annual precipitation in the mountains is 120 inches (3m) or more, much of it falling as snow. The snow cover typically is very deep, and, like the Olympic Mountains, the Cascades boast some of the deepest snow in the world, ranging from 360 inches (9m) to 1,140 inches (29m), with an annual average of 659 inches (16.7m). We do not have lots of cities and towns in this area, but Coquitlam and Abbotsford, BC; Concrete, Darrington, the area along Highway 2 and I-90, Issaquah, Morton, and Orting, WA; down to Mount Hood Village and Elkhorn, OR; and the mountainous area along McKenzie Highway are all within this region.

Columbia Plateau: East of the Cascades, in Washington, Oregon, and southern British Columbia, the climate is considered continental and fairly dry. The land looks different—flatter, with rolling hills instead of mountains. The soil changes to support types of vegetation and wildlife that tolerate temperature extremes and reduced rainfall. This subclimate or ecoregion contains Kelowna, BC; Moses Lake, Othello, Richland, Lake Chelan, Spokane, and Pullman, WA; and Burns, OR—really all of the cities and towns from the eastern foot of the Cascades to the western edges of the Rockies.

How can this area be considered one large region if the subclimates or ecoregions within it are so geologically and atmospherically different? The answer is, they are connected by overall large-scale global weather patterns. These patterns are influenced by the slow but constant, deep currents of the Pacific Ocean, by the high peaks of the massive Cascade Range, and by the vast, flat surface of the Columbia Plateau. This is what makes the Pacific Northwest one region—intimately connected and defined by seasonal patterns in temperature and rainfall.

THE EFFECTS OF CLIMATE CHANGE

If you noticed that we've been discussing the weather with repeated terms such as "typical" and "usual," that's intentional: Our climate is changing. Weather patterns are in flux all over the planet, and the Pacific Northwest is no exception. Summers and winters are either getting sunnier, warmer, and drier, or colder and wetter than "typical." Some scientists predict that normal patterns will be completely altered, with both more sunshine and heavier rainstorms, in an overall pattern combining more rainfall with warmer temperatures and longer dry periods. Longer El Niño and La Niña cycles may become the norm in the near future.

Maybe we Northwesterners won't complain about extra sunshine, but climatologists at the University of Washington predict that climate change in the Pacific Northwest will bring more rain than snow in the winter, resulting in less snowpack and higher winter stormwater runoff pollution, and drier, warmer summer seasons that increase the threat of long-term drought. Snowpack is the principal means of precipitation storage to provide continuous stream flows, which are essential to salmon health. It is also the source of potable water for most people in Washington, Oregon, and Idaho. Reduced snowpack alters the hydrology of the soil; when paired with increased temperatures it can cause drought, even if rains are heavier.

In what is perhaps a preview of the coming changes, the Cascade and Olympic mountains experienced the lowest snowpack ever recorded in 2014–2015, and this combined with drought to create a devastating wildfire season. And yet the record drought year of 2015 ended with record precipitation in just its last two months. Such heavy winter rains increase the burden on undersized urban combined stormwater systems, triggering the release of more sewage and runoff contamination into Puget Sound and freshwater lakes and streams. The fear is that this will become the new normal climate condition.

Scientists do not have all the answers about what to expect from the changing climate. We may at some point need to retire our ski equipment and embrace mud runs as a new sport! Humor aside, however, one lesson to draw from all this is that rain gardens are more important than ever for helping reduce the negative impact of climate change, from both extremes: They not only mitigate the consequences of heavy rains, but also, by moving the water into the soil, they reduce the severity of droughts.

THE GEOGRAPHY OF SOIL

The Pacific Northwest's other great regional divider/uniter is its random and often violent geologic history. Let's geek out with some geology to understand the soil throughout the region!

The Northwest straddles a convergence zone of tectonic plates (sublayers of the earth's crust, or hard surface, that are in continuous motion, afloat on the earth's mantle), two of which, in particular, affect our geography and soil: the North American Plate (the continent) and the Juan de Fuca Plate (offshore of British Columbia, Washington, and Oregon). These enormous plates press and grind where they meet and, as the Juan de Fuca plate bends under the North American Plate (known as subduction), its leading edge hits lava and melts. The speed of this melting pushes it forward as the other plate floats on top.

The products of this motion (in addition to

earthquakes) are mountain formation—sometimes violently fast and sometimes painfully slow—and intense volcanic activity, all of which helped create the Cascade Range, as well as some of the Insular Mountains and all of the Coast Mountains in British Columbia. As erupting volcanos spewed ash and lava, these materials settled in layers on the ground. The lava cooled, sometimes quickly and sometimes slowly. Fast-cooling lava led to the formation of granite layers, which are seen frequently in the western parts of our region, along with ash layers (which compacted easily under the weight of other layers). Slow-cooling lava became basalt, a common sight in the eastern Northwest, where lava flooded flat areas.

Glacial Activity

Other factors besides seismic and volcanic activity worked collaboratively to create the landscapes here. Scientists estimate that about a million years ago the earth's climate cooled, and over the succeeding millennia snow and ice accumulated over most of the landmasses. In the area we now call Canada, this ice was over a thousand feet thick! The weight of this massive layer flattened much of the landmasses—if engineers had been around to see the process, they might have come up with some clever way to capture the colossal power involved. Building pressure caused the continent-size ice sheet to slowly move southward, and as it did, it blocked rivers and built lakes in the same way our man-made dams create reservoirs today.

For thousands of years, miles-thick ice moved back and forth over the entire upper North American continent. This slow-moving, heavy ice ground boulders, rocks, and stones like the coffee beans Seattle is known for now, turning them into particles from fine to coarse: sand, silt, clay, gravel, and cobbles.

GLACIAL ERRATICS

Sometimes soil testing turns up giant boulders, called glacial erratics. This glacial erratic was discovered by the city of Edmonds, Washington, in fall 2015. Wanting to move it to a site outside the city, they advertised it as "free to a good home" under specific conditions, including easy yard access and promises that the recipient would clear it with their significant other and wouldn't ask the city to move it again! However, most glacial erratics stay put—moving them can be more expensive than the construction they are blocking.

(Courtesy of the City of Edmonds)

Soil Types

Our soils formed on top of what the glaciers and other geological forces left behind.

Silty Loam

These prehistoric flood events left behind fine silty loam soils, which are wonderful for agricultural use. Silty loam soil is able to hold on to moisture and nutrients so plants can access them over longer periods of time. As the soil still allows water to infiltrate, it drains well. Also, it has an almost ideal 50 percent void space between the particles, so roots can grow into it easily and access everything they need, including air.

Glacial Outwash

Every so often the weather "improved" during the Ice Ages—going from "icy as hell" to just "cold as hell"—and the ice shrank, melted, and turned to water at the ever-changing edges of the glaciers. As the ice moved north again, faster-moving meltwater deposited primarily gravel, and slowly moving meltwater laid down more sand. These layers, called glacial outwash, were deposited by the meltwater one on top of the other, and didn't mix due to the differing sizes of their main particles. In other words, gravel tended to stay with gravel and fine sand with sand of a similar granularity. Gardeners will recognize that such soil usually drains well—the more sand in these mixes, the easier it is to work with when you are digging.

Lacustrine Parent Material

As the topography changed, many temporary lakes were formed, and the melting water settled into these ponds. Very fine silt and clay particles settled at the bottom. When these areas dried out they left behind what is called lacustrine parent material. Because of their clay content, these soils are much less permeable than glacial outwash, but they are still able to infiltrate water at a slow rate.

Glacial Till

Along the coastal Pacific Northwest, glacial till is prominent. Its colorful ingredients—beautiful rocks and gravel, mineral-filled sediment, and dust—were stirred by the force of the glaciers into a mixture with the finer materials of sand, silt, and clay. Then it was all rolled around a few times and compacted together; this is the basic recipe for glacial till. The process takes thousands of years and the results vary greatly. Soils made of these layers contain all sorts of materials of different sizes mixed together in unpredictable ways and proportions.

Hardpan Layers

Over many millennia, the weather never stayed "warm" for long. Volcanoes would choke the sky with ash, which blocked sunlight and caused the air to cool. The ice formed again and again and again, its weight compressing the materials left behind by earlier glaciers and/or deposited by volcanoes. In places, that compression compacted random outwash and till mixtures to the density of concrete. These are called hardpan layers.

Hardpan can be a few inches or many dozens of feet deep, but might as well be miles thick—anyone unfortunate enough to have dug it understands. There is no rhyme or reason for the size and location of these layers. Planting even just a rosemary twig can require a pickaxe and a rock bar.

The action of ancient glaciers and volcanoes created unpredictable soil conditions throughout the Northwest. The only way to tell what is where is by testing the soil everywhere. In chapter 3, we'll talk about how to do your own soil testing.

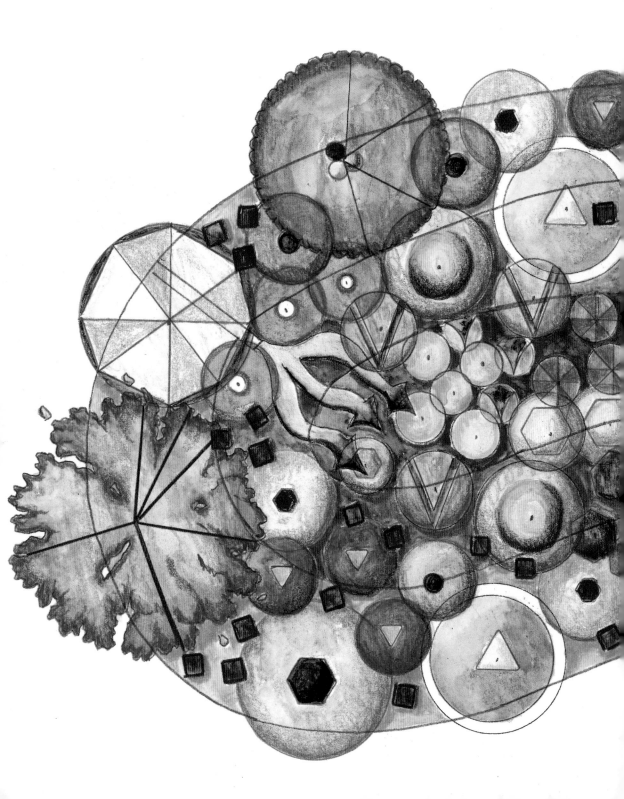

CHAPTER 3

JILL NUNEMAKER

Siting Your Rain Garden: Get Up Close and Personal with Your Yard

Planning a rain garden takes time. When we get calls from potential rain garden clients, it can be six months to a year before we implement the design. Even if you design and build the rain garden yourself, you're not going to wake up one morning wanting a rain garden and have one a week later.

Before you get out a shovel, you have to start with a site assessment, which can sometimes take several months. You must understand your region and its jurisdiction requirements, how runoff flows through your yard based on your neighborhood's topography, where utility lines are located, and what types of soil are in your yard. Designing the garden takes time too—especially if you have never designed a garden or planting plan before.

You can have a rain garden planned, designed, and built for you, which will likely cost several thousands of dollars. But you can also plan, design, and build one yourself, which will cost you almost no money but will take a lot of time and effort on your part. Most people end up in the middle somewhere, getting advice from a professional on some of their questions and renting some equipment, yet doing as much as possible themselves. While this book offers everything a DIYer needs to know, it also points out where professional help may be desirable or necessary, depending on the scope of your project.

We cannot emphasize enough that the secret to a well-functioning and beautiful rain garden is its design, and a good design starts with knowing the variables of your site. The introduction to the Northwest's hydrology and geology provided in

Rain garden site before construction

chapters 1 and 2 should give you some insight into the unique climatic and geologic conditions influencing your site.

Site assessment is the first and most important step in any project design: It defines project goals and objectives for a design based on current, observable information. The goal is to ensure your rain garden fits into the surrounding conditions and works well with the site's very specific parameters. This critical information can be influenced by the timing of the data collection and the methods used to collect it. To make sure the rain garden works as intended, the planning process must be diligent and detailed.

While there is time, energy, and, yes, math involved in siting and planning your own rain garden, we want to help make the process as easy as possible. Done well, your rain garden will be beneficial to you, your yard, and your neighborhood. It will not be an overnight process, but the results will be worth it.

—————— • • ——————

TIP Record your planning process, observations, and calculations in a notebook. You'll be referring to these throughout the life of the project.

—————— • • ——————

IDENTIFY YOUR JURISDICTION

In chapter 2, you identified your specific Pacific Northwest region and the conditions found in this location. Your next task is to find out who regulates environmental planning in your area. Ask your city, county, or province's planning and development department (or the surface water department or local conservation district) about their rain garden requirements.

Generally, in Washington and Oregon, rain gardens fall under the Low Impact Development

This pretty rain garden was built with a Snohomish County grant.

CRUNCHING THE NUMBERS

Costs for a rain garden can vary greatly, depending on how you answer the following questions. If you don't know the answers yet, this chapter will help you figure them out.

- Are you going to DIY or seek professional design and/or installation?

- What is the quality of the soil at the site, and how easy is it to work with?

- How big will the rain garden be?

- How many rain gardens are you building?

- Will you use machines or do it all by hand?

- Will drainage systems have to be disconnected and reconnected?

- Is the site easy or difficult to access?

- How far are your rock, soil, and/or other suppliers from the site?

- How are you going to acquire plants?

A TIME TO PLAN, A TIME TO BUILD

The rainy season (late fall and winter) is typically the best time to assess your site, design the garden, and start sourcing plants. At that time of year we can generally get a better picture of soil type, water table, and runoff movement. However, if the ground freezes in the winter where you live, you must test the soil before or after freezing weather, and take note of what happens to melting snow on the site and in the neighborhood. Runoff from sudden melts can be worse than record rainfalls in terms of creating flash flood conditions.

Installation of the garden usually takes place during spring, summer, or early fall, although with climate change producing more sunny and dry days during the winter, we are seeing more installations done during those bright and cold periods.

standards of the states' Department of Ecology (WA) and Department of Environmental Quality (OR), while in British Columbia the Ministry of Environment controls overall provincewide regulations and incentives.

Rain gardens are sometimes regulated, and the rules can vary widely from jurisdiction to jurisdiction or even year to year. Regulations might cover a rain garden's distance from a structure, or its overflow direction—for example, in some cities or counties a rain garden cannot overflow into a right-of-way area or a sidewalk, and in others it must overflow into the original drainage system. Most jurisdictions will want to see at least 100 feet (30m) between the rain garden and a steep slope.

If the contributing area is larger than 9,999 square feet (929m²), a civil engineer may need to oversee or complete the design. Since all jurisdictions are different when it comes to codes and limits, and can change them often, we strongly recommend that you contact your jurisdictional authority. The best policy is to ask before you start working on your plans and design.

When you contact your jurisdiction's relevant department, ask them a few basic questions:

- Does a residential rain garden require a building permit?
- Is a permit required to disconnect the downspout?
- Are there recommendations or requirements for rain garden design?
- What happens to runoff in the neighborhood? Is it collected in pipes and channeled to a sewage treatment facility, or into a natural waterway directly?
- Do they have information regarding local water tables?
- Can they tell you what watershed you are in?
- Are there plant height restrictions?
- Do they offer any incentive programs for rain garden implementation?
- Are they aware of any local incentive programs offered by other organizations?
- Do they offer any free classes about rain gardens?
- Is your property near any critical areas and/or steep slopes?
- If you're near a slope or a bluff, what is the required distance to build from it?

Once you have answers to these questions, you can continue with your site assessment using your jurisdictional requirements as guidelines. Even if local jurisdictions do not require a permit for a rain garden, they may be able to share information about previous projects they've worked on. They will know which watershed your property is in, what your soil and water table's important aspects are, and even what local nurseries sell quality plants.

RESEARCH YOUR LOCAL RESOURCES AND INCENTIVE PROGRAMS

Where you live will help determine just what resources are available to you. Generally speaking, local conservation districts and university extensions are good sources for plants and information about rain garden professionals in your area. Some conservation districts, like the one in Snohomish County, Washington, even have an engineer on staff who helps property owners with site assessment and rain garden design free of charge.

Cities and conservation districts may also offer incentives to help your rain garden project along, either on your own or with professional help. These might include matching funding, cash rebates upon project completion, and/or free education programs. Some programs require that the rain garden be designed and built by a professional, but others ask that only the design be done professionally.

A few jurisdictions allow the property owner to design and implement the project, as long as the jurisdiction is allowed to evaluate and approve the design before installation begins. The list of these is changeable, but at the time of publication it included, among others: Bellingham, Everett, Lacey, Mount Vernon, Olympia, Port Angeles, Puyallup, Seattle, Shoreline, Tacoma, Tumwater, and Vancouver, WA; Portland, OR; and Vancouver, BC. Portland, OR, and Spokane, WA, offer education around public right-of-way stormwater projects completed by the city.

Note that incentive programs sometimes have their own limitations or specific requirements for a project to qualify. That is the case with the RainWise program in the Seattle and Portland areas (see "RainWise Rebates" sidebar later in this chapter). With RainWise, the city determines which addresses can even apply for the program, typically areas that suffer from CSOs. Then, once an address is okayed, the project has to meet specific conditions, which are different from the city's general rain garden specifications, including:

*   minimum contributing area size
*   specific design and installation qualifications
*   minimum soil drainage rate
*   rain garden mix type
*   prescribed inflow and overflow parameters
*   five-year commitment to keep the rain garden

Pros and Cons of Incentive Programs

Working with incentive programs has pros and cons, of course. Some typical conditions and constraints of an incentive program might be:

*   Time frame: Some programs are only offered until a certain date, or you may have to finish your rain garden within a certain time period.
*   Tax: Reimbursement may count as income, with the property owner required to fill out an IRS W-9 form.
*   No DIY options: You may need to hire a professional and not be allowed to handle the project yourself.
*   Paperwork: Grant- or tax-based programs can involve extensive paperwork, not only to qualify but to document what happened when and why.

However, these programs have upsides, too:

- Free training and classes: A program may offer education not only about rain gardens but about good stewardship of urban land, sustainable practices, and community development.
- Networking: These programs are most often created as partnerships between the government, the public, and private industry.
- The funding itself: If you qualify and can complete the process, you will be able to get back some of the money you spent on your rain garden.

OBSERVE YOUR SURROUNDING TOPOGRAPHY

Topography affects how the water flows, because water always flows downhill! What is going on with the topography in your neighborhood? What do the surrounding few blocks look like? Through the siting and design phases, we must constantly think about the flow of water. Water must get to and from the rain garden without the assistance of a pump. In other words, it must move only by the power of gravitational flow.

It's not necessary to create a complete topographic map of your entire neighborhood (although with software such as Google Earth that is possible), but it is important to develop a sense of the neighborhood's characteristics, to refer to during the design phase.

————— • • —————

TIP Take photos as you walk around your neighborhood, to remind yourself of its conditions and aspects when you reach the design phase.

————— • • —————

If the area around you is hilly, it makes a big difference whether slopes are running *from* or *toward* your future rain garden. For example, if your home is lower than the neighboring properties, it will receive surface runoff from those lots as well as from your own roof and driveway. Your design will have to deal with this by diverting the runoff from adjacent lots, having a foolproof overflow system, and/or sizing the rain garden to handle the excess contributions. (Or consider multiple, smaller rain gardens; see Terraces in chapter 4.)

Conversely, if a slope directs water *away* from the future rain garden location, does the flow go

RAINWISE REBATES

The RainWise rebate program is a joint effort by King County and the City of Seattle to reduce combined sewer overflows by building rain gardens and rain tanks to lower runoff flow during heavy precipitation events. David Hymel of Rain Dog Designs says that about 45,000 private properties across sixteen Seattle neighborhoods are eligible, and most installations are at no or minimal cost to the property owners. The City of Seattle is also aiming to process 700 million gallons (2.6 billion liters) of stormwater by 2025 using LID techniques such as rain gardens, green roofs, and more. While RainWise program managers and staff at first focused on smaller residential properties, now the program is also targeting owners of roofs larger than 5,000 square feet (465m^2), which more measurably reduce peak runoff flows.

Account for extra runoff from hills and slopes.

The rain garden at the base of this bluff collects and mitigates runoff.

toward the house or another structure? Where will the water go when the rain garden overflows and/or is absorbed into the ground? Subsurface water still flows, and it continues to flow downhill.

While observing the topography in your neighborhood, chat with your neighbors (rain gardens also help to build community!) and ask some questions:

- Find out if any of the nearby homes experience seasonal flooding and soggy yards. If the answer is yes, when do they have these problems—during the rainy season only, or year-round?
- What happens when water collects? Does it flow somewhere or just sit there?

Sometimes pre-development conditions can haunt an area for a long time. The previous presence of wetlands or bogs can seriously affect how the water table behaves at various times during the year. Believe it or not, in the not-so-distant past, these areas were allowed to be built on. You can always ask your jurisdiction for historical information, and Google Earth now can show you aerial images from times past. Research your neighborhood's history. Talk to neighbors who have lived there longer than you have.

———— •• ————

TIP Remember that, due to the Northwest's crazy geology, just because your neighbor has poorly draining soil doesn't necessarily mean you will too. However, take note of these areas so that you aren't inadvertently directing runoff toward them.

———— •• ————

ANALYZE SLOPES AND BLUFFS

Does your property include or is it near a slope, bluff, or ravine? Increased infiltration into the ground near bluffs, ravines, and very steep slopes can result in a *blow-out failure* of the slope. And what is a blow-out failure? Exactly what it sounds like: Water builds up underground, the hydrologic pressure increases, and suddenly the soil on the side of the bluff or the slope blows out and gives way, resulting in very severe landslides. Check the slope of steep areas to determine whether it is advisable to install a rain garden on them.

How to Measure the Grade of Your Slope

You will need:

- string
- line level
- measuring tape
- plumb line or leveling bar

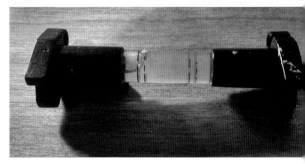

Line level

1. First, find the *run* of the slope. Thread a string through the line level, and run the string out horizontally over the length of the slope from a fixed point. Adjust the string so the level shows it to be flat. Measure the length of the string and write it down. (You can use easy-to-calculate numbers, such as 3 feet, 91cm, or another round number.) Leave the string and level in place for the next step.

2. Next find the *rise* of the slope. With your measuring tape, measure from the far end of the string down to the ground. Use either a plumb line or a leveling bar to make sure the measuring tape is vertical and that the two lines are at a 90-degree angle to each other. By placing the leveling bar vertically next to the string, you can determine whether the string is truly vertical or not. If the bubble lines up in the middle, the line is vertical. If you use a plumb, make sure the plumb matches the string exactly. That means the string is vertical. Record the distance.

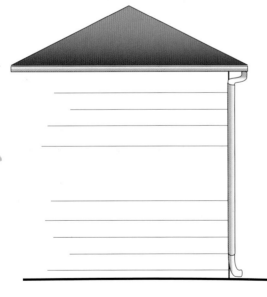

RUN OF SLOPE

RISE OF
SLOPE

Calculating slope grade

Rain garden built on a gradual slope, bermed with soil and Gardensoxx

3. Now calculate the grade of the slope by dividing the rise by the run and multiplying the total by 100. For example, for a run of 20 feet (6m) and a rise of 4 feet (1.2m):

4 ÷ 20 = 0.2 x 100 = 20

The grade of this slope is 20 percent.

Generally, if a slope is more severe than 10 percent, it is considered too steep for a DIY rain garden. However, engineers can often come up with great design solutions for such places, so call in a professional to help with the siting and design. If the governing jurisdiction says it is OK to build a rain garden near your steep slope or bluff, be sure to site it at **a minimum distance of 100 feet (30m) from the steep area. More is even better.**

If the grade change is low enough that you do not need a permit and engineered design, your options include creating either a *berm* (a raised bank of soil) or a terraced rain garden. A berm requires digging deeper on the higher end of the rain garden and forming the berm on the lower end, to create a level water surface. Terracing, or building multiple rain garden cells on several levels, will require some structural planning such as incorporating weirs (a barrier to slow the water's flow) or a retaining wall system. (See Berms and Terraces in chapter 4.)

MAP YOUR YARD

Now that you know your region, your jurisdiction's requirements, and the lay of your neighborhood and any sloping areas, it is time to plot out your yard (back, front, and side). You don't necessarily have to create your own map: You may be able to obtain a plot plan layout drawing from your jurisdiction, if they have it on file. Another option is to print an aerial view of your property from Google Earth large enough to make notes on, but nothing is stopping you from developing your own map, and the instructions below will walk you through the process.

The foundation for mapping your property is the creation of a measuring grid on the ground. The grid's reference lines, called *baselines*, will allow you to position everything correctly on the map. To establish baselines and begin your map, you will need:

- Notebook (graph paper is handy), colored pens and pencils
- Two measuring tapes 50–100 feet (15–30m) long, for baselines
- A third measuring tape or a measuring wheel, to measure from the baselines
- A large triangle or carpenter's square, to establish perpendicular angles (optional)

- A camera, to document tape readings and how the tapes are placed

Your first step is to form a general idea of where you want your rain garden to go. Your goal is to map out your entire property so you can find the best location for your future rain garden. You will be able to make this decision based on what you find when mapping your site; you want to locate healthy vegetation, hard surfaces, structures, easements, and utility lines, as well as map the topography.

In the process of the assessment you will be able to eliminate areas as potential rain garden locations: too steep, too wet, too close to property lines or structures, near or on top of utility lines, within the root zones of healthy trees and native or sustainable vegetation, or maybe too far from the roof, driveway, and/or lawn you want to collect the runoff from. To make these decisions, you will need measurements of where things are on your property.

Once you've narrowed the property down to the location your rain garden will call home, you

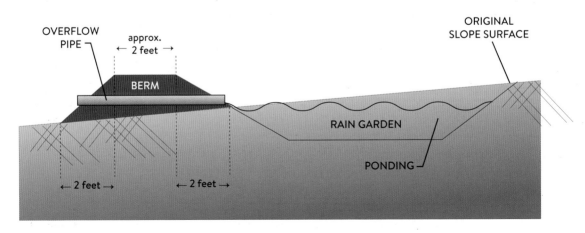

Adding a berm to the downhill side of a slope to create a level ponding area

will need to create a detailed map of that section of your property. That means you will have to measure it more thoroughly than the rest of the property. Once again, grab two long measuring tapes. It's best to use a nearby structure or fence line—something straight—as a reference, so you can use it as one of your baselines.

Place the zero point of the tape at one of the edges of the future rain garden area, and run the tape out along this baseline (the side of your house or the edge of a straight driveway works very well usually), staying as close to it as possible, till you reach the other edge of the area you want to measure. Anchor the tape there. This is your first baseline, or BL1.

Starting at that endpoint with the other tape's zero point, create the second side of a rectangle by running out that tape perpendicular to the first, all the way to the opposite boundary. This is your second baseline, or BL2. Anchor it at both ends. Draw the two tapes (Baselines 1 and 2), in your notebook, label them, and mark measurements on them that correspond to the ones on your tapes (every 2 feet, for example).

With your preliminary grid now set up, you can walk around inside the area with your measuring wheel or third tape measure and pinpoint individual items in your landscape. Anything there can be located using a combination of measurements from the two baselines: You'll want to mark areas of vegetation, locating larger plants that shade your future rain garden, where the buildings and their features begin and end—for example, where windows and doors begin and end, and where downspouts are. To locate a specific feature, measure out to it perpendicularly first from one baseline and then from the other (a triangle or carpenter's square will help keep those right angles true). Photograph or jot down the two measurements. Find the meeting point

Jill uses a measuring wheel within the established baselines.

of the two corresponding measurements on your map (paper already laid out in a grid makes this easier), and you've found the right spot to sketch in that feature.

With your grid and your plotting method established, your map is off to a good start. Now it's time to discuss what specific things you should put on it. Following is information on some important planning considerations that should ultimately be reflected in your map.

Utility Lines

With our easy access to natural gas, water, and electricity, we sometimes forget how those things find their way to us in the first place. The fact is, their various conduits are all around us, and no rain garden project can afford to ignore them.

You can find buried utility lines on your property with the help of public and/or private utility locating services. There are usually free services offered by utility locator companies to prevent expensive and often very dangerous accidents—it's easy to cause a major evacuation of the

Utility markings in standard colors

power, it is often overhead but not always. Hitting a power line, even with a shovel, can kill a person, so take locating and marking these lines seriously.

Once the utility lines are appropriately, colorfully marked, it can't hurt to take pictures of the markings to remind you later where the lines are. You should also transfer those indications to your map, assuming there is overlap between the area your map covers and the locations of the lines. Note that, by law, you will have to contact the utilities again before any digging 12" or deeper takes place, if work lasts longer than 45 days, or markings were done for design, assessment, etc. and excavation does not start until 45 days or more have passed, or the markings are no longer visible, paint has worn off and flags are missing (in which case the utilities must be marked again). Call the "call before you dig" hotline (811 in the United States and Canada) before you dig. It is the law.

With the combination of your map and the markings on your property, you've got a good

neighborhood with just one dig, if the utility lines aren't marked. In the Pacific Northwest, dial 811 or go online to call811.com. If you do not have a public utility locator program or if the lines are private, call a private locator. It takes about three business days to get the lines marked, and it does cost money, but repairs cost a lot more. If you do not want marks on permanent surfaces such as concrete driveways, ask them to only mark only nonpaved surfaces. (The paint does wash off over time, however.)

It's also a good idea to call the utility companies directly and see if they allow rain gardens near their lines. Natural gas companies often have regulations about water infiltration around their lines, since gas can easily travel through water and create a huge fire and explosion hazard. Phone and cable companies do not typically have these types of limiting regulations. As for electric

	WHITE: Proposed Excavation
	PINK: Temporary Survey Markings
	RED: Electric Power Lines, Cables, Conduit, and Lighting Cables
	YELLOW: Gas, Oil, Steam, Petroleum, or Gaseous Materials
	ORANGE: Communication, Alarm or Signal Lines, Cables, or Conduit
	BLUE: Potable Water
	PURPLE: Reclaimed Water, Irrigation and Slurry Lines
	GREEN: Sewers and Drain Lines

Standard utility marking colors and their meaning

idea of where *not* to place a rain garden! Specifically, over the the colored markings, or within 2 feet (61cm) of either side of them. The garden also cannot be situated over any septic fields or "reserve fields" (an extra area on the property set aside for use as a new drain field).

There is an exception for your *inflow* and *overflow*, which can usually be safely channeled through pipes over utility lines excepting natural gas. But certain guidelines must be followed. (See the Tip about excavating by hand in chapter 5.)

Last, watch out for unseen irrigation systems or landscape lighting lines. You may want to eliminate them, but there are good and bad ways of going about it. See if you can reroute existing underground systems around the rain garden site, or remove them carefully so the materials can be recycled into another project rather than being thrown away.

If you have questions about utilities as they relate to the placement of the rain garden or any of its elements, consult a professional designer or engineer, who may have more experience with utility companies and be more familiar with the regulations.

Structures

It's very likely that your prospective rain garden site is in close proximity to at least one structure, whether it's a house or a garage. Distance from structures is an important factor in siting your garden. We recommend keeping rain gardens as far away from buildings as possible. If there is enough space, allow for a gap of 3–10 feet (91cm–3m) from the rain garden's top edge; whether it is a berm or just Zone 3 plantings, it is still the same.

JURISDICTIONAL NOTE: In some cities, rain gardens must be at least 10 feet (3m) from any basement (measured from the *bottom* of the garden—the deep, inside edge of the dug-out area), which is also the Zone 1 planting area. If the house does not have a basement, it is acceptable to place a rain garden bottom within 5 feet (1.5m) of the house. Most jurisdictions, however, require a 10-foot (3m) minimum distance from all buildings, while some areas allow for a distance of as little as 3 feet (91cm) from a driveway. NOTE: These distances are usually measured from the bottom of the rain garden to the structure, not the top planting edge, and

On your map note locations of trees and their distances from structures and each other.

Pacific madronas (*Arbutus menziesii*) can live next to water as long as their roots aren't wet.

trees already mitigate runoff and offer a multitude of ecosystem services, as does flourishing vegetation, especially native plants. Rain gardens can destroy the roots of these beneficial plants and kill them. Some trees will die if the amount of water around their roots is increased: Pacific madrona (*Arbutus menziesii*), for example, will not tolerate increased infiltration into its root zone. (See Top Plants for Pacific Northwest Rain Gardens to help identify beneficial native plants that will thrive in a rain garden.)

CONSIDER INFLOW AND OVERFLOW

In our wanderings around the yard looking for the best rain garden spot, we should also think about *inflow* (how water will flow from different areas into the rain garden) and *overflow* (where excess water will be diverted to).

————————• •————————

TIP Avoid cutting through tree roots just for the sake of facilitating inflow or overflow. Damaging a tree's roots always stresses and weakens it, and can sometimes kill it.

————————• •————————

bottom vs. top can make a big difference! Ten feet from the bottom means you can have a rain garden next to a house. The same distance from the top means you probably do not have enough space in an urban yard.

Once you have determined the distance of all nearby structures from the proposed site, make sure to add the structures to your property map.

Trees and Vegetation

Trees and other sorts of vegetation have their own vital hydrologic roles to play, and you will want to site your rain garden somewhere where it and the vegetation don't interfere with each other. Avoid putting a rain garden in an area with large, mature trees or healthy native vegetation. Big

Inflow

Because water flows downhill, it has to be routed into the rain garden by the force of gravity. An inflow system should meet the following conditions:

- Has a slight slope, 2 to 4 percent, either natural or built in
- Minimizes erosion and soil disturbance
- Is safe for all of the structures it routes the runoff from (see the Structures section above for particulars)
- Is predictable and easy to maintain

- Is higher than the elevation of the overflow
- Does not run over utility lines (unless the line is a pipe and the company agreed to this placement)
- Is not within a septic field

If it is a *swale*, it is not located in a high water table area (a swale is a built, open surface channel, shallow, sometimes lined with pond liner and sometimes soil based, allowing infiltration, with the purpose of moving water from one place to another; ditches are very simple and rough swales) (see Swale in chapter 4).

If any of these inflow design conditions cannot be met, the rain garden may need a professional consultation or design.

On your property map, mark the areas that seem suitable for the inflow route; there may be more than one if you are directing runoff from multiple places, such as several roof downspouts. We'll calculate the specifics when we get to chapter 4, Planning and Design.

JURISDICTIONAL NOTE: If you are planning to disconnect the downspout for the inflow (see Types of Inflow in chapter 4), check whether your jurisdiction requires a permit for this. Some cities do not have a permit requirement for the entire rain garden, but they do for the downspout disconnection. The jurisdiction will let you know if you need to hire a professional to design the inflow or complete the disconnection, or if you need to have an inspector check the work.

Overflow

Overflow determines the depth of the ponding area. ("Ponding" refers to the formation of standing water on top of the rain garden when the ground has been fully saturated, such as by a storm.) The placement of overflow needs careful

This rock wall was kept low to facilitate overflow.

consideration because, just like inflow, overflow moves water. In order to maximize the surface area of the rain garden—and thus the time the water spends being filtered by the rain garden's natural processes—the overflow should be situated as far as possible from the inflow. It does not need a particular grade of slope, but it has to slope away from the rain garden. It can simply allow water to exit the rain garden at a specific location and spread across a larger landscaped area, such as a lawn or sidewalk, or it can be a pipe that channels the excess water back into the original drainage system.

Overflow must meet the following conditions:

- Be in an area that is easy to see and maintain
- Be as far away from the inflow as possible to maximize filtration
- Be lower than the inflow
- If sloped, slope away from the rain garden and not into it
- Not directly move water onto a neighboring property or into a building
- Not be over a septic field
- If a swale, not go into a high water table area

Overflow may be positioned over utilities, depending on local regulations, the type of utilities, and the type of overflow: If it will *sheet-flow* (slide across the landscape in a thin sheet rather than infiltrate) into the existing landscape, it is OK to place it over utilities. If it is piped to a specific area away from the utilities, most utility companies will allow you to place it over their lines. Infiltrating swales should not be placed over utilities, especially gas lines.

JURISDICTIONAL NOTE: Some municipalities, such as the City of Seattle, don't allow you to discharge water onto the sidewalk. Ask your planning department before designing this type of overflow.

MEASURE AVAILABLE YARD SPACE

As you can see, it is as important for your map to indicate the *wrong* places for your rain garden as the *right* ones: These include septic fields, reserve fields, utility lines, healthy trees and lush vegetation, and slopes with a grade greater than 10 percent. By now you should be forming an idea of what will work and what won't.

With the various obstacles taken into account, it is time to measure the suitable areas and pinpoint them on your map. If the suitable areas have unusual shapes, or geometry is not your strong suit, break them up into easily measurable segments or just approximate their outlines.

DETERMINE SOIL TYPE, DRAINAGE RATE, AND WATER TABLE

Now you have a pretty clear idea about where in the yard you will place your rain garden, so it's time to get dirty: We need to dig a test hole in order to assess our soil's texture and structure. Once we do that, we'll know if we have rocky soil or a hardpan layer for a yard! Which means we'll know whether we want to hand-dig the entire garden, use a machine, or ask the teen next door to do it in exchange for pizza (costs less than renting a machine!).

JURISDICTIONAL NOTE: Different jurisdictions have different soil and drainage requirements for projects needing a permit. In Oregon, because the soils are generally so well draining, the process for design and installation is typically less complicated than most places in Washington State or British Columbia.

Incidentally, if the utility locator marks have faded or the flags got moved, go ahead and call 811 again. There's nothing worse than deciding on a rain garden location only to find out later that it's on top of a utility line or the septic field.

It may be a pain to dig test holes, but it is not uncommon to have several going in different areas of your yard. Remember how funny the geology is here in the Northwest: Soils can vary greatly just a few feet away from each other. If one area is simply blue clay or concretelike hardpan, much better soil may be only five or six feet away. Persistent people often end up finding a good spot—not always, but often enough to inspire others to keep digging.

So put on your boots and rain hat. It's time to go outside and do some real-world testing!

——————•·——————

TIP Rite in the Rain offers weather-resistant paper and notebooks so you can take notes and make your calculations outside during the wet season, when most of the testing takes place.

——————•·——————

Dig Test Holes

There's a lot to know about the soil on your site. Is it consistent throughout, or does it randomly change? If your soil has often caught you by surprise when you gardened, you should plan on digging two or three holes across the width of your planned rain garden. If your soil fails any of the following tests, it is a good idea to dig another hole and redo the test. If, on the other hand, your first test is acceptable (assuming you followed the steps exactly), and you know that your site is fairly consistent, one hole may just do it.

You will need:

- Pointed shovel
- Posthole digger
- Rock bar
- Trowel
- Camera
- Notebook and pencil
- Gardening gloves

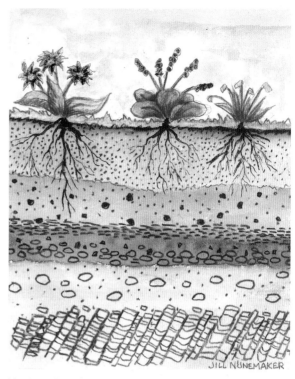

Varying colors indicate the soil type and health of each of the soil layers, or horizons.

A test hole with visible soil layers

The test hole should be at least 24 inches (61cm) deep, but preferably 30–36 inches (76–91cm). Fully excavated rain gardens are typically 30 inches deep for DIY and 36 inches deep for professional excavation, so if you want to get a good understanding of the soils all the way to the bottom of the rain garden, you need to dig down at least that deep.

The hole should be wide enough to show the soil's horizons, or a cross-section of its layers, between 10 and 24 inches (25–61cm) wide. If you use a posthole digger and shovel, you will get a hole you can see into easily.

Keep your excavated soil in a bucket or on a tarp near the test holes, grouped in clusters by layer so you can see, smell, and touch each one. Take a few pictures of the soil layers in the hole. Now we'll carefully study what we've exposed to understand what layers are present in this cross section of the yard.

Soil Color Test

First, examine what you have dug up, looking at the soil to get a basic sense of what you're dealing with.

Most people think of soil as brown, but there's actually a lot of variety within that spectrum that gives clues as to what's in your soil. The darkest brown or even black soils have the highest levels of organic matter (humus) in them, smell like the forest, and can be pressed into loose balls and shapes. The lighter brown the soil, the less organic matter it has. Colors tending toward red and yellow indicate high levels of iron or aluminum that have oxidized (interacted with oxygen), while mottled light colors and red and yellow blotches show that iron and minerals interacted with moisture. Soils high in oxidized iron can be too acidic. Lighter, whitish colored soils may be high in calcium, which can make soil too alkaline and/or indicate the presence of salts.

A grayish, clayey soil can signal an anaerobic condition—in which the soil has been saturated for long periods of time without exposure to air. These soils often smell rotten, or even moldy. These are the soils you can actually make pottery from!

Soil Jar Test

A simple "jar test" is one of the best ways to get an overall picture of the *texture* of soils within the rain garden zone. Soil particles can take a couple of days to separate in this test, so set it up first, then let it sit while you continue with the other tests.

After a couple of days, we can identify the soil types in the jar.

You will need:

- Wide-mouth canning jars (one for each test hole dug)
- Dishwashing liquid
- Windowsill, or out-of-the-way shelf space
- Notebook, pens, and pencils to record results
- Camera to take pictures of your results

To perform the test:

1. Combine soil from the different layers within a single test hole and fill a wide-mouth canning jar one-third to halfway full. Repeat this step for each hole you dug.

2. Add a few drops of dishwashing liquid and fill the jar with water, leaving a good inch (2.5cm) gap at the top. The dishwashing liquid will help to separate the soil particles faster; plain water works too, but the test takes longer.

3. Screw the lid on tightly, and shake for a good 5+ minutes. (This may be a good time to ask a buddy to prepare a rewarding cup of coffee or cocoa—whichever will bring feeling back into your arms after the shaking!)

4. At the end of the 5+ minutes, put the jar on the windowsill or shelf, and drink the cocoa or coffee you just earned. After only a few hours have passed, you will see that any sand has started to settle out. The finer particles will take longer: Clay can take up to a couple of days, and organic matter sometimes remains floating indefinitely.

5. The test is complete when the water at the top of the jar clears up to an acceptable level. Organic floaters are OK, but the water should be mostly transparent.

To measure the results:

Sand, silt, and clay are the three soil particles that we are testing for. Sand, the heaviest of the three, settles out on the bottom as visible sand, usually within a few minutes. Silt is the second to drop out, and if you have any in your soil, it will be in the second layer up. Clay is the finest material and will sit on the third layer up; individual clay particles are too tiny to make out with our eyes alone. Any organic matter will settle on top of the clay as uneven and random particles and doesn't need to be considered in this test. Sometimes (not too often) clay stays in suspension for a very long time. If your jar does not clear up for days, you may have suspended clay floating in the water. You will have to take this into consideration when you are thinking about what soil you have.

Once we can see each individual layer of soil particles in the jar, we can calculate the percentages for each type of particle. Not all samples will have all types of materials. So you have an idea of what to expect, do the soil ribbon test, described below.

Measure the thickness of each layer. If there are 6 total inches (15cm) of soil in the jar, and the sand layer on the bottom is 3 inches (7.5cm) thick, the middle layer of silt 1 inch (2.5cm), and the clay on top 2 inches (5cm), we can figure the percentage of each particle type by dividing the individual measurement by the overall number:

Sand: 3/6 = 0.5 = 50%
Silt: 1/6 = 0.17 = 17%
Clay: 2/6 = 0.3 = 33%

We can now look up these numbers on the Soil Triangle, shown here.

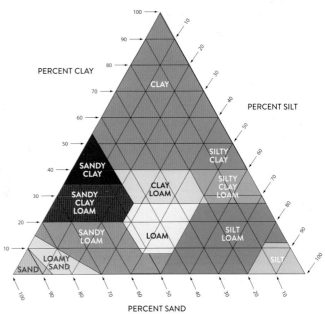

Based upon our percentages, the Soil Triangle says you have sandy clay loam. This is an almost perfect soil—you own a great property!

Soil that is 40-55 percent clay is considered clay soil even if it has another 45 percent sand or 60 percent silt. This is because clay is so influential for water retention and structure of soils. Pure clay has a bathtub effect in the garden—any hole we dig becomes a water container. Sand, on the other hand, does not define soil conditions this much, so only 90 percent or more sand with no or very little clay is considered pure sand soil. Pure sand is very hard to maintain; it does not hold water and does not compact. The less sand soils have, the better they cling to moisture and nutrients.

Silt is categorized as *pure silt* only if the mixture has a minimum of 80 percent silt, with less than 20 percent sand and/or less than 10 percent clay. Silt holds moisture and nutrients while allowing for some drainage. It is fine material and can compact, forming crusty layers on the surface.

Loam soils are a mix of sand, silt, and clay in a ratio that may vary; however, no one type of particle is dominant. It is generally loose, yet it holds a shape fairly well when moist and retains nutrients and water just enough to enable plants to draw them as needed. Loam soils drain well. Variants of loam soils include *clay loam*, which has more clay than the other two ingredients but is still a loose mix; *silty clay loam*, with more silt and clay than sand; *sandy clay loam*, with more sand and clay than silt; and so on. The more clay the loam has, the less it drains.

It is often said that loam soils are the best, but this depends on the soil's purpose. Clay and hardpan are best for building foundations on. For agriculture, though, loam soils are indeed the best. The sandier it is, the more irrigation it needs. Adding compost can reduce the need for watering,

as it will help hold the water in the ground. Clay loam, on the other hand, may be too slow to infiltrate and needs compost to improve the drainage. As you will see later, quality compost is a "magic" ingredient in the right amount, filling the gap in soil function.

Now that you have an idea of the soil texture from your jar test, try the ribbon test while on your site, to see if it matches your jar results and how it influences the structure of the soil.

Soil Ribbon Test

You'll need:

- Camera
- Garden gloves
- Your notebook, pens, and pencils

Pick up a small handful of your excavated soil in your bare hand, so you can feel the soil, moisten it, and try to sculpt it. If it forms a nice little sculpture and keeps its shape well, you might consider opening a pottery shop! If that wasn't your plan, however, don't despair: We'll let you know what to do with clay soil (see Bog Gardens in chapter 7).

The soil ribbon test reveals your soil type.

If the soil falls apart, try one more test. Slightly moisten the soil again (if it has dried out), and squeeze it between your thumb and index finger, creating a ribbon. If it forms a ribbon 2 inches (5cm) or longer, it is mostly clay. If you cannot shape a ribbon that long, that's your silty loam or loam. If no ribbon forms at all, it's sand or sandy loam. (See the Soil Triangle, above.)

Record the results in your notebook. The ribbon test's results are not as informative as those of the jar test, but this test will help you know what to expect from your soil.

Water Infiltration Test

This test establishes your soil type's rate of infiltration when it is wet, or the amount of time it takes for the soil to drain standing water, which will tell you what size your rain garden will need to be. The best time to do it is during the rainy season. Depending on your soil and its moisture level, drainage tests can take several hours to complete.

The jury's still out on the best and most foolproof technique for testing infiltration, but we prefer the PVC pipe method described below whenever it is possible. It ensures that you're measuring only the gravitational infiltration of the water and not side seepage from the surrounding soil. This method will give you a lower infiltration rate than you would get without a pipe, which means you will know that the final rain garden can infiltrate only better than expected and never worse. Consider that sometimes a rain garden's sides get altered: A road is built close by, or the nearby areas get very wet, even saturated, for one reason or another. When that happens, side seepage no longer functions, so if we based our plan on a measurement that included such seepage, the rain garden would likely overflow more and pond longer than we planned for.

———— • • ————

TIP People often tell us they have the perfect spot for a rain garden: a wet spot that is mucky even in July. Actually these are not good rain garden sites! The fact that the ground is wet even in the dry months tells us this spot's soils are draining less than 0.1 inch (3mm) per hour and/or the water table is very high. The area can still be used to filter runoff and add a functional garden to the landscape, but it should not be made into a rain garden.

———— • • ————

You'll need:

- PVC pipe 6 inches (15cm) or wider by 30 inches (76cm) or longer, so it can be placed into the hole and removed easily
- Yardstick, or measuring tape that can be locked when extended
- Timer or watch
- Garden gloves
- Hose or bucket
- Notebook, pens, and pencils
- Camera

To do the test:

1. Insert one end of the pipe into the test hole, securing it firmly in the loosened soil.
2. Using the hose or bucket, fill the pipe to the top, three times. Each time, let the water fully infiltrate, i.e., drain away.
3. Place the yardstick or extended and locked tape measure in the pipe, and fill it a fourth time. Record the initial height of the water.
4. For the first hour, record the water level every 10 minutes.
5. After the first hour, record the water level every hour, until the whole pipe is drained.

6. Repeat the entire process two more times, and record the results.

To calculate your results:

For each of the three measuring cycles, divide the distance the water dropped by the number of hours it took. For example:

1st Test: 12 hours to infiltrate / 12 inches (30.5cm) of water: Your soil infiltrated water at a rate of 1 inch (2.5cm) per hour.

2nd Test: 12 hours to infiltrate / 11 inches (28cm) of water: Your soil infiltrated water at a rate of 0.92 inch (23mm) per hour.

3rd Test: 12 hours to infiltrate / 10 inches (25cm) of water: Your soil infiltrated water at a rate of 0.83 inch (21mm) per hour.

Test hole, PVC pipe, yardstick, and hose—you're ready for testing!

The three numbers from the three separate tests may vary, as they did here. You want an average, so add them up and divide the result by three.

1+0.92+0.83 = 2.75

2.75 ÷ 3 = 0.92 (23mm)

If you find that infiltration is very slow (less than 0.3 inch, 8mm, per hour) or very fast (over 6 inches, 15cm, per hour)—possibly suspicious, in other words—move 5 or 6 feet (2m) from the original drainage test hole if you can, dig again, and repeat the testing processes to ensure you really are looking at a suitable location. This is especially recommended if you are on a site with high clay content and poor drainage.

———— • • ————

TIP **The amount of time it takes for the water to infiltrate depends on the texture of your soil: A sandier soil will drain faster, possibly within a few hours, while a more clay-heavy soil could take up to 12 hours to drain completely. Be sure to fill the pipe completely each time—as the water infiltrates the soil, the soil becomes more saturated, potentially slowing the total drainage time.**

———— • • ————

In the Northwest, especially around Puget Sound, soil with a rate of 0.5 inch (13mm) or greater infiltration per hour is considered well-draining soil. Less than that is considered poorly draining soil. This test hole has an infiltration rate of 0.92 inch per hour and is therefore well-draining soil. This is the figure you will use to size your rain garden in chapter 4, Planning and Design.

What Does Your Infiltration Rate Mean?

Well-draining soil is considered to have an infiltration rate of 0.5 inch (13mm) per hour or higher. Soil that drains at 0.25–0.5 inch (6–13mm) per hour is considered *poorly draining*. An infiltration rate

Measuring infiltration rate

of 0.15–0.25 inch (4–6mm) may be OK but may also mean that water will pond for extended periods during the wet season.

A rate of 0.1 inch (3mm) per hour means your soil is *non-draining*. If the infiltration rate is that low, the site is really not a good rain garden location. Sometimes a professional engineer can help improve challenging soil conditions with innovative technology, but for DIY rain garden builders, a spot with a rate of 0.1 inch per hour is not suitable for a rain garden. Consider using it for a built wetland or wet bog garden instead (see chapter 7, Smarter Gardening and Other LID Techniques).

Water Table

The water table is formed by water seeping into the ground and saturating it; it is essentially standing water within the soil. The depth of this layer can fluctuate, depending on the weather and the season. In clay or poorly draining soils, the

INFILTRATION TEST RESULTS

Less than 0.1 inch (3mm) per hour	0.1–0.25 inch (3–6mm) per hour	0.25–0.5 inch (6–13mm) per hour	More than 0.5 inch (13mm) per hour
Non-draining	Very poorly draining	Poorly draining	Well-draining
Soil is not draining enough to build a rain garden. A non-infiltrating bog garden can be created for habitat interest.	Very slowly, very poorly draining soil. A rain garden here may function as an infiltrating bog garden; during the rainy season it will regularly overflow and continue to pond.	Poorly draining soil. The rain garden will regularly pond and infiltrate, occasionally overflowing during the rainy season.	Well-draining soil. The rain garden will infiltrate and may never or rarely pond. Overflow may never occur, but is still necessary as a backup for the design.

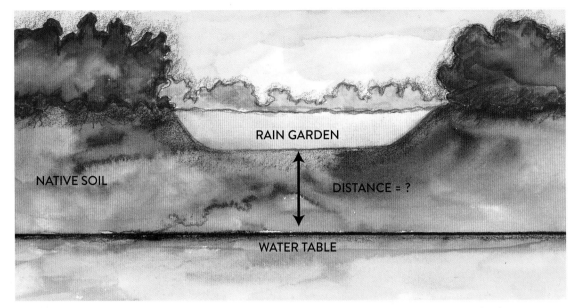

NATIVE SOIL

RAIN GARDEN

DISTANCE = ?

WATER TABLE

The distance from the bottom of the rain garden to the top of the water table is critical because saturated soil cannot infiltrate water from the rain garden.

water table is sometimes right up at the surface during rainy seasons or snowmelts. Knowing where the water table's highest level is during the wet season is important, because soil that is saturated cannot absorb more water. Building the base of the rain garden too close to the top of the water table can lead to failure, because the water will have no place to infiltrate to. Your jurisdiction may have regulations about this. So be sure to conduct the following test during the wet season or during snowmelt.

JURISDICTIONAL NOTE: Some jurisdictions require the excavated bottom of the rain garden and the top of the highest water table level during the wet season to be a specific distance apart. It can vary from 3 to 5 feet (91cm–1.5m), depending on where you are in the Northwest, but it is important to get this number from your local authorities. Keep in mind, also, that

your jurisdiction may make information available about water table depths. If so, it is safe to rely on that data—you do not need to test the water table yourself.

You'll definitely want to check the water table if:

- You are near a creek or a lake
- You are at the bottom of a slope or in a valley
- Your or your neighbors' property often has standing water during any season, or drainage is a problem
- The planning department says you may have drainage problems
- A wetland or bog existed in the area before development

Note that if you are on a hill or hilltop, or a site where everything is always dry and plants never seem to get enough water, this test is not necessary.

You will need:

- Pointed shovel
- Posthole digger
- Rock bar
- Trowel
- Auger (optional)
- Camera
- Gardening gloves
- Bucket or piece of plywood

To do the test:

Your rain garden will likely not be deeper than 30 inches (76cm)—the ideal DIY depth—so dig your original test hole an additional 1–3 feet (30-91cm) deeper, depending on your jurisdictional water table regulations and how clayey or sandy your soil is. For example, if the rain garden must be 3 feet above the water table, your hole should be 30 inches + 3 feet deep (total 1.7m).

If you feel like digging a hole 5.5 feet deep with a posthole digger or auger is a daunting test, you are correct—it takes time! If your soil is mostly clay and/or rocks, having the neighborhood teenagers help you makes a difference, so order that pizza! In sandy soils this will not take that long, but the hole may not hold up very well, since sandy soils are loose and will likely keep falling back into the hole.

Cover the top of the hole with an upside-down bucket or a piece of plywood, and wait to see whether the hole fills with water over a period of a few days. Reviewing your soil layer colors should also provide clues to the presence or lack of water. Water table levels may be fluctuating. It is possible that at the time you are digging the test hole, the water table is low, but during heavy rains it moves up. You can see evidence of this periodical inundation if the soil in the test hole is mottled, meaning discolored patches and blotches are present all over the soil layer you are excavating.

If you are testing during a dry period (maybe the winter is a dry one, or you are testing before or after the rainy season), you will have to study the soil carefully for color, smell, and other signs of periodic flooding. Again, review your soil test notes. You might want to hire a professional for this step if you are uncertain about what you are looking at.

What Does This Mean for Your Rain Garden?

If water pools 4 feet (1.2m) below the surface, your water table is 4 feet below ground and will be 18 inches (46cm) below the bottom of a 30-inch-deep (76cm) rain garden. If your jurisdiction allows that distance between the water table and rain garden, you can go ahead and design your rain garden for this site. If a minimum distance of 3 feet (91cm) distance is required, you will need to come up with another plan, such as turning the rain garden into a bog garden that infiltrates (see Bog Gardens in chapter 7).

If your jurisdiction does not have an applicable code, use your judgment. In soils with high clay content, we recommend keeping the distance to 3 feet (91cm) and in sandy soils to 1 foot (30.5cm). Rain gardens with the water table very close to them will not drain fast and will behave as bogs.

DETERMINE RUNOFF AMOUNT FROM CONTRIBUTION AREAS

Once you have your soil data, take another really good look at the entire site. You now understand how topography is influencing water flow, where the utilities are, what soils are in the yard, and how the soils infiltrate. But what is the total water flow-contributing area? In other words, what surfaces will the rain garden be collecting the water from, and how big are they?

Contributing areas could include the entire roof of the house and/or garage, or just part of it, the driveway, even the lawn. Urban lawns are typically compacted areas, unlike healthy meadows, and are almost as impervious as a compacted gravel driveway. This causes rain to sheet-flow across them instead of being absorbed into them.

You'll need:

- 50/100-foot (15.2/30.5m) measuring tape or a measuring wheel
- Anchors (e.g., rocks or a helper) to secure the ends of the tape
- Notebook, pens, pencils

Unfortunately, not every surface whose area you need to calculate will be in the shape of a neat rectangle. For easier calculating, you may want to divide irregularly shaped areas into approximate triangles, rectangles, or circles whose area can be computed separately and then all added together.

Typical contributing areas are shown in brown.

Roof

If you will be utilizing any rooftop runoff, for example, by capturing it through your (permitted!) disconnected downspouts (downspout disconnection means that you physically remove the gutter section from the in-ground downspout

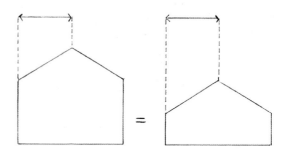

How to measure the area covered by the roof. The pitch does not matter, just the area covered.

connector and channel the water into another structure, swale or pipe, to use it as your inflow for the rain garden), you'll need to determine the amount of that contribution. So, is there any difference in measuring a flat roof vs. a peaked one? Nope! The reason is that you're not measuring the area of the roof itself, which would be greater for a peaked roof, but rather the amount of ground area it covers, which is equivalent to the footprint of the building the roof is on, *plus any overhangs such as eaves*.

Ground Surfaces—Lawn, Driveway, Walkways

Measure the driveway, the lawn, and every other ground surface whose runoff you plan to direct into the rain garden. Remember, these flows must be propelled by force of gravity alone, so the surfaces need to slope toward the rain garden if you are to collect runoff from them.

If you have any paved areas such as walkways or driveways that slope away from the rain garden, but you would like to capture that runoff as well, one design option is to cut a trough into the concrete to collect and channel the water toward the catchment area. Perhaps add a decorative grate to the top of the trough.

Adding a decorative grate to cover a channel

There are other ways to direct runoff from a driveway that does not slope directly toward the rain garden, but you should consult a professional about them. These scenarios may include a site where the rain garden is at a higher elevation than the in-ground downspout connection, or where the topography between the house and the rain garden is mounded. A professional can help you find a suitable solution and design it for you; we do not recommend that you tackle such scenarios on your own.

Once you have totaled up your surface area numbers, you can settle on the size of rain garden you will need (see Calculating Rain Garden Volume in chapter 4). Most people would like to filter all of the runoff they generate on their site. If this is too complicated for one garden, or if there is not enough space for a rain garden of the required size, you can always think about dividing the rain garden into two or more individual ones.

YOUR SUMMARY SITE ASSESSMENT

All of the data you've collected throughout this chapter will provide you with the basic information you'll need to move forward with design. To review, make sure you have done all of the following:

- Contacted your relevant local jurisdiction, conservation district, etc., about requirements that apply to your project
- Researched resources and incentive programs
- Documented *everything* with photos
- Walked around your neighborhood, talked to your neighbors
- Measured the grade of any slopes
- Mapped and measured the yard, including structures and substantial vegetation
- Called 811, located utility lines, and added them to your map
- Assessed your prospective site in terms of inflow and overflow, and determined the size of all contributing areas
- Measured the available yard space
- Determined the site's soil type and drainage rate (perform soil tests and drainage tests, check the water table)
- Determined permitting needs

Now let's get to the creative part—design!

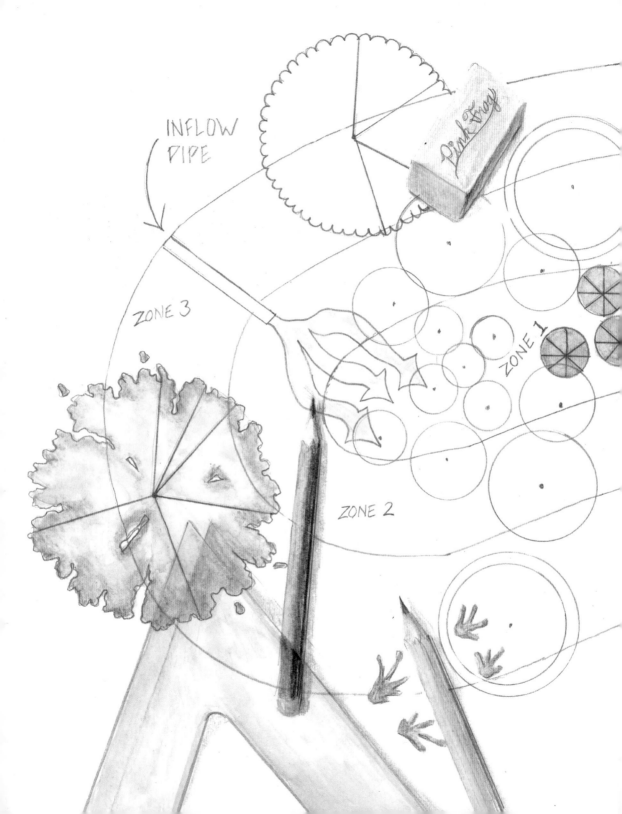

CHAPTER 4

ZONE 3

ZONE 2

OVERFLOW

Planning and Design: Get Your Pen and Paper Ready

The planning and assessment process outlined in the previous chapter helped you understand your neighborhood and yard, and how a rain garden sited there would behave. Designing will fill in the specific details of your rain garden's dimensions and shape: You will integrate all the information and data you have gathered, and it will finally all make sense to you. You will also calculate exactly how much material you need to bring in, such as soil, compost, and rocks, as well as material for any retaining walls, piping, or swales, and order the materials. You don't want to be running back and forth from Lowe's on installation weekend!

CALCULATING RAIN GARDEN VOLUME

The first step in designing your rain garden is to calculate its volume and how much stormwater runoff it will be able to filter. To do this, refer to the following information you've gathered in your notebook:

- The measured total area of your roof(s), your driveway, and any other surface you want to direct runoff from
- The average infiltration rate as measured with your test hole, and whether your soil is poorly draining (less than 0.5 inch, 13mm, per hour) or well draining (more than 0.5 inch per hour)

- The size of the area available for a rain garden.

How to Use the Rain Garden Sizing Table

The rain garden soil mix depth for each possible garden in this table is calculated at 18 inches (46cm). This is the minimum required depth for the soil mix in the rain garden, because pollution removal happens best if the water has time to sit (for more on soil mix, see Rain Garden Mix later in this chapter). Without at least this much soil, the water may not be maximally filtered. An 18-inch soil layer also allows for better root development, which means that plants can use the water below the surface for transpiration faster, since plants need well-developed root structure for adequate transpiration to take place, or they will not be able to pull the water from the ground.

The first column shows the size of the top of your rain garden's ponding area (Zone 1) as a percentage of the size of the contributing area made up of roof(s), lawn, and/or driveway. (Remember, the rain garden will have sides, Zone 2, and a top edge, Zone 3, and will be larger than the ponding area itself.)

Using 1,000 square feet (93m^2) as a sample size for the total contributing area, we end up with a 100 square foot (9.3m^2) ponding area. Moving right, we see that if your soil is poorly

RAIN GARDEN SIZING TABLE

All percentages apply to a rain garden soil mix 18 inches (46cm) deep and a ponding depth of 6 inches (15cm).

Size of ponding area as a percentage of total contributing area	Percentage of annual rainfall held in the rain garden in poorly-draining soils (less than 0.5 inch per hour)	Percentage of annual rainfall held in the rain garden in well-draining soils (0.5 inch or more per hour)
10%	70%	99%
20%	90%	100%
50%	99%	100%
80%	100%	100%

This table is based on data created by Curtis Hinman in 2003–2005 at Washington State University's Puyallup Extension and the Stormwater Center. It is a good reference guide for many DIY projects across the Pacific Northwest, and for other locales with similar site conditions, soils, and precipitation amounts and patterns.

draining, your 100-square-foot ponding area will infiltrate 70 percent of the annual precipitation. The overflow will function often during heavy storm events and large snow melts. If, however, your soil is well-draining, the same size ponding area will infiltrate 99 percent of the annual precipitation, which means the overflow will be active only intermittently. This is true whether you're on the east or the west side of the Cascades (see sidebar, Seasonally Heavy Loads, in this chapter).

What if you decide to make the ponding area 50 percent of the contributing area, or 500 square feet (46.5m²)? This means even your poorly-draining soil will infiltrate 99 percent of the annual precipitation. The overflow may or may not ever kick in, as most of the runoff will be absorbed (though you still need a well-designed overflow,

just in case). If your soil is well draining, your 500 square foot ponding area will infiltrate the full 100 percent of the annual precipitation. But again, to be on the safe side, don't skimp on the overflow design and size.

The sizing given in the table provides for a rain garden that will drain the water away from the ponding area in a maximum of three days (72 hours) *once the rain stops*. Note the word "stops": In a weekslong stormy period, the rain garden may in fact pond for that whole time, but that does not mean it's failing. That also does not mean it will never overflow; overflow drainage is there for exactly this purpose. The calculations in this table provide lots of buffer room within the percentages established, however, so rain gardens using this table will be slightly oversized and will function well even in record rain events.

FURTHER RESOURCES FOR DETERMINING RAIN GARDEN VOLUMES

The 2013 *Rain Garden Handbook for Western Washington: A Guide for Design, Installation, and Maintenance*, produced by Washington State University Extension, is a good additional resource for property owners needing to meet the minimum rain garden sizing requirements for west of the Cascades; its tables are easy to use and consider the different precipitation amounts. If your project is a small construction requiring a permit, use this handbook for reference in order to comply with Western Washington permit requirements.

Portland area rain garden builders should consult *The Oregon Rain Garden Guide: Landscaping for Clean Water and Healthy Streams*, published by Oregon State University, when sizing the rain garden.

Eastern Washington property owners can reference the *Eastern Washington Low Impact Development Guidance Manual*, or Stormwater Management Manuals available through their local jurisdictions.

It is really amazing what a difference it makes whether soils are well or poorly draining. And yet, even in poorly draining soils, a rain garden sized at just 10 percent of the contributing area, with soil mix only 18 inches (46cm) deep, can absorb 70 percent of the annual rainfall. Nature is truly remarkable.

SEASONALLY HEAVY LOADS

Remember that while the west of the Cascades is rainier, the east receives more snow. This snowpack is an important difference. When the weather warms and the snow suddenly melts, rain gardens on the east side of the mountains receive large volumes of runoff all at once, volumes similar to a "pineapple express" storm (lots of atmospheric moisture coming north from the warm waters near the Hawaiian Islands, often referred to as "atmospheric rivers" by meteorologists). Therefore, rain gardens on the east and west sides of the Cascades will have similarly intense loads overall, although these happen at different times and seasons.

Remember, the ponding area is only *part* of the overall rain garden, so now you can play with the sizing. For a 100 square foot (9.3m²) ponding area, you will need a 5 foot (1.5m) or wider Zone 2 section all around it. As you will see in the next section, that means a 20 foot (6m) by 20 foot or larger center for Zones 1 and 2. Zone 3 is still additional to this center size.

Do not despair if you have a smaller yard. The sizing charts in the handbook provided by your local jurisdiction may allow for smaller rain gardens. For example, in some areas in Seattle, you can use as little as 2.8 percent of the contributing area for your ponding area. Check with your planning department and their reference sizing charts as you design your rain garden.

CALCULATING TOTAL AREA: FROM THE BOTTOM UP

It is easy to confuse the overall size of the rain garden with the size of the ponding area, and sizing tables refer to the ponding area only. Now you will learn to calculate the size of the *entire* rain garden—ponding, sloped sides, and top edge included.

Depth

From the bottom up, the rain garden is made of several layers:

Bioretention or rain garden soil mix: 12–24 inches (30.5–61cm), ideally 18 inches (46cm). If your soil is very well draining (several inches per hour) and is mostly sand, you can use 12 inches of bioretention soil mix; if it is mostly clay and drains around .3 inch (8mm) per hour only, you should plan on using 24 inches of bioretention soil mix.

Woody mulch: 3–4 inches (7.5–10cm) deep, mimicking the forest duff layer.

Ponding: 3–6 inches (7.5–15cm). The typical ponding depth used is 6 inches (15cm), but in some scenarios, such as a rain garden at a daycare center, where little ones will be tempted to run around in the water when ponding, 3 inches (7.5 cm) is used.

Freeboard: Usually 3 inches (7.5cm). This extra height above the ponding surface provides backup protection in case there is a very, *very* large storm or snowmelt event.

Berm: A mound around the top edge, if needed. This means that the overall depth of the rain garden excavation, even if no berm is needed, is somewhere between 21 inches and 36 inches (53–91cm) deep. That is a good-sized hole!

JURISDICTIONAL NOTE: Deeper is not always better, and beyond a certain depth it doesn't provide more benefits. The deeper the soil mix layer, the deeper the hole you will have to dig, and, depending on your jurisdiction, that depth

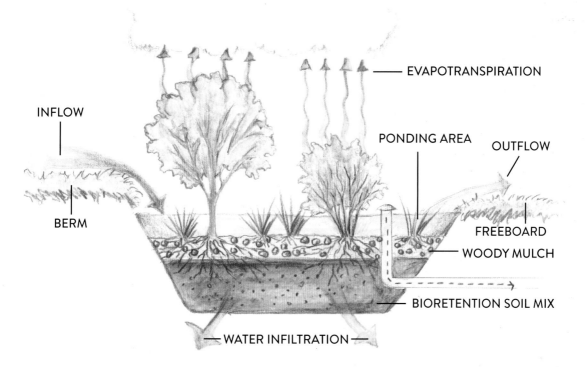

INFLOW

BERM

EVAPOTRANSPIRATION

PONDING AREA

OUTFLOW

FREEBOARD

WOODY MULCH

BIORETENTION SOIL MIX

WATER INFILTRATION

Proper material depths are critical to sound rain garden function.

may trigger the need for a grading permit. We usually recommend that if, because of jurisdiction, slope situation, or site conditions, the soil mix layer needs to be more than 24 inches (61cm) thick, the rain garden should be designed—and, if necessary, built—by a professional.

Sloped Sides

Now that you have determined the ponding area of the rain garden as well as its depth, you can figure out the slope of its sides. Remember what we said regarding the size of the rain garden? If the bottom of the rain garden needs to be 100 square feet (9.3m²), how big is the rain garden actually going to be in the yard?

It is not recommended to dig vertical sides for the rain garden, unless it is being done by a professional who understands how to ensure that the sides will not collapse. Your DIY rain garden will have sloping sides.

A comfortable slope is 3:1, meaning for every 3 horizontal feet (91cm), the slope rises by 1 foot (30.5cm). (In the percentage method we used earlier, this is expressed as a 33.3 percent grade.) This is a shallow slope, so the rain garden will be large, even with a small ponding area. The steepest slope we recommend for a DIY project is 2:1, which elevates 1 foot (30.5cm) for every 2 horizontal feet (61cm)—in other words, a 50 percent slope. If you have room in your landscape, you can always make the rain garden larger by extending

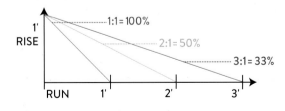

Slope ratios

the sides with even less of a slope than 3:1. But this is only a good idea if there is enough space for it.

Let's say that you are calculating the total size of the future rain garden with a 10 foot by 10 foot (3m × 3m) bottom area. You want to keep the garden to the minimum possible size, so you've chosen a slope of 2:1. You also know it will be filled with 18 inches (46cm) of rain garden mix and 3 inches (7.5cm) of mulch, and it will allow for 6 inches (15cm) of ponding depth with 3 inches (7.5cm) of freeboard. That equals 30 inches (76cm) total depth. Therefore, we need 60 inches (1.5m) for the sloped sides, or 5 feet (1.5m) all around the ponding area.

Adding up rain garden zones 1 and 2, then, you will need to allow 20 feet (6m) by 20 feet.

Top Edge

Again, the top edge plantings, or Zone 3, are an additional area added to the size of the rain garden (such as the sloped sides example noted just above). But for those you can choose a size that fits your landscaping, unless the area is a berm with a fixed size. The zone can simply fit with what looks good in the rest of the landscape.

Berms

If your site slopes less than you need to create the bowl that runoff can fill at level (water always seeks level!), you will need or want a berm around your rain garden.

In your design, the berm should be wide enough to be stable. If the soil can be compacted well, with high clay content (clay loam or more clay), this usually means at least three times as wide as it is high, with the sides sloping toward ground in a ratio no steeper than 1:1, which elevates 1 foot (30.5cm) for every 1 horizontal foot (30.5cm)—in other words, a 100 percent slope. The top of the berm should be established based on how steep the slope is; it will be higher on steeper sites. You will have to calculate the rise of the slope and build a berm that provides the needed rise to hold the runoff when it is ponding. This, too, will add to the overall size of the rain garden.

The best berms are made of soils with high clay content. What is your soil type? Maybe you can use the soil excavated from the rain garden basin for this berm.

Terraces

If you are building your rain garden on a slope that is steeper than 5 percent (1:20) but less than 10 percent (1:10), it is best to *terrace* the rain garden rather than building a very large berm on the lower side of the slope. A terraced rain garden is made of multiple cells, of which the upper one (or more) flows into the lower: you will essentially build two (or more) smaller rain gardens instead of one larger one. These will need smaller berms, and you'll end up with a

By using terracing, this small urban site became a large, multi-celled rain garden.

shallower rain garden that often better fits the scale of a typical urban site. Because of the smaller scale, it is also easier to maintain and care for.

As long as your slope is less than 10 percent and your jurisdiction does not have any limiting codes relating to terraced rain gardens, you will be able to build one yourself. If you feel unsure about the design, however, ask a professional to look over yours or create a design for you.

THE POWER OF ANNUAL INFILTRATION

How much rain will this rain garden of ours treat, filter, and infiltrate? For an example, the urban Puget Sound area just outside the city of Seattle has an average rainfall of about 40 inches (1m) a year, or 3.3 feet. If your rain garden is collecting runoff from a 1,000 square foot (93m^2) roof surface, that equals 3,300 cubic feet (94m^3) of runoff. One cubic foot is 7.48 gallons (28.3L), so 3,300 cubic feet equals 24,684 gallons of rain. That is more than 100,000 liters of rain a year.

Terracing has a few tricks to it. Think about the following as you design the system:

- The overflow from the lowest rain garden should be as far as possible from the inflow into the highest one.
- The vertical underdrain (see Vertical Underdrain in chapter 4), if used, should be placed in the lowest rain garden.
- The overflow from the upper cell to the lower cell(s) has to cross through the terrace. Pay attention so the pipe or rock-lined opening at the top of the berm really drains from one to the other as intended, is straight and predictable, and is easy to maintain on both ends.

This terraced rain garden has overflow pipes and a vertical drain in the lowest cell.

This slope was too steep for a rain garden, so it has been reinforced with CompostSoxx and made usable for planting.

Terraced rain gardens need solid walls to separate each cell from the next. Terracing can be done with rocks, concrete blocks, or DuraSoxx (a variety of "compost soxx" solution, see Resources). Freestanding terraces are best built using concrete, DuraSoxx, or, if those are not available, logs. Most rocks and blocks require backfill behind them and typically have to lean against something, unless the wall is very low. Terrace walls can sometimes double as weirs to slow the water flow.

Terracing Materials: Rocks or Concrete Blocks

If you use rocks, their size depends on the type of rock they are, and the size of the terrace wall being built. They have to be able to stand solidly, essentially forming a berm. Your rock supplier should be able to provide the details

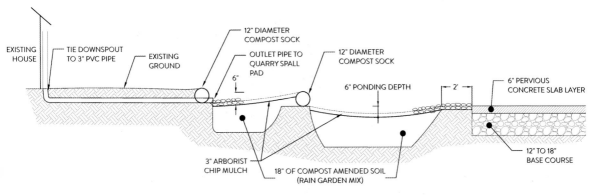

Cross-section of a terraced rain garden using CompostSoxx to berm (Rendering by Derek Hann, P.E.)

and reference material you need, but remember, you need angular and large enough rocks to build a wall with. Cobblestones will not be good for this purpose. The same goes for concrete blocks: The type of block and the size of the wall determine the number of blocks needed and the pattern they will have to be stacked in.

Terracing Materials: DuraSoxx

DuraSoxx are tubes filled with compost, compost and sand, or a specified soil mix. The tubes' textile material is basically stable, but it is susceptible to UV, which can break it down in six to eight years if not planted. This is why these Soxx are always planted with vegetation, in some areas with grasses and in others with woody groundcovers. *The plant cover will ensure that the material lasts indefinitely.* They stack fairly easily, particularly if you can get them prefilled. If you can't get them prefilled, you can purchase them from Filtrexx, the manufacturer (see Resources) and fill them at home. Use your own homemade rain garden mix or order soil mix (see Rain Garden Mix, later in this chapter).

To fill the Soxx, you will need a large, utility-size wide-mouth funnel (you can make this yourself using an empty 2-liter, or larger, plastic bottle) and lots and lots of patience. You will also need friends to help you maneuver the sections as you fill them. One-piece sections for each layer are best; shorter blocks work but must be placed in a crisscross, staggered fashion. As the rain garden plants grow roots over a few years, they will anchor the Soxx in place while shading them from UV rays. If you have a way to purchase or get the Soxx to you prefilled, take advantage of that option!

Do not use straw tubes (also called straw wattles) as terracing walls, because they break down within weeks and will not hold the rain garden behind the line. Burlap will also break down within a few months.

Logs

You can use logs to create terraces. Plan on securing them to the ground with rebar drilled and hammered into them so they do not move by the force of either the backfill or the water. This means you have to drill through the logs and, using rebar longer then the diameter of the log, hammer it through the hole and into the ground at least as deep as the log is wide. Wooden stakes will rot away fast. We recommend using rebar in the logs for longer-lasting solutions.

If you use Soxx for the terracing, you have to secure them as well. The Soxx must be planted so they are protected from UV. The plants will grow roots through the Soxx in a few years and anchor the Soxx in place. If you cannot afford rebar or have stakes on hand already and your Soxx are just one row high and water does not move against them, you can use wooden stakes securing the Soxx in place and plant deeper-rooted woody groundcovers of even small shrubs into the Soxx for stronger root structure. As the wooden stakes rot away, the roots will take hold in the ground and anchor the single-layer Soxx in place.

Shape

We can of course play with the exact shape of the rain garden. It can be an oval, a bean, a circle, a rectangle, or even a triangle, as long as the specific areas remain the right size.

When drawing and measuring your rain garden shape into your design plan, breaking down oddly shaped areas into more regular (and easier to measure) shapes such as squares, triangles, or circles will help you maintain the correct proportions. You can fudge the corners between them if you are not a confident illustrator.

DESIGNING INFLOW AND OVERFLOW

In Chapter 3, we considered inflow and overflow in relation to the natural contours of the site and where we might place each. At this stage, it's time to calculate the dimensions and determine the exact location of the inflow and overflow.

If you are channeling runoff from multiple surfaces, perhaps from a roof with several downspouts, you can consider creating multiple inflows. We've seen condo owners create inflows from every stall in a small parking lot into the rain garden.

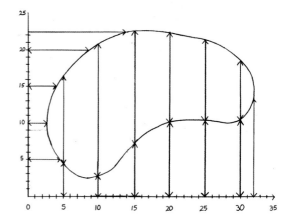

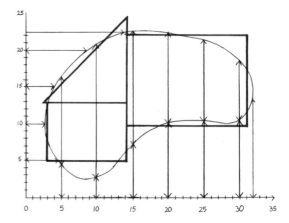

To make calculating an area easier, break it down into geometric shapes that roughly fill the space. Calculate the area of each shape and add the areas together. This will give you a good estimate of the area.

Likewise, you may have two or more overflow systems, such as a vertical underdrain overflow control structure (see Vertical Underdrain, below) paired with a simple, wide, rock-lined area allowing the water to spread out into the landscape, to help during very heavy rain or sudden snowmelts. Dividing the overflow into multiple channels will minimize erosion, the load on the sewer system, and the amount of water flowing across the sidewalk or street. If the rain garden soil is poorly draining and the garden receives runoff from roofs, driveways, and lawns totaling more than 1,500 square feet (139m²), and it sits close to a sidewalk or a right of way, having two or more overflow exits can help during very heavy rain or snowmelt events.

Sometimes tight space or other constraints require complicated solutions. If you feel unsure about the decisions you are making, you do not see a practical way to move runoff into the rain garden, or you just cannot find a good overflow location, call a professional to help you with the design.

Inflow

The route water takes to the rain garden, whether it's from drainpipes, the lawn, or impermeable surfaces, needs to have a slight slope or the water will sit and not flow well. The slope should be 2–4 percent, which will ensure that the water flows fast enough and does not clog the pipe or the swale. A 2 percent slope means the grade drops .25 inch (6mm) for every foot (30.5cm) of horizontal distance; a 4 percent slope drops .5 inch (13mm) for

Inflow pipes coming into the rain garden with a vertical overflow control structure in place

every foot. With just 2 percent slope to the inflow, you can safely move your runoff into the rain garden and your inflow will not have to be dug in too deeply. Four percent will not increase velocity (the speed of the water) to the point of severe erosion, but a drop in the inflow steeper than 4 percent may require flow control, weirs, or other means to slow the water.

In your design you have to consider how far the rain garden is from the various contributing areas. Given a slope to our inflow of up to 4 percent, and the requirement that the overflow be lower than the inflow, the farther away we are from the contributing surface, the deeper the rain garden will have to be. In some cases this can mean a very big pit in the yard. It can even become too deep for safe excavation and function if it leads to a ponding area deeper than 12 inches (30.5cm).

Here is an example for how deep inflow can be sometimes: If you are calculating the slope for the inflow at 4 percent, and your rain garden is 30 feet (9.1m) away from the house, the inflow will be 15 inches (38cm) deep from the yard's surface level with no site slope. (If your site slopes, this depth is

Inflow trench running from disconnected downspout to underneath the concrete walkway

Driveway inflow created by a gap designed into the metal barrier

going to be less of course.) That means that even if we only use 12 inches (30.5cm) of rain garden mix in the rain garden, the overall minimum depth of the dig will still be 45 inches (114cm). And the finished rain garden will have a minimum of 21 inches (53cm) between the ground level and the top of the mulch layer.

Calculate your inflow based on both a 2 percent and a 4 percent grade. If you have a longer distance from your contributing area to your rain garden, using a 4 percent slope for the inflow can make your inflow arrive in the rain garden very deep. Since your rain garden will be at least 30 inches deeper than your inflow elevation, such depth can make for a very deep rain garden basin. In these cases, use only 2 percent slope for the inflow, to reduce the overall depth of the excavation and finished rain garden.

Types of Inflow

Ways to move water into the rain garden can include in-ground pipes (necessary if installing over utility lines), open-planted or rock-lined swales, or a combination of these methods. To decide what type of inflow is best to use, think about the type of surface you are connecting to. Are you disconnecting a downspout for the project? (Remember, you may need a permit for that.) And is the rain garden fairly close to the downspout? If yes, it is best to use a pipe for the inflow. Will the area between the downspout and the rain garden be used as a walkway? As a lawn? Another type of landscaping? You may need to use a pipe so as not to interfere with the other uses for this area, and tunnel underneath an existing walkway or driveway. If, on the other hand, the rain garden is farther away from the downspout and there is no other planned use for the space, you may want to create more interest and use a swale.

If the rain garden will collect roof runoff, the water will enter the inflow from the home's gutter system through the downspout disconnected from the sewer. The disconnected flow must be channeled away from the building in a pipe or in a swale. A swale, near the building or structure, must be lined with an impervious layer, such as a pond liner with felt underlay above and below it. The felt underlay is a thick material manufactured to protect the expensive pond liner from puncture damages and cuts. The pipe or swale must carry the water at least 10 feet (3m) away from a building with a basement and 5 feet (1.5m) without a basement—or whatever your jurisdiction requires. This means that a swale inflow should not be infiltrating the water until this distance from the building is reached. Past this point, the swale no longer needs a liner.

If pipes move the water into the rain garden, plan to install *cleanouts* for maintenance if your inflow pipe is longer than 40 feet (12.2m) or has curves in it, or if the roof has lots of debris on it regularly. A cleanout is a T built into the pipe with a removable cap. You can easily open these caps, run a hose into the pipe, and flush it out, preventing clogging. Mark these cleanout spots on your design, and place them where they will not be in the way and can easily be used.

The best inflow systems help remove fine particulates from the runoff using rocks, plants, and/or maybe even grass or other low-growing groundcover vegetation. The fine sediment particles will cling to the rocks and the plants and stay within the inflow area instead of washing into the rain garden.

It is always a good idea to incorporate some art into your inflow if you can. Consider channeling water onto hard surfaces first, so there is

A "dry creek"–style decorative swale moves water while improving the area next to the walk.

PIPES TO LAST

If your inflow or overflow will use pipes, the best pipe material is Schedule 40, 4-inch (10cm) diameter. These pipes are thick enough that they will not crack under foot traffic or even personal vehicles. Do *not* use the black corrugated pipe that is sold for drainage work: This piping ages fast, starts to crumble, collapses under regular walking or small-vehicle traffic, and clogs up easily with sediment.

Inflow pipes are connected to two downspouts to capture maximum roof runoff.

feels like a seasonal creek. You can add metal or ceramic fish, or colored garden balls, some garden statuary—whatever your creativity calls for, really. A bridge or large rock steps across it is not only fun but useful if you need a path over the inflow. Connecting the different parts of a landscape with paths creates interest and involvement, fosters ownership, and simplifies maintenance.

————— • • —————

TIP There are alternative ways to shrink the distance between a rain garden and the runoff source. Several smaller rain gardens may be connected to each other in what professionals call a *treatment train*, or a narrower rain garden, also called an *infiltrating swale*, can be created.

————— • • —————

Overflow

No matter how well functioning a rain garden we build, overflow will happen; it is truly just a matter of time and record rainfall. Typically, overflow is dealt with by directing it in one of four ways: through a pipe; through wide areas, allowing for sheet flow; through a swale; or through a vertical underdrain. The choice depends on what you are draining the overflow into.

Pipe

If you want to route overflow *into* a pipe, perhaps connecting back to your original downspout drainage system, use a pipe for the overflow. The pipe can simply be placed at the right elevation in the side of the rain garden and directed to the drainage system. Make sure the pipe slopes to the drainage system and not the other way around—you don't want the drainage system to fill your rain garden!

a wonderful sound effect every time it rains. Or, if the rain garden is farther away from the house, add an open swale as part of the inflow design, planted with low-growing or grasslike plants and with rocks placed in the rest of the swale so it

A footbridge over a wide swale adds interest and utility to the rain garden design.

The overflow pipe can also be installed as a vertical pipe connected to an elbow (a bend in the pipe) and then a horizontal pipe out to the designated overflow area. A vertical pipe allows you to adjust the level of ponding in very tight places, thus reducing the length of an overflow pipe.

Sometimes pipes also just move the overflow out into the landscape somewhere, such as through a retaining wall into another garden section, or into a rock-lined area where the water can safely spread out and sheet-flow.

CAUTION FOR PATHS THROUGH THE RAIN GARDEN

If walkways with large rock steps are planned through the rain garden, remember that these surfaces will take away from the infiltration area, which means the rain garden area will need to be enlarged by the total area of the large rocks. Also, because the rain garden soil is loose and should not be compacted, such rock steps need to be large columns that sit on the bottom of the rain garden, surrounded by the soil mix rather than right on top of it.

In Portland, an overflow pipe drains through the retaining wall and onto the sidewalk, but sidewalk overflow is not allowed in Seattle.

into the rest of the landscape. This is an acceptable solution as long as the water is flowing into a landscape that thrives in such conditions; anything that needs and loves dry conditions, such as a madrona tree, is not a good candidate for the overflow path. Also, it's very important to make sure you are not letting water flow and spread out into a neighbor's yard.

Swale

A swale overflow can feel like a dry creek bed if you plant it with appropriate low-growing or grasslike plants and arrange varied-size rocks in a natural way. There is no mathematical formula for sizing a swale overflow; position it as it fits best and looks best in the landscape. If the swale is long, you may want to add a bridge over it. How long is long? You decide—let's just say *long* means long enough that you wish you could cross over it instead of having to go around it!

Sheet Flow

A sheet-flow overflow moves through an opening in the downslope side of the rain garden. Line the opening with rock, and allow the overflow to spill

Vertical Underdrain

One simple overflow design that can be used in certain jurisdictions by DIY gardeners is the

STANDARD UNDERDRAINS

One option for overflow is a standard underdrain, a horizontal pipe placed near the bottom of the rain garden and usually connected to the sewer or stormwater sewer system. These are used in rain gardens that are built on very slowly draining sites and/or where ponding needs to be limited to just a few hours. Note that underdrains shorten the time the water spends in the rain garden, and therefore they often lead to unsatisfactory filtration and reduce infiltration and soil recharge, while increasing overflow. They can be installed as a turn-on-turn-off system, however, allowing the creation of rain gardens on sites where they otherwise would not be possible.

Installing horizontal underdrains is *not* a DIY project. They must be designed and installed by a professional—adding significantly to the price—and require specialized maintenance to keep them working well.

An overflow swale should move water to plants that don't mind an occasional drenching.

vertical underdrain overflow-control structure. Derek Hann and Zsofia Pasztor designed and patented this system a few years ago, and it is now part of the design standards for Snohomish County, Washington. You might want to choose this overflow if your soil is clayey or poorly draining (an infiltration rate of 0.3 inch, 8mm, per hour or less), or if space for creating another type of overflow is limited.

This structure prolongs the time the water spends in the rain garden soil by providing additional void space. It also allows an observer to actually see the level of saturation within the soil, which is not only fun but sometimes, in a research context, provides important information about the speed of infiltration. The structure is an overflow as well, connected to the original drainage system or to another safe overflow location.

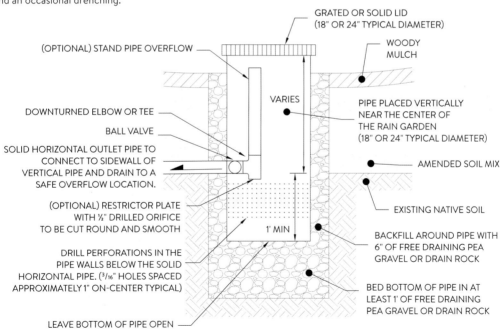

This vertical underdrain was designed by Zsofia and Derek Hann to be installed by the homeowners. (Rendering by Derk Hann, P.E.)

This vertical underdrain is hooked up to an injection well, a setup that must be permitted and professionally installed.

The benefits of the vertical underdrain over a standard underdrain are:

- **DIY installation.** With only a professional consultation about the design, homeowners can install a vertical underdrain themselves.
- **Cheaper cost.** It requires fewer materials, less labor, and less excavation to create the assembly.
- **Easier maintenance.** If a standard underdrain becomes plugged, the entire rain garden often needs to be excavated to clear the pipe. If a vertical underdrain becomes plugged (which is very hard to do), clearing it is simple.
- **Easy to access and observe, manage, and control with the valve.** If cost is limiting, the valve can be left out.
- **Runoff can sit in the rain garden much longer.** A standard underdrain typically has the runoff sitting in the system for 1.5 hours, because infiltration paths to the perforated horizontal pipes are very short. The vertical underdrain forces water to travel horizontally through the soil of the entire garden

before it enters the overflow. This increases the "residency time" of the water within the rain garden, for a small rain garden 15 feet (4.6m) in diameter, by between 15 and 30 hours. Residency time is what engineers call the duration the runoff spends within the rain garden soil mix before it is moved out of the rain garden through horizontal underdrain systems, or is absorbed through roots and infiltrated into the ground below.

Armoring

The areas where inflow and overflow meet the rain garden must be protected from flowing or splashing water with what is called *armoring*. Essentially, it involves nothing more than placing drain rocks or cobblestones around and slightly beyond the area where the water flows in. This prevents erosion at the entrance area and helps the sediment settle. Drain rocks are typically smaller, round rocks, sized between 1 inch and approximately 4 inches (2.5cm–10cm) in diameter. They are often called out as *1-1/5" +/- drain rock* or *4"+/- drain rock*. Cobblestones are larger than 4 inches in diameter, roundish, meaning some are oblong while others are globe shaped. Those are called out as *4"+ or 8"+, etc. cobblestones*. You can use a mixture for interesting effect, making the area look like a dry creek bed during the dry season.

We recommend designing this area to look as natural as possible: Rocks of all the same size and shape, arranged neatly in a line, can take away from the beauty of a rain garden. Rocks typically vary in size in the natural environment, so if you can, use large drain rocks, 1.5 inch (4cm) combined with cobblestones. You can even bring in a couple of even larger half-man rocks (see sidebar, below) to make the armoring look like part of a creek bed. Do *not* use pea gravel; it will simply wash away.

Overflow armoring in various configurations, clockwise from top left: rock armoring; rock and stone armoring; rock terrace and armoring

ROCK OUT!

Originally the terms "half-man," "one-man," "two-man," etc., referred to how many men it would take to move a rock into place using their muscle and maybe a rock bar. Because not all men are equally strong, these categories are simply weight ranges. A one-man rock can range from 60 to 350 pounds (27–158kg). A two-man rock can be between 360 and 900 pounds (163–408kg).

To calculate how much rock you will need, begin with an idea of how wide your inflow and overflow areas will be, plus an additional skirt around them. Plan on also lining the length of the sloped side below the inflow, 6 to 8 inches (15–20cm) deep. So, if your inflow area is a half-foot-wide (15cm) pipe and your sloped side is 6 feet (1.8m) long, in order to cover two-thirds of this sloped side and have additional rocks for the wider area around the pipe (usually at least another 6 inches on either side, which makes the inflow 18 inches, 46cm, wide), you will need 5–6 cubic feet (.14–.17m³) of armoring. If your overflow is similar to this inflow, you will need about 10–12 cubic feet (.28–.34m³) of rock. That is about .4–.5 cubic yard (.3–.38m³). It is best if you assume a rectangle for the shape when you make your calculations, but make it look natural when building the rain garden.

Bring these numbers to your rock supplier and ask how much you will need of each particular rock. Depending on the rocks' sizes, she will be able to calculate this number for you. Don't forget, rock is heavy and you may need to have it delivered. Only .4 cubic yards of cobblestone can easily weigh 3,000 pounds (1360kg), so half a yard or just a little less will still be over 1,000 pounds!

PLANNING FOR EXCAVATION AND FILL

Even if your rain garden is small relative to the site, it is going to be a much bigger dig than you probably think. What about all the soil you'll remove? And what about the rain garden mix you'll need for the bottom of the garden?

Excavated Soil

How much soil will be excavated, and what are you going to do with it? If your rain garden is 100 square feet (9.3m²) and 30 inches (76cm) deep in the bottom area with 2:1 sloping sides, the overall volume of soil excavated will be about 21 cubic yards (16m³). That is a lot of soil. The amount of soil needing a new home depends on how good or bad your soil is. If it is filled with rocks, for example, even if the drainage rate is good, it is tough to use it and have fun while doing it.

However, much of the soil can be reused in the rain garden, as long as it is not mainly silt or clay. Silt does not compact as tightly as clay does, but it can generate lots of sediment in the overflow system and can sometimes compact enough to develop a crusted barrier layer within the rain garden. Therefore, only soils that contain some sand and that infiltrate faster than 0.3 inch (8mm) per hour should be used as part of the rain garden mix (see Rain Garden Mix, below). Refer back to your soil test notes and the soil triangle to find out whether your soil type can be reused in the rain garden.

If your excavated soil is rocky or full of clay and silt, you will have to think about hauling it away. Think creatively to reduce costs. Is there room in the garden to use this material as a new landscape bed base? Buying soil is just as expensive as hauling it away; you can save a lot of money by using the excavated soil as your base for landscaping projects you are planning. Another

Be prepared to move much of the soil by hand.

quickly become a major headache that you can't ignore. Pay attention to soil, because repairing soil failure is a *big* undertaking. If a plant dies, you can easily replace it. If the mulch is not good, you can rake it out and put in a new layer. But if the soil is bad, you have to dig it all out.

For the rain garden mix, you will use either a combination of your own soil and high-quality compost, or readymade soil mix that you purchase. You should purchase premade bioretention mix if any of the following conditions apply:

- Your soil is too rocky or high in clay
- Your infiltration rate is slower than 0.3 inch (8mm) per hour
- Your jurisdiction requires it

Rain Garden Mix

Soils make or break a rain garden! If the soil is good, the rain garden will thrive, function without problems, and require little maintenance. If the soil is not the right mix, the rain garden can

possibility, particularly if the soil is clayey, is to use it to build a berm, if your design calls for one, since that requires soil that can be compacted.

Pre-engineered mix contains specific-sized aggregate particles and high-quality compost (in about a 65/35 to 70/30 percent mixture based on volume, not weight). These soils typically have infiltration rates of 2 inches (5cm) or higher per hour.

The Golden Ratio

If you cannot get readymade soil mix from a nearby supplier, yet your own soil is unusable,

ORDERING MATERIALS

During the design process, you should already be contacting your suppliers to find out what rocks, compost, and mulch they carry and how much notice they need usually for an order. Order the materials for pickup or delivery the day before installation or, if installation will span several weekends, order in phases based on the requirements of each weekend's project. You do not want compost, soil mix, rocks, mulch, and other bulk material sitting too long in the driveway, but you need to have them on hand once you are ready to work.

Plan ahead, and talk to your supplier to see what they recommend, especially if they have to deliver the materials. They need to schedule drivers and are not always able to deliver with just twenty-four hours' notice.

you can mix large aggregate washed sand with compost at a ratio of 65 percent sand to 35 percent compost. The supplier should certify that the aggregate is washed and is in fact large-particle-size clean sand. If you have tough clay soil in your garden, use a sandy loam mix and compost rather than pure sand and compost. Clay plus sand and water makes adobe—brick, in other words. You really don't want a brick layer at the bottom of the rain garden!

If you mix compost with your own excavated soil, use a volume ratio of two-thirds native soil to one-third compost in each batch. For 18 inches (46cm) of rain garden mix in your 100 square foot (9.3m²) by 30 inch (76cm) deep rain garden with 2:1 sloping sides, we will need approximately 10 cubic yards (7.6m³) of rain garden mix. Two-thirds of 10 is about 6.5 cubic yards (5m³) native soil; one-third of 10 is about 3.5 cubic yards (2.7m³) of compost. It's always better to plan on getting more rather than less, and the excavation is rarely going to be precise, so round up 10 to 20 percent when you order. You can give away good soil and compost to neighbors if you have leftovers that you do not want, or put it on Craigslist. But if you don't have enough to begin with, it becomes a logistical mess.

Soil Is Not Enough

Our goal is to create rich and well-infiltrating soil that resembles the forest floor. You might read in some books or reference materials that sometimes as little as 10–20 percent compost in your rain garden mix, based on volume, is enough, or even better. We disagree: Natural, healthy soil usually contains 5–8 percent organic matter based on *weight*. That is very different from volume, because organic matter is lightweight. In the words of our good friend, restoration ecologist and educator Rodney Pond, "Compost is fluffy!"

Urban soils are usually nutrient poor and depleted, so when we add one-third volume in compost, we are actually not enriching the soil too much. We are merely getting it ready to be the great soil it will become. The newly planted plants will initially grow a lot, like they're on steroids, because of the high level of available nutrients. But as they use up the nutrients provided by the compost, they will slow down. Since rain gardens are not tilled or amended with new compost year after year, organic material is only replenished through the natural buildup of plant debris and mulching in layers, just like in natural soils. Eventually, in just a couple of years, organic matter content will balance out at 5 percent by weight, or even less.

If you do not add enough compost in the beginning, the plants will struggle in the long run and the soil will have less life in it. Less life, or fewer microorganisms, means less runoff filtration. Rain gardens are not simply giant shower drains but sophisticated living systems. They are designed and even, yes, engineered, but they are complex symbiotic networks and functioning ecosystems. The soil mixed with the compost is what makes it all possible.

The Secret Ingredient: Compost

Not all composts are created equal. Understanding how compost is made, what it is, and how to buy it is very important for a successful rain garden project: Compost is the heart of the rain garden mix. Read this section carefully, because, again, if your soil mix is not good because of the compost, repair means digging it all out!

There is a big difference between one compost and another, based on what they are made of and how they are produced. A compost that is wonderful in a food garden or orchard might not be good in a typical rain garden or Low Impact

Development setting. For example, compost high in manure content, which is great for agricultural use, usually has higher salt levels from the licking salt provided to the animals. But because compost is used in the rain garden in very heavy concentration (unlike in agricultural practices), the salt will draw water out of the plants and kill them. Also, if the manure is not aged enough, it can leach compounds such as nitrites that are not desirable in groundwater. Manure also contains lots of weed seeds and, depending on the animal it is sourced from, may actually still have viable seeds. Even if the compost is just from landscape waste, if it was not processed at a hot enough temperature, it can still contain viable weed seeds and plant pathogens, which can cause fungal infections and bacterial diseases.

When sourcing your compost, make sure it conforms to the following checklist (for a list of recommended compost producers, see Resources):

- It feels like humus, smells earthy, and is made up of mixed-size particles. The particles should all be broken down or on their way to being almost fully broken down, soft and pliable yet not uniform in size. It should be dark brown or black in color.
- It was made with controlled internal heat, and the temperature was tracked for the duration of the manufacturing period.
- It was, if possible, made with yard waste, perhaps with food waste, and shredded woody material, without manure or with only a small amount of it.

Healthy, rich compost provides the appetizers, entrées, and desserts to all the plants feeding on it.

- If it is manure based, or carcasses have been used in the composting process, it has been heated long enough to meet the standards as prescribed by the EPA and your state regulators, as well as the US Composting Council.
- The composter is a member of the US Composting Council and can provide you with a certification for the material's content.
- It is salt and weed free.

If you are unsure about the compost for any reason, verify the salt- and weed-free claim before you deposit a ton of it into a rain garden. Ask for or buy a small amount to test. Bring it into the house and keep it moist for a few weeks; see what comes up. Then plant some pea and radish seeds in it. If the peas come up and look good, but the radishes do not, the compost may be too low in nitrogen. If nothing comes up, neither seeds nor weeds, the compost may contain something that actually kills seeds and will harm plants. If the seeds germinate but dry up despite your watering them, the compost is probably high in salt.

If no weeds are growing in three to four weeks, and the peas and radishes are doing well, the compost is likely safe to use. If mushrooms pop up too, this is a good thing: It means the compost is not sterilized and dead, but was treated just hot enough not to be a challenge for the garden.

———— •• ————

TIP Remember: Whatever goes into compost is what comes out. If people put trash in the compostable loads, the compost will have trash in it—it's that simple. It's up to all of us to keep our compost clean and usable.

———— •• ————

Mulch

Mulch mimics the natural duff layer in the forest or the meadow. It's a deep layer in nature and should be thick in the rain garden too, keeping the soil moist and cool in the dry and warm season, warm in the cold winter, and protected from heavy rains. It also prevents erosion and breaks down into great plant food. If you ever have to walk into the rain garden, the mulch layer will help distribute your weight and protect the rain garden soil from compacting. It is also makes a good weed barrier layer.

Use woody mulch made of chipped or shredded mixed wood. *Do not use ornamental bark.* Bark floats; it is designed by nature to repel water, and it breaks down very slowly. It can create a cake layer in the garden, keeping water out and leading to poor, dry, lifeless soils. It is best to use wood chips or hog fuel (ground-up wood from sawmills) in *all* garden beds, not just the rain garden, rather than bark.

DON'T DIY

We don't recommend using homemade compost when it comes to your rain garden. For one thing, it's not easy to make and can take up to two years to produce at home! The volume you will need for the rain garden mix is much more than a homemade compost pile can produce. You're better off seeking out good compost from nearby and having it delivered to your site when needed. However, composting at home is a great thing to do, and the material you are making will be excellent for your home gardening. Everything counts when it comes to reducing what goes into the landfill. Learn how to do it well and experiment with different methods.

Cover the entire rain garden—all the zones—with a layer of mulch 3 to 4 inches (7.5–10cm) thick. To calculate how much you need:

1. Figure out the total size of the entire rain garden in square feet or square meters.
2. Multiply that:
   A. (*American*) by .3, to get the number of cubic feet of mulch you will need to cover the site with 4 inches' worth. Then divide that total by 27 to get the amount in cubic yards.
   B. (*metric*) by .1, to get the number of cubic meters you will need for the 10cm equivalent depth of mulch.

We often place burlap bags under the mulch to further reduce the chances of weed growth until the desired plants get established, especially if we sheet-mulch for a berm area. Sheet mulching is essentially creating a lasagna-style garden system,

HOW COMPOST IS MADE

How compost is made determines whether the compost is good quality or not. Here is how good compost is produced: The raw ingredients (food waste and yard waste materials) get ground up, mixed with shredded wood, and gathered into huge piles that will be black gold in just a few weeks or months. Modern facilities usually cover the piles and check them for oxygen and moisture content, adding extra oxygen and moisture by running air through the material and spraying water on it as needed. The idea is to allow the pile to breathe, keep out rain and excess water, and control temperature and odor. Meanwhile, bacteria is busy breaking down the raw material and producing a substance that looks more and more like humus.

Burlap is great for berms because it conforms to the mounded shapes. (Photo by the Hanson Family)

layering materials on top of one another. Burlap or cardboard layers can be placed on top of the lawn or other unwanted herbacious and cut vegetation, and that layer can be covered with woody mulch to keep the barrier layer in place and provide more weight and shade, helping eliminate weeds. Cardboard can be slippery, however, so it is not a good sheet mulch on slopes.

If you can get enough burlap, place the bags on top of the amended soil layer in every zone under the mulch. Burlap can go under the armoring as well, but that can require a few more rocks to look natural; if you have just enough rocks to do the armoring, don't put any burlap underneath it.

JURISDICTIONAL NOTE: When wood breaks down, it leaches a small amount of phosphate. If nearby water bodies, like Washington's Lake Whatcom, are sensitive to phosphate levels, any phosphate leaching can be a problem and woody materials—and even plant debris, leaves, and branches—should be minimized in rain gardens. For this reason, in some jurisdictions, rocks are required as a cover layer for the bottom of the rain garden instead of woody mulch.

If there are no other options, it can be done, but rocks present huge challenges for long-term maintenance. It is difficult to weed between rocks, for instance. Rocks also heat up in the summer and cool off in winter, so instead of mitigating the temperature swings of the environment, they amplify it. They do not break down into humus and will not feed the plants as time goes by. But they are also habitat features, and with clever design, rain gardens can function well even with rocks on the bottom. If you are obliged to use rocks, you may want to consult a professional about plant material choices and long-range maintenance.

SELECTING PLANTS

And now, the really fun stuff: selecting the plants for the rain garden design! We're not afraid to admit that we're plantaholics. We've tried lots of therapy, but we've finally accepted that we will not recover from this condition. In fact, we are also enablers, since you are definitely going to want to get some after this chapter!

As you start to think about plants, take a step back and look at your whole yard. Ask yourself the following design questions:

- How will the rain garden feel and look in relation to the house, the driveway, the walkway, the street, the rest of the garden?
- Is it in a sunny or a shady spot?
- What colors are around the future rain garden?
- Do I want the plants to fit and meld into this background, or stand out?
- Will the entire rain garden become the focal point of the space, or just a certain area within it?
- Do I want to use the plants as a screen?

AN ENTHUSIASTIC ASIDE FROM ZSOFIA

I got into this field many years ago because of the plants. I simply loved the idea that a small space can have such diversity: Because a rain garden's three zones are such different microclimates, it's possible to combine plants that would never pair in nature. Where else can I plant marginal sedges, typically found on banks and beaches of lakes, a few feet away from a mountain hemlock?

Seattle rain garden with lots of plant variety (Photo by Holli Margell)

- Do I want a seating area for spending time with my rain garden, or it is enough just to know that it is there?
- Do I want to attract specific birds and insects?
- What is typical weather in my locale?
- What USDA zone am I in?

Take some walks in the neighborhood and see what plants you like or dislike in other people's yards. Go and visit a nursery to see what they have during each season, both what they look like and what environment they need. Once you've read about the planting zones of the rain garden below, you can start sketching plants into the design, consulting the plant lists at the back of this book

(see Top Plants for Pacific Northwest Rain Gardens) as you go. Take a photo of your rain garden area, and start playing with different arrangements of plants on a sketch pad or the computer. Do you want evergreen plants in a specific area, or deciduous and flowering ones instead? Start thinking about the different plants in the rain garden as they will relate to the surrounding area.

Design Elements and Principles to Consider

Landscape designers, when imagining a new space, think about a variety of design elements and principles. You may not be a designer by trade, but you can incorporate the following ideas into your planting plan.

Average Annual Extreme Minimum Temperature

Temp (F)	Zone	Temp (C)
-40 to -35	3a	-40 to -37.2
-35 to -30	3b	-37.2 to -34.4
-30 to -25	4a	-34.4 to -31.7
-25 to -20	4b	-31.7 to -28.9
-20 to -15	5a	-28.9 to -26.1
-15 to -10	5b	-26.1 to -23.3
-10 to -5	6a	-23.3 to -20.6
-5 to 0	6b	-20.6 to -17.8
0 to 5	7a	-17.8 to -15
5 to 10	7b	-15 to -12.2
10 to 15	8a	-12.2 to -9.4
15 to 20	8b	-9.4 to -6.7
20 to 25	9a	-6.7 to -3.9

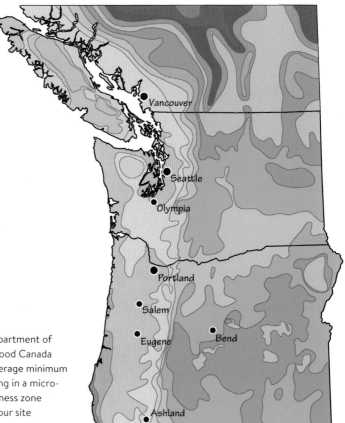

Map and key developed from United States Department of Agriculture (USDA) and Agriculture and Agri-Food Canada (AAFC) hardiness zones, which are based on average minimum winter temperatures. Note that you may be living in a microclimate colder or warmer than the typical hardiness zone around you. Choose your plants with care for your site specifically, suitable to your property's characteristics.

Design elements can be objective qualities like these:

- **Color:** How do the colors of the different plants relate to one another? If you like red-leaved plants, you might want to choose red-leaved ninebark or heuchera, and red-leaved grasses for the garden. These will look wonderful, but only if you also use other colors around them. If everything is red leaved, the effect of the individual foliage will be lost.
- **Shape:** In the plant world, leaves, flowers, stems, and complete plants come in defining, varied shapes, and if you plant too many similar ones together, they will not be readily visible. Yet you can spread out repetition of a certain shape in the garden for a very significant design trait.
- **Texture:** From fine leaves to massive robust foliage, plants offer it all. Combine different textures to create interest that draws people into the space.
- **Form:** Some conifers are giant triangles, other trees look like a candle flame. Some shrubs are almost a perfect globe. Play with these shapes so you can direct the observer's focus.

- **Space:** This refers not only to the very area you are building the rain garden in, but also to empty areas between plants. Use space between certain trees and shrubs purposefully to define them as focal points.

But design principles are sometimes more subjective qualities too:

- **Harmony:** This is not the same for everyone. What feels harmonious to me may feel very chaotic to you. Create the harmony, or disharmony, that you desire for your garden.
- **Balance:** This, too, is subjective. It is defined as even representation of all elements, meaning that if you use something very big you will also use something very small, and no one element overpowers another. But every designer interprets balance differently.

- **Scale:** This is about how things relate to each other in size. For an out-of-town visitor, a large, mature western red cedar tree may seem out of scale next to a small craftsman home. But for many people who live in the Northwest, these trees are common occurrence, so we do not think of it as off scale at all.
- **Importance and Hierarchy:** What is important to you in the garden? What element or concept matters more than others? Are you primarily interested in function, or is it all about aesthetics—or both? Which is your favorite feature, the path or the trees? Or maybe an artwork you want to incorporate, or a rock? If you have lots of similar plants, is one group of them more significant than the others? If you have purple coneflowers and black-eyed Susans near anemones, are they

In autumn, black-eyed Susans feature interesting seed heads that provide seasonal interest as well as fodder for birds. (Photo by Holli Margell)

Dwarf conifers add year-round texture to rain gardens.

- **Similarity:** What it sounds like: how plants look and feel alike. For example, you might use this principle to create a "white garden," where plants tend to have something white about them, whether that be leaves, bark, flowers, berries, etc.
- **Contrast:** Plants can be similar, but they can also be dramatically different from one another. You might pick two of the same species, like ninebark shrubs, but one with light golden-green foliage and the other with deep black-red leaves. Put together, they will create an interesting effect.

equally important or do you want to bring attention to just one? If you want to really draw attention to, say, a special shrub, you will use smaller, less interesting plants as backdrop around it instead of other unique plants that only compete for attention.

Importance and hierarchy are not the same, however. Similar plants grouped together create a feel of importance, especially if repeated, while a few well-defined and focused plants will dominate the overall view and seem to rank higher in the hierarchy than the rest of the plants around them.

We like to achieve variety in texture, shape, color, and form in the garden by choosing plants based on what their foliage looks like. Flowers fade fast, foliage remains. That said, flowers do matter: If certain plants flower at the same time, pay attention to the colors and how they will interact with each other.

Make sure the garden looks good in the winter. Many plants offer nice colorful bark, seed heads, or other features for the winter months, such as red osier dogwood, mahonia, and evergreen emergents.

Evergreen plants have benefits that all rain gardens can use. Since they have leaves all year, they evapotranspire year-round. This lets them

RESPECT EXISTING TREES AND NATIVE VEGETATION

You should not be removing healthy trees or healthy native vegetation for the sake of your rain garden. You may move a small tree, if you absolutely must, but otherwise it has the right-of-way. Rain gardens aim to mimic forest or meadow ecosystems, and existing trees and healthy native plants are the forest ecosystem. When it comes to strictly ornamental plantings, you may move or alter them to place a rain garden, especially if they include any invasive species. In general, however, we usually place rain gardens where an existing lawn is not needed or is simply a problem child, and it is time to make a change.

move water out of the rain garden faster during the winter than dormant deciduous plants do, and better reduce phosphorus levels in the water.

Never forget that beauty is in the eye of the beholder. What matters in the end is that *you* are happy with your rain garden and the way it looks and feels in your yard!

Rain Garden Planting Zones

When you are thinking about a planting plan, you have to consider the different micro-environments that exist within a rain garden. These zone-specific circumstances are additional to basic garden-specific situations and conditions, such as light and wind exposure, prevailing regional climate and weather, and distance from structures and roads. Understanding plants and what they need

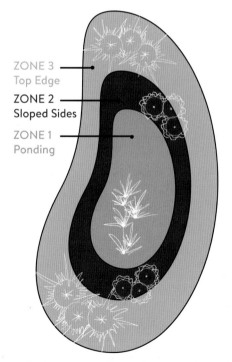

ZONE 3
Top Edge

ZONE 2
Sloped Sides

ZONE 1
Ponding

Each zone has its own microclimate. Be sure to choose the correct plant types for each.

EDIBLE RAIN GARDENS?

People often ask us about planting edible plants in a rain garden. The question we respond with is, Would you lick your roof or driveway for breakfast? Runoff enters the rain garden unfiltered, and the Zone 1 and 2 plants absorb that water as is—so they're not really good to munch on. Roof runoff contains *E. coli* and salmonella from birds pooping on the roof. Other runoff could contain copper, zinc, heavy metals, coolant and oil from leaky cars, and fertilizer residues. So our answer is that *normally* it's not a good idea to plant an edible rain garden. (And leafy greens should be watered only with potable water.) However, most edible plants will do fine in Zone 3, because this area does not come into direct contact with unfiltered runoff, and therefore the plants won't either.

in order to do well in a garden is essential for a good planting plan and successful rain garden vegetation. Rain garden zone labels vary around the country; make sure you know what system your reference materials are using (see the jurisdiction note in chapter 1).

Zone 1, where the ponding happens, is going to get very wet and be saturated very often during the rainy season. The plants will be sitting in water that is 6 inches (15cm) deep—or however deep you have designed the ponding to be—during heavy rains and long wet seasons. The plants used here must love, or at a minimum tolerate, this condition. In nature, these plants occur around lakes and streams, close to the water's edge. Red osier dogwood, sedges, and rushes are common plants in these areas and work well in the rain garden too.

But there's a catch: They must also love or tolerate drying out during the dry season, because rain gardens do dry out completely! This zone resembles seasonal marshes or vernal pools where water consistently ponds only during the wet season. (Remember that rain gardens are meant to be low maintenance and need very little extra care after a few years, so they are not supposed to be designed with permanent irrigation.)

Zone 2, the sides of the rain garden, will take after river banks where the water level fluctuates frequently. Sometimes it is very wet and other times it is very dry, and there is no standing water around the plants. Red-flowering currant, Oregon grape, salal, and ferns are just a few possibilities for this zone.

Zone 3, the top edge of the rain garden, including any berm, is not supposed to get any wetter than any other landscaped area in the yard. It should not be irrigated permanently, and the plants in general should be drought tolerant. We love using alpine plants here just for the fun of it. People who know plants stop and look a couple of times, wondering how on earth it's possible to mix such plants so closely? Dwarf conifers, such as dwarf mugo pine (*Pinus mugo* var. *pumilio*) and weeping Snow Sprite Deodar cedar, if combined with colorful noninvasive grasses such as blue oat grass, are real showstoppers.

JURISDICTIONAL NOTE: Rain garden zone labels vary around the country. In some places the zones are identified as A, B, and C, starting at the bottom. Other areas use A, B, and C starting at the top. Washington State manuals and handbooks refer to the zones as 1, 2, and 3 starting at the bottom of the rain garden (while some places use 1, 2, and 3 but in the opposite direction). When using rain garden reference material, check which label refers to which physical location within the garden, or the plantings may fail.

Plant Types

A rain garden benefits from a wide variety of plant types that each contribute different qualities both above and below ground. Root systems create networks that support the plants as well as microbial life and soil health. Flowers and foliage varying in height, color, and shape provide habitat for wildlife as well as visual interest. The Plant Lists at the end of this book offer detailed information about plants for each zone of the rain garden. Remember that if you're near a coastline with salt spray, or in an area that uses salt or deicer on the road in winter, you'll want to select plants that are salt tolerant.

Trees

Typically, trees are the largest plants in an ecosystem and have only a few woody stems that we call trunks. But, as with everything else in the world,

Red osier dogwood in summer (Photo by Holli Margell)

there are exceptions. Some trees have dwarf, weeping, or even creeping forms and remain low, yet their trunks over time can get very large. Trees have varied root systems, and generally speaking they are wide and far reaching, extending way past the edge of the canopy (unlike a carrot). The root system of a large tree in a small yard will grow into the entire yard.

Keep this in mind when looking at existing trees or planning to plant one. It is important to understand not just what the tree will look like as it grows, but what the roots will be like underground, and choose the tree wisely. Since trees use a lot of water once they mature, the rain garden will likely pond less often, due to the tree's work.

You can plant trees in a rain garden if you have enough space in your yard overall and if the rain garden is large enough. In many suburban yards, especially in eastern Washington and Oregon, rain gardens can be quite large. These DIY rain gardens are perfect locations for one or more trees.

Shrubs

Shrubs are plants that have multiple stems originating from their base, and they generally remain smaller in size than trees in the same habitat. Over the years, shrubs often lose their canes or stems to old age, while new fresh growth keeps the plant going. Some shrubs should be pruned of old canes as part of routine maintenance (see Pruning in chapter 6).

Perennials

Perennials are the best surprises you can give yourself. You plant a beautiful, flowering plant with great foliage and it "dies" in the fall. As winter goes on, birds take any remaining dry seed heads, and eventually the plant disappears. But as spring rolls around, new shoots come up and the gem is

EDIBLE PLANTS

Many plants are edible, even though we do not think of them as food anymore. Traditionally people used to forage for food throughout the year and ate much more wild vegetation than we do today. New shoots, mature leaves, roots, flowers, bark, and berries were collected and made into meals regularly. So, in reality, many of the plants not generally recognized as food sources were and are important foraged foods for Native Americans and others who still remember.

back in full glory—only this time, slightly larger than what you planted! We often forget where our perennials and bulbs are and are pleasantly surprised by these garden gifts each spring when they sprout up again.

The word *perennial* does not mean only plants with showy flowers; grasses and ferns that are not evergreen are referred to sometimes as perennials as well. But in the nursery industry, if you ask about perennials, they will usually take you to the section where the flowering plants are.

In a rain garden, perennials will need to be matched to the specific zones similarly to all of the other plants. Perennials will have varied root systems: Some are shallower than others, some will spread wide and others will stay close to the plant's crown. Think about seasonal interest and year-round function when selecting these for the rain garden. Keep in mind that leaving spent flowers and seed heads supports wildlife and minimizes the need to walk around in the rain garden.

Emergents

Emergents are grassy-looking plants (but not grasses) that usually grow at the edges of marshes and ponds, where the water level fluctuates. Even when flooded, though, emergents have their foliage out of the water. Some prefer moist or even wet soils year-round (these are not good candidates for rain gardens because of the summer dry season), and others can tolerate bone-dry conditions as long as periodically they get very wet.

Emergent root systems are fibrous and very different from typical woody tree and shrub roots. All the roots grow from the base of the plant and spread as individual threads with no branches, or fewer branches than most trees and shrubs, yet they grow deep into the ground. They filter sediment from the water through their leaves and pollutants through their roots. Not all species are suitable for all climates; west of the Cascades, it is particularly important to use either evergreen emergents or ones that keep their spent foliage for a long time in winter. This is because our rainy season is during the winter, when deciduous emergents would do little work buffering and cleaning the runoff, yet it is when we need it the most. Evergreens also look better on cloudy days, especially if deciduous shrubs are growing in the rain garden. However, the real cold-tolerant emergents are not always evergreen. The right emergents, even deciduous if maintained well, provide lots of winter interest.

East of the Cascades, the emergents will remain evergreen until the real cold starts. The plants will go dormant under the snow, and then their leaves will regrow nice and big as the snow melts in spring. Their work is essential as the snow melts, so the timing of their growth works well with the timing of the rain garden.

If emergents are maintained with care and a holistic understanding of habitat, the seeds feed animals during the cold months and foliage (dead or alive) is used for nesting in the spring.

Groundcovers

Groundcovers are an essential part of the ecosystem. These plants function as living mulch. They are usually no taller than 12 inches (30.5cm), have woody or herbaceous (soft) stems, and spread around the garden following its contours. Groundcovers have great diversity. Some are evergreen, some are not; some have deep roots, others have shallow and fibrous roots, and others form a net-like root system in the ground. Many flower and some have berries, but many will have no visible flowers and simply offer foliage for the garden.

In the natural environment, groundcovers create one of the lowest canopy layers before the duff and moss layer. They may be small, but they are powerful! They help prevent erosion, control soil temperature, keep moisture in the soil, and protect the ground from weeds proliferating. In a garden they are also a beautiful contribution to the overall aesthetics.

Some groundcovers need more shade than others. Remember that a sunny site can still provide dense shade for groundcovers if the upper story is thick and fully planted with trees, shrubs, and taller perennials. If groundcovers are the only plant in an area, they will be in full sun unless the site receives other shading from nearby trees or buildings. For example, if you plant kinnikinnick in a DuraSoxx terracing wall within the rain garden, the groundcover may be in full sun.

Plant Size

It is very important to know how big plants will get. They can look deceivingly innocent in their tiny containers at the nursery, but look closer and read the tag: It says 35 feet tall and wide! And the labels give the *average* size in ten years—plants

In the right conditions, this innocent-looking salal (*Gaultheria shallon*) can grow into a 5 x 5-foot shrub.

keep growing past that anniversary! Rain garden soils are full of nutrients and life, and plants often grow like teenagers in the first few years, reaching their mature size quickly before they slow down. Thanks to the abundance of horticultural varieties, you can usually find a favorite plant in dwarf form. We normally recommend using only smaller native plants, but for ones that grow much larger, use a hybrid or variety (a naturally occurring variation of a plant species) or a cultivar (a horticulturally developed variation of a species) instead. Cultivars are usually smaller and easier to manage, while they still offer many of the same qualities the original native species did for wildlife.

JURISDICTIONAL NOTE: Determine whether there are any height limits that apply to your site. Sometimes traffic nearby can mean that the plant material cannot exceed a specific height. This is to ensure that the plants do not block visibility. The plant selection is almost always limited if the rain garden is in the right-of-way (ROW) area, because these spots are typically maintained by the jurisdiction's generally nonselective maintenance crew (particularly mowing) and the plants need to be able to withstand that.

PLANTING TREES IN RAIN GARDENS

The typical urban DIY rain garden project may be too small to include planting a tree. However, because this book covers the entire Pacific Northwest, where there are many suburbs and rural areas in which people have huge yards and large roofs—and will thus build larger rain gardens—this book's plant lists include trees suitable for each zone. These trees may also be useful to plant *instead* of a rain garden if it turns out you cannot build a rain garden for some limiting reason. If a tree is too big for your site, try larger shrubs.

In larger, especially commercial-site rain gardens it is OK to plant trees in the ponding area. Many trees, such as willows and birches, tolerate very wet conditions and thrive in this zone. However, rain gardens on this scale are what we usually call *bioretention systems* and are designed by engineers.

Layering

Because we are mimicking a healthy forest floor in nature, planting larger plants to grow over smaller ones is important. This is called *layering*. Knowing the mature size of the plants you are thinking of using will allow you to calculate how many of each plant you need. They need to be spaced at least as far apart as they will be measuring at maturity. However, layering means that you can plant a larger, taller plant next to a smaller one. At the top area you can plant a tree, for example a mountain hemlock, and plant a huckleberry shrub close to it, with an even smaller fern near the huckleberry. This is what happens in the forest.

Layering also happens underground. In fact, it is a good idea to use a variety of plants to create a complex and diverse root system that supports diverse organisms. Different roots reach different depths and interact with the soil differently too. Some deeper-rooted shrubs, such as red osier dogwood (*Cornus sericea*), have aggressive root systems. These plants slowly push against the compacted layers of soil, including hardpan layers, to find or create new cracks. Water starts seeping into the crevices and eventually breaks up previously solid soil layers.

Grasslike plants, such as sedges and rushes, have roots that form intriguing web structures in the ground. They soak up and filter water too, but in somewhat different ways than the larger shrubs.

Using Native Plants

Native plants are plants that grew here before European people arrived. Because they evolved with the natural ecosystem, they typically are more resilient and resistant to diseases and pests than exotic imported plants. The native plant palette is diverse in the many areas of the Pacific Northwest.

CAN NATIVE PLANTS BE INVASIVE?

At times you may hear complaints about native plants, too: Have you ever heard your neighbors gripe about spreading snowberry or salal, about how they just can't get it under control, how it just keeps growing and widening each year? Sometimes I get asked why I am not upset about these "invasive" *native* plants? My answer is because that is an oxymoron; a *native* plant cannot be invasive. It can be overly happy in a spot, but not invasive. To illustrate the difference, picture looking out the kitchen window and seeing your son setting up a tent in the backyard. He is not invasive—although he may trample your flowers. But if a kid from down the street does the same thing, that's invasive! —*Zsofia*

We love using native plants whenever we can, but most native shrubs and trees are too big for an urban rain garden. This is why we often end up using the cousins of natives. "Cousins" is not an official term for plant relations, but we use it anyway! We define them as hybrid varieties and cultivars of native plant species that are a better fit for an urban site because they are smaller, less vigorous, and slower growing than the native origin species. These hybrid plants also often offer other interesting qualities, such as colorful foliage, brighter bark hues, fragrant or larger flowers, etc., which make them really wonderful in a rain garden.

It is important to know that not all hybrids are recognized by the local wildlife as habitat. Some plants will be utilized in the same way, but others may not be; this is particularly true when it comes to berry color. If birds eat the white snowberry, they may not know to also eat the pink hybrid form. If you want to attract specific wildlife to your garden, you may have to either use the original native plants or place additional feeders in your garden.

Do not allow invasive plants into your rain garden! Resilient nonnative plants can take over the natural environment, causing costly problems. Always check with your local noxious-weed board or agency for the most recent list of noxious weeds, and avoid using plants that are on the list.

———————— •• ————————

TIP We offer several planting plan ideas in the back of this book. None of these are meant to be the only way to design a planting plan for a rain garden. They are simply ideas and a guide for those who have never worked with plants before. If it makes the project easier, you could consider hiring a landscape designer for the planting plan phase.

———————— •• ————————

Placing and Sketching Plants

Now it's time to pull out the colored pencils and start a simple art project: placing your plants on the page so you have an organized planting plan. When you add plants to your design, you should outline them showing their *mature size* to scale. Use graph paper, or use a ruler to create the scale. One easy scale system represents every foot in real life with one-quarter inch on the paper (if necessary, come up with your own scale for metric measurements). Under that ratio, a plant that will be 8 feet wide at maturity should be represented by a circle 2 inches in diameter.

We usually use circles to represent plants because they grow in all directions. A circle

When sketching a planting plan, try to envision how plants will look when full and lush.

template from your local office supply store can be very useful for this. Then, in order to know which circle stands for which plant, you will have to use some symbol system (you can also color them). We often use a circle with a small triangle in it to symbolize Oregon grape, for example. A circle with a star in it can mean ferns, or swamp or sweetbay magnolia (*Magnolia virginiana*) maybe—you decide. Because memory only takes you so far, create a legend for your plants. Write down the plant name and draw its symbol next to it. This way you will always remember what you were thinking of in the middle of that rainy night. It can be a really fun and creative process.

SOURCING AND PURCHASING PLANTS

The best time to design the rain garden is during the wet season (which in the Pacific Northwest is generally winter). Nurseries are slow at this time of year, and they often offer very good sales on plants; if you hunt for them, you can find the plants you need during this time.

To keep the plants from drying out with minimal maintenance, place them in a kiddie pool and water them from below, filling the pool with a couple of inches of water every few days. Don't drown your plants, though—do not keep them in saturated pots, and allow the water to run out before adding more to the pool. Allowing the water to run out also eliminates the risk of mosquitoes.

Other good plant sources are ethical salvaging by local habitat restoration groups, and sales of baby plants in early spring by local conservation districts and university extensions. You may also get plants as divisions from friends, but check their pots for weeds before planting them in the rain garden.

Out of its pot, a 4-inch plant will be about the size of your palm. (Photo by Sindea Kirk)

Pot Size

Plants come in all shapes and sizes. You can purchase pot sizes of 4 inch, 1 quart, 1 gallon, 5 gallon, all the way up to 25 gallon. (Beyond that, the plants are usually sold in burlap wraps with very large rootballs.) Note that these are not really correct volume measurements. A 4-inch pot is typically 4x4x4. A gallon pot, however, normally only holds 3 quarts of soil, and a quart pot holds less than a quart! You may also see just pots labeled #1, #2, etc.; these mean 1 gallon, 2 gallon, etc.

Plant Quality

If you see a letter after the pot size, such as P, G, or L, it refers to the quality of the plant in the container. P is premium, G is generic, and L is "landscape grade," the smallest and lowest-quality plant. But you shouldn't necessarily reject

1-gallon, dibble, and 4-inch pots (Photo by Sindea Kirk)

an L plant: If you are searching for plants early in the season, a still-small L plant, transplanted not long ago, may be perfect for planting later in the year and could save you some money. However, if it is labeled L because it is already pot bound (or root bound), it will only get worse and may even die before you get to plant it.

Buying Small vs. Large Plants

Small plants that will stay small for a while are fine for Zone 3, but in Zones 1 and 2, where plants will get wet and even flooded during the rainy season, tiny plants may drown or get washed out. Again, if you are buying the plants early, in the spring, you can buy as small as 4-inch pot plants, transplant them, and grow them out for the fall planting. If you are buying the plants close to the planting project's start, however, you may need to buy larger plants.

There are good and bad things about buying larger plants. The garden will feel grown-in sooner, yet they cost more and will have more non-rain-garden soil mix on their roots. If you plant enough large plants, the large volume of nursery soil can effectively alter the overall soil mix. If you buy plants early in the year, wash the nursery soil off their roots and transplant them into bioretention soil mix or sand and compost mix; grow them out in this soil instead of the nursery soil. Bioretention soil mix is rain garden soil mix, typically manufactured by soil companies, following the specifications of their local jurisdiction and the US Composting Council.

Fertilizers

If nursery plants have colorful crystals and fertilizer granules on top of the soil, remove these before planting. The blue crystals are likely copper sulfate, and copper, even in small amounts and even though it is certified organic material, is

PLANTS WITH SPUNK

"Hardiness" and "tolerance" refer to the conditions species can withstand and live with. But plants, like all living beings, are individuals, and their specific tolerance may not always be the same as the species' average. Where seeds and starts are from can make a big difference. If you raise a plant in a mild climate from a seed that came from a mother plant living in a mild climate, chances are the new plant will not be as cold hardy as the species' average would indicate. Even if a species is generally capable of surviving –50°F (–46°C), if it was grown in the mild climate of Portland, Oregon, it may not be able to acclimate to the severe cold temperatures of the Columbia Plateau successfully.

Plant sizes from left to right: 4-inch and 1-, 2-, 5-, 7-, and 10-gallon pots

deadly to fish and bad for aquatic life. Fertilizers can leach nitrogen and phosphate into the water as well. Nursery mixes often contain other ingredients that can float or crust in the rain garden.

Bound Roots

If the plants have been sitting in their pots for a while, they are likely to be *root bound*. This means the plant's roots have grown completely, filling the container and now growing in circles. These roots will eventually *girdle* the plant (kill it by impeding the flow of its water and nutrients) because they will constrain the rest of the root system from spreading out and growing into a healthy open structure. Healthy roots grow in an open fashion, each root taking up space away from the other.

Check the roots of plants you buy at a nursery, and transplant them into larger containers if they seem like they need more room. If the roots are showing all around, if they are starting to grow in circles, it is likely they need a larger home. When planting root-bound plants, spread the roots out. You may have to cut through some of the girdling roots (the ones growing in a circle). Use a sharp, clean tool and do it without tearing the root tissue. Never plant a root-bound plant, because the roots will continue to grow in circles and will girdle the plant over time.

Root bound (Photo by Sindea Kirk)

Not root bound (Photo by Sindea Kirk)

Plant Health

In nature, plants of the same species will graft onto one another's root systems if their roots touch. They will send nutrients and information to one another through the roots this way. However, they can also share diseases, so keeping every plant healthy is important! Plants have immune systems the same way we do. Since you are storing them for a few weeks or maybe longer, you may need to add some food to their pot. Compost spread around the plants in the pots can provide much-needed nutrients. You can also dilute the compost in water and water the plants with this weak-coffee-looking mixture once a week.

If you want plants that can cope well with your specific conditions, get your seeds, starts, and nursery material from your own area, from plants that have been performing well in your climate and have proven that they in fact can tolerate it.

CHECK YOUR DESIGN PLAN

Do a final review of your plan before digging in.

- Calculate rain garden size.
- Consult rain garden handbooks specific to your area.
- Calculate rain garden area from the bottom up.
    - Depth
    - Sloped Sides
    - Top Edge
    - Berm, if necessary
- Determine any terracing needs.
- Determine shape of rain garden.
- Determine whether underdrain is needed.
- Design inflow and overflow.
- Design armoring.
- Plan for excavation and fill.
- Contact suppliers for rock, soil mix, mulch, pipe supplies.
- Select plants, contact nurseries for availability, determine storage.
- Ensure all necessary permits are gathered.

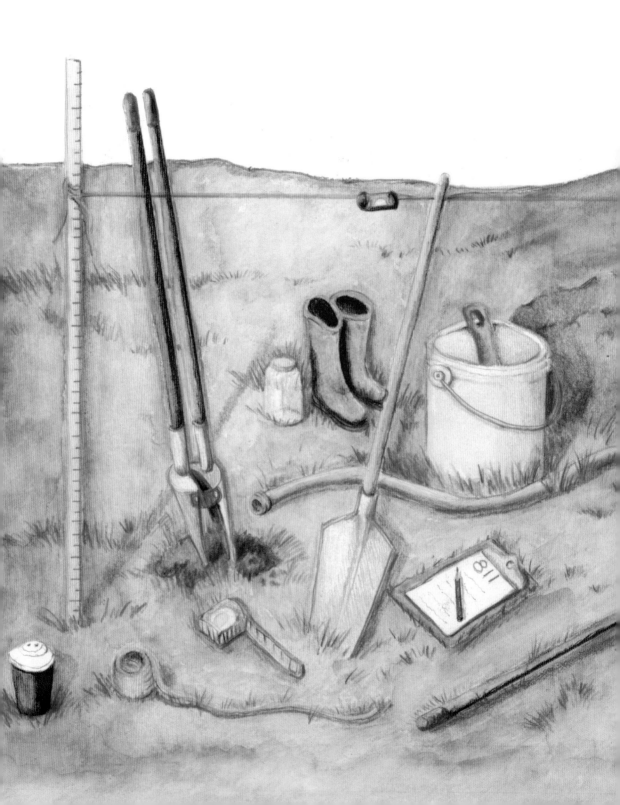

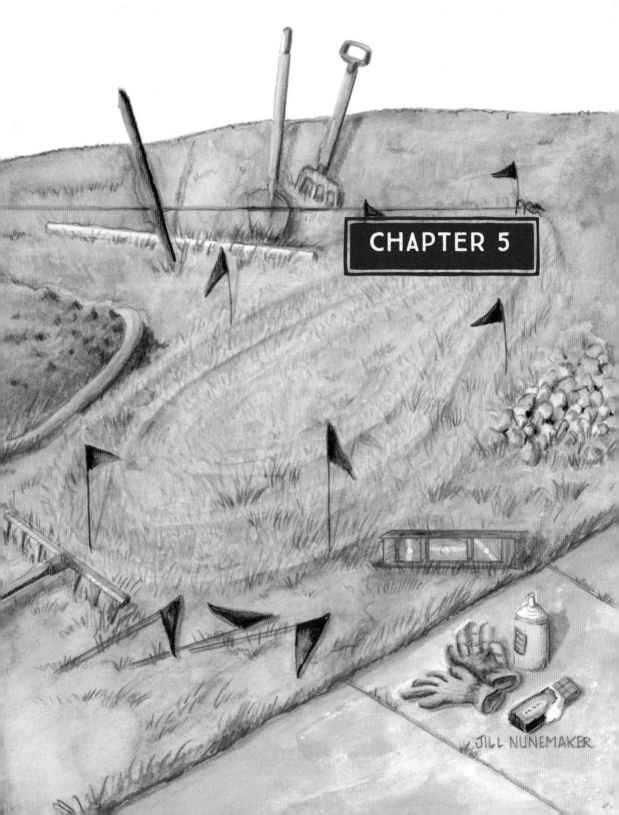

CHAPTER 5

JILL NUNEMAKER

Time to Build: Let's Get Dirty!

Got a design? Got plants? Got compost? Got mulch? Got permits? You're ready! The best time to install a rain garden, however, is during dry weather. In the past we used to say "during summer," but with climate change turning our weather patterns upside down, now we just say do it when it's dry for a longer period. Give yourself plenty of time for the installation so it's not rushed; this is hard work and requires lots of thinking, being present, and making decisions at each phase. If you will be building an average urban rain garden by yourself with one helper, it may take you three or four weekends. If you have help with the digging, friends or a pro with a machine, you might shrink this time to three long days. If you are building a larger rain garden, the work will take longer.

BEFORE YOU DIG

Before you get started, whether you're doing all the work yourself or with help, you'll need to gather the following equipment and supplies:

- Gloves, eye and ear protection, sturdy closed-toe shoes
- Hand tools—shovels (pointy, trenching, and flat), pickaxe, hori-hori, tamper, rock bar, garden rakes, wheelbarrows, handcart, and garden hose

—— • • ——

TIP Get yourself a "hori-hori." It's a fantastic Japanese garden knife designed to dig, chop, and saw through a great number of things in a garden, all in one, fitting perfectly into a beautiful leather case.

—— • • ——

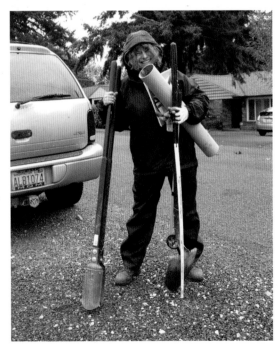

Zsofia is armed and ready for rain garden work!

- White spray paint, to mark out the rain garden outline
- Wooden stakes (three bundles of 10 or more each, as needed), to mark out the rain garden zones, 18 inches (46cm) minimum length
- Orange marking flags
- Sod cutter, to remove lawn
- Leveling equipment: transit and leveling bar to check elevations during the excavation to keep the bottom of the rain garden level, string level and plumb if building a berm
- Measuring tapes and anchors for the ends, measuring wheel
- Excavating machine, to dig out the rain garden
- Cardboard and/or burlap (ask around for cardboard at your local appliance store, and

Keep tools handy, but out of your way.

check for burlap at the nearest coffee roaster), to sheet-mulch
- Mechanical plate compactor machine or hand tamper, to build the berm
- Truck, to haul extra soil away
- Pipes as designed for inflow and overflow, plus glue, primer, etc.
- Vertical underdrain and accessories, if used
- Compost or bioretention soil mix for the rain garden refill
- Wood chips or hog fuel for woody mulch
- Drain rocks and/or cobblestones for armoring
- Pond liner and felt underlay to line the swale inflow, if there is one
- Plants as specified in the design
- Art and other accessories for fun

Have materials delivered before you start.

CAUTION!

Most of the time, utilities are buried deeper than 6 inches (15cm) in the ground, but sometimes phone, cable, and even gas lines can be just a couple of inches below the surface. Be very cautious if you work around utility lines of any kind—and don't forget to call 811!

Figure out your equipment plan before the installation phase begins. Using machinery can save time and chiropractor visits, but it also costs money and may require some expertise, or at a minimum some practice beforehand. Any kind of machine is much more powerful than a person with a shovel; it can also do much more damage in inexperienced hands.

Whether or not you dig by hand or rent machinery, plan on always having at least two people at the site. It gets lonely by yourself, plus it's safer—if you get hurt, it's good to have another person on hand.

MARKING OUT THE RAIN GARDEN

Before you do anything, make sure the utilities are marked out in your yard (see Utility Lines in chapter 3). *If the markings from your first 811 call have faded, call again!*

Mark the rain garden site area on the ground by painting its outline with white spray paint. Now check the location of the rain garden, and its inflow and overflow placement, against the utility layout one more time. Are these elements close to any utility lines? Do you have overhead wires? If yes, watch for them when using a machine, and choose equipment that clears the lines by a generous margin. Generally, 13 feet 4 inches is the maximum height for any vehicle or equipment that does not require a special permit around and under wires. Are you running inflow or overflow over in-ground utilities?

Once the utility lines are marked and the rain garden is outlined, it's time to grab some wooden stakes. These will come in handy several times during the installation, so get a bundle or more of ten or twelve stakes.

TOOL TIPS

Keeping a tidy job site not only saves time, because you can find the tools when you need them, but it is also safer. Here are a few tips for keeping the job site safe and organized:

- Always keep rakes, forks, and shovels with the pointy ends toward the ground and out of the way, or leaning up against a sturdy surface, so people cannot trip over them easily.
- When you are done with a rented tool, return it promptly and save money on the fee.
- Put tools back in a tool pile spot when not in use.
- Once you are done with the job, clean your tools.
- Mark your own tools with a bright duct tape strip, especially if you're doing the project with friends who are bringing their own tools.

Flags mark where the excavator will sit and how far it can reach. The center white line marks the placement of the overflow pipe, the edge of Zone 1, and the bean shape represents the edge between Zone 2 and 3, the garden's overall shape. Zone 3 in this yard is the entire surrounding area around the rain garden.

Use the stakes to mark out the edges of the three rain garden zones. If the excavation is done by hand, the paint marks will not be visible once you remove the lawn and start digging, so these stakes will be very helpful. For machine excavation, the stakes come out as soon as the machine starts working, so be prepared to measure often to make sure your zones have the right dimensions.

Use the stakes to indicate where you want the excavated soil to go as well. It needs to be moved into the correct spot as it is excavated; just piling it by the rain garden will create a really big mess.

Use white painted stakes for visibility.

REMOVING SOD AND VEGETATION

Begin by removing the lawn or other unwanted plant material from the entire rain garden area. If you are using an excavator, the machine will take the grass up with the soil. This is fine if you do not mind it mixing sod and soil, but if you'd rather not mix them, you will need to use a sod cutter and remove the grass separately.

If the sod is not completely infested with weeds, you can use a sod cutter. You can rent one at most big-box hardware stores. And what should you do with the sod once you're finished? Try these:

- Compost: Sod is high in nitrogen and good for worms, too. Start a new compost pile in the garden or add it to an existing one.
- A base for new landscaped beds. If you are going to use the excavated soil to build mounded landscape beds, place the sod with the grass side facing down as the base of these mounds and cover with sod-free soil.

The stakes are helpful marking the zones, signaling where the sloped sides will be. Use even placement, three steps apart or whatever similar measurement works for you.

Sod cut and rolled

An excavator mixes sod and soil during removal.

The grass will decompose, and over time the mound will shrink as the grass becomes a great nutrient source for new plants in the bed.

- Roll it up and put it on Craigslist for free.

Sod is not good for building the berm: It will break down over time, causing the berm to shrink and possibly lose its ability to contain ponding water.

When taking out plant material, save expensive plants—even if you don't like them, your neighbor might love them! Give them away on Craigslist or visit a website like Plant Amnesty, which has a page where people can find new owners for unwanted shrubs and small trees.

USING LEVELING EQUIPMENT

Leveling equipment is key to ensuring that the rain garden is dug to the proper depth, the slope grading is correct, and the shape of the berm is as you calculated it to be. Leveling and elevation measuring tools vary greatly. If you want to play with high tech, you can rent precise remote-controlled equipment for the day (consult the source of those gadgets for instructions on how to use them). A simpler and lower-cost option is a mechanical transit, which requires two people to use. Since transits are easy to find, rent, and use, we recommend them over more basic leveling equipment like water lines, which are not as simple as they sound. You will want to set up your leveling equipment before the big dig.

Using a Transit to Level

A transit is a precise, tripod-mounted tool that sets a reference line and gives angle measurements. Read your transit instructions thoroughly, and then set it up at a spot where you can safely leave it for a few days during the installation. You must be able to see the entire rain garden site from this spot, as you will need to take measurements in many places *without* moving the equipment. Be sure to level the tripod base *and* the transit itself before starting to measure!

The height of the transit is called the *zero spot*; you will relate all other elevations to this spot. Zero is not really at zero elevation, though, since it is above the ground. To find your zero, measure the height of the transit using the calibrated pole that comes with it. For the sake of this example,

Finding the levels with a calibrated pole

Setting up the mechanical transit correctly is key to a successful dig.

let's say that the transit is 3 feet high (91cm), so your zero spot is 3'00", or 36" (1m).

Before you dig, measure the existing ground level at the rain garden site, following the instructions in your transit manual. If the ground is fairly flat between the transit and the rain garden, it is likely going to be the same as your zero. If the ground slopes, this number will be higher or lower depending on where the transit sits in relation to the measured spot. Write this number down in your notes.

If your design calls for a total depth of 30 inches (76cm), your excavation will be finished when the transit measurements from the bottom of the rain garden read 30 inches plus the elevation reading at the original topography at the

In order to measure the elevation difference between the zero point and the ground level before excavation, one person looks into the transit while another person holds up the calibrated measuring pole.

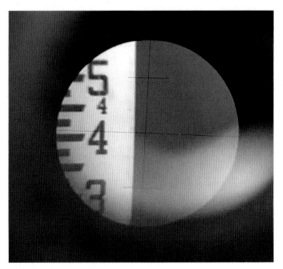

Looking through the transit to measure the elevation where the rain garden is going to be

edge of the rain garden. In our example, if the ground is fairly flat and our zero point was 3 feet (36 inches), it will read 5.5 feet (66 inches; 1.7m): 3 feet (36 inches, your zero elevation) + 30 inches (or 2.5 feet, the depth of your rain garden). Take the measurements for the entire bottom depth to ensure the bottom of the rain garden is fairly flat. It should all read the same.

EXCAVATING SOIL

Depending on the soil conditions, the size and location of the rain garden, and the location of the property, you may decide to hire an excavation professional for the day. Make sure the company you hire is licensed, insured, and qualified to do the work. Ask for references and have a contract in hand.

Machine digging

Tire marks left by the machine. They will be repaired later, and the grass will regrow well. The excavated soil is arranged here into a new raised bed. This is what 10 yards (7.6m³) of soil looks like: 18 inches (46cm) high, 8 feet (2.4m) wide, and 20 feet (6m) long.

But sometimes the only choice is to dig by hand, and if you have lots of friends who want to help you, digging by hand may just be easier. One of our projects involved a fence that the client did not want to take down to bring in a machine. Our

THE PROS AND CONS OF HIRING A PROFESSIONAL EXCAVATOR

PROS:

- The excavation will be done in a timely and efficiently manner, without the risk of damaging the property, and according to the design.

- If you don't need the extra soil, the company can haul it away.

- You can just sit back and relax!

CONS:

- Not every landscape and excavation contractor has heard about rain gardens; even fewer have had any training in designing and installing them.

- The cost can add up quickly. As of this writing, the hourly rate for an operator and equipment is often $125 or higher, and an average urban rain garden will require six to eight hours of work, including mobilization time (perhaps expensive to us, but often these operators barely make any profit after paying all their own costs).

- Digging equipment, as much help as it is, needs specific-sized openings for access and can be difficult to manage on small sites without lots of practice. It also leaves tire or track marks.

crew ended up hand-digging the entire 4-feet-deep rain garden in fairly clayey soil. Because we all have a sense of humor, we had a good time, but it was a tough day. So, if this is a Dig It Yourself project, have the chiropractor and massage appointments scheduled for right after the work is done!

————— •• —————

TIP If any utility lines are within a few feet of the rain garden, the law requires that anyone, even a professional excavator specialist, excavate there by hand. Exposing any of the utilities by hand can be a slow and difficult process.

————— •• —————

Keep measuring the depth during the excavation.

Start at the center.

Have the machine back out of the site, leaving the remaining soil uncompacted and loose inside the rain garden.

Finishing up by hand allows you to create a nice, well-defined shape and a solid slope for the sides. This rain garden is built near larger shrubs, but we made sure no roots were in the area, so the shrubs were not damaged.

The berm is built and the bottom is scarified, ready for refill.

For inflow construction over utility lines, use only hand shovels to dig and place the pipe as close to the surface as possible (see Utility Lines in chapter 3). Usually the overflow area simply allows water to flow out and spread widely into the landscape, which does not interfere with utilities. If you need to place a pipe, make sure you dig with care and use only hand tools.

Whether you use a shovel or a machine, start the excavation in the middle of the rain garden and dig away from the center to avoid compaction. Compacting the ground as you go is counterproductive to the purpose of the rain garden. If an excavating machine has to drive into the rain garden area, back it out of the site in a way that ensures it never drives over loose, freshly excavated bottom or side areas. It has to leave the site as loose (or fluffy, if you like) as possible. The excavated soil should be moved and piled in the designated areas, not in messy piles, during the dig.

Measure the elevation as the excavation progresses, making sure the hole reaches the intended depth. Remember, the bottom needs to be flat! To make sure it is, walk around the top edge of the hole with the calibrated pole, and check with the transit to ensure the measurements are similar everywhere within an inch (a couple of centimeters).

As the sides are excavated, measure the slope of the sides, checking them against your measurements for each 1 foot (30.5cm) distance from the ponding area. Try to maintain continuous slopes on the sides. Curving them slightly is OK, but too much curving, especially if it undermines the top area, can cause the top edge of the rain garden to collapse.

SCARIFYING THE BOTTOM

Before the bottom of the rain garden is considered done, make sure you scarify it: Keep it messy and roughed up. If you are using a machine to excavate, run the bucket over the bottom and loosen it up. If you are hand-digging, dig in deeper with a shovel but do not lift out the soil. It should be flat, fairly level, but with the soil on the bottom and sides broken up. This is to ensure that the fill soil and the native soil mingle to interact, allowing the microorganisms to develop live and active transition between the layers. A smooth garden bottom can easily become a crusty separation where roots and water have a hard time transitioning. This can cause the rain garden to infiltrate poorly and the plants to struggle or eventually die.

BUILDING THE BERM

The next phase of installation after excavation is to build the berm, if your design calls for one. The berm area should be ready before the digging starts, especially if you're using excavated soil for its construction.

Sheet Mulch

If the berm area has plants, groundcovers, lawn, or weedy growth you don't want, sheet-mulch it the day before the excavation to choke out and eliminate unwanted vegetation and to prevent weedy growth. First, cut the existing vegetation very low, as close to the ground as possible. If it is woody material, dig the plants out; if the stems are soft and herbaceous, just use a weed eater. Wet the surface so it is easier to place the cardboard or burlap. Cardboard is best, as this layer needs to be thick and strong, keeping out the weeds. You can use burlap as well, but you will need multiple layers to have the same effect.

Next, place sheets of cardboard or burlap over the area, overlapping tightly. Secure the sheets with rocks or other heavy objects, so the wind will not blow them away. Water the sheets before the soil is piled on it to build the berm; this helps it to better contour with the ground.

SAFE SHOVEL PRACTICES

People can injure themselves by overdoing it during the dig phase. Following are some tips for safe shovel use. But above all, do not overdo it—it's not worth it to pay for the rain garden with the health of your back.

- Do warm-up exercises before digging.

- Avoid lifting, twisting, and turning at the same time. Do only one thing at a time: Lift, then twist, then turn. *One movement at a time!*

- Lift by squatting and using your legs instead of bending down from the waist.

- Keep your back straight when you stand up.

- If it hurts, stop! Stretch and take a break. Listen when your body tells you it has had enough.

Filled and mulched, the rain garden is ready for plants. (Photos by the Hanson Family)

TREE-SAFE EXCAVATION PRACTICES

Placing a rain garden close to a tree is generally not recommended. However, if a pipe has to run across a tree's root zone, the line needs to be dug by hand, using the smallest shovel possible, and the pipe has to be tunneled and woven into the root area as much as possible, without damaging tree roots and still allowing for a slight slope in the pipe.

Consult a certified arborist before the installation, in order to preserve the health of the trees and not create a hazard. It may be possible to cut small roots without creating a risk of lasting damage, or it may even be possible to tunnel under the roots, but these decisions are best made by a professional who knows and understands trees and their root systems.

If during the excavation you accidentally damage a root, stop the work and take care of the injury. Recut the wound with a sharp saw or pruner disinfected with rubbing alcohol or hydrogen peroxide. Cover the root with soil right after the new cut. If the root is larger than 3 inches (7.5cm), you may want to ask the opinion of a certified arborist about follow-up care to help the tree recover.

Do not use an AirSpade to expose tree roots yourself! An AirSpade is a machine that forces air into the ground at high speed. It is usually used with an industrial vacuum or vacuum truck so the soil is contained and does not blow all over the site. This tool can expose roots and remove the soil from them very effectively and very fast. But while blowing the soil off of the root system sounds like fun and does leave the roots intact, it dries them out and can completely destabilize the tree. Soil holds the root system and the tree in place; without soil, the roots have nothing to grip. You will never be able to replace or refill the soil in the same way as it was in its natural state, and you risk root failure, especially in windy weather. Only certified arborists should use AirSpades for root exposure.

If trees are planted in or near Zone 3, the roots will grow around the pipes. If the right pipe—schedule 40 or stronger, and not black corrugated—is used the right way, it is not easy for the roots to get into them and block them (see section on pipe types in chapter 4 for more information). They will just cling around the pipes as they grow.

Compaction

Mark out the berm on the ground before the work starts, just as you marked out the rain garden. Because berms need to be holding in ponding water, they have to be fairly water-tight. As you build the berm, compact every 6 inches (15cm) of soil using a mechanical plate compactor, which you can rent at a big-box hardware store. Alternatively, you can work with a hand tamper, but it is very difficult and quickly becomes tiring. A rake will be important to have if you are shaping the berm by hand. If a professional excavator is on site, he may be able to use the bucket for compaction, but a mechanical plate compactor is still the best tool for this job.

Move the soil bit by bit and measure often. You will need to check the level of the top with the leveling equipment. To make sure the berm sides slope as you designed them, use a string with a level on it and a plumb to make sure it is the ratio you want.

As you are building the berm, don't forget about your overflow design. Do you need to leave a gap in the berm to create the overflow area? Do you need to place an overflow pipe within the berm as it is being raised?

TERRACING

If you're building a terraced rain garden, start your excavation at the upper rain garden and shape it, forming the ground as needed for the retaining wall or weir structure. Then dig out the lower rain garden, complete with the sloped sides. Build the retaining wall or weir between the two rain gardens. Place the overflow of the lower rain garden as far as possible from the inflow of the upper one coming in from the upper rain garden cell.

Make sure the overflow of the first rain garden really does move into the next cell by testing it with a hose, running water through the system. Check that the placement allows for the water to sit long enough in both cells by measuring the elevation of the installed inflow and overflow pipes, making sure it is per your design and allows for 6 inches (15cm) of ponding in the rain garden. Adjust the pipes if needed.

Professionals from Applied Organics fill a compost sock on site.

Here, prefilled socks were delivered and put in place.

The terraced rain garden has been permitted to overflow onto the sidewalk.

Rock armoring is used for both the inflow and overflow.

INSTALLING INFLOW AND OVERFLOW

When the excavation is close to being complete, it's time for the inflow and overflow installation. If you are installing pipes, they will need to be glued together using a two-part plumbing glue. The primer is purple and the glue is blue. Make sure not to breathe it in closely; use a mask and do the work outside. If you find similar alternative materials, just make sure they comply with any applicable regulations. Make sure to install the cleanouts if you use a long run of pipe (40 feet, 12.2m, or longer) or if it has multiple tight 90-degree bends in its run.

Inflow

Remember, do not connect the inflow to a downspout until the rain garden is ready to receive water. Right now, construct it offline.

You may need to wrap the piping around footings or other foundation structures.

To construct the inflow slope you will need a shovel and hand tools. We recommend digging it with a machine only if you are running a pipe longer than 10 feet (3m). The equipment will dig a larger hole, and you will have to fill it back in carefully after the pipe is placed. So it is easier to hand-dig these routes if the soil is not too hard or rocky; you have more control over the size of the trench.

Make sure the trench and pipe or swale have the minimum 2–4 percent slope to them. This is very important so that the water moves at a good speed, not too fast and not too slow (see Inflow in chapter 4).

Check with a level to make sure the pipe slopes 2 percent or more.

If your inflow uses a swale, line it as you designed it, with pond liner sandwiched between two pieces of felt underlay, so that it will not allow infiltration until the water is far enough from the structure you are protecting. You can place the cobblestones and rocks on the liner once it is in its final position.

The inflow is in place in a gap within the walkway. This inflow connects the overflow from a rain barrel into the rain garden.

Here liner is placed on felt for a much longer run than in most DIY projects. Liner is heavy, though, even in smaller sections, so have enough people on hand to help with it.

If your inflow uses a pipe, do not put rocks back into the hole when you backfill. A rock will rub against the pipe and eventually break it. Only use a hand tamper, working it very lightly, or boot-pack—gently walk around on—the area once the soil is filled back in.

Tunneling

If the inflow has to cross a walkway or drive-way, it will have to run through a pipe under the hardscape, which means tunneling. This is a big job—tunneling under walkways is probably the toughest part of rain garden construction.

Start by using a rock bar to loosen the soil. Hitting the ground with the rock bar, especially the pointy or sharp end, and moving it as fast as you can, you will be able to loosen up the soil effectively. Then dig it out with a trenching shovel. If you run into a large rock, you may have to move your tunnel over. Sometimes the ground below the driveway is very hard due to heavy compaction before the concrete pour; if so, attach a PVC pipe to the end of a garden hose and run water into the hole until the soil softens. Use the pipe as you used the rock bar, while the water is running, keep hitting the ground in front of the pipe. If all else fails, you can rent a "mole," a machine designed to tunnel, but its strong vibrations can crack the concrete. It's sometimes easier to cut out the concrete above the tunnel, dig out the rock or very hard soil that's causing the issue, run the pipe, and

Tunneling under the sidewalk

The pipe was placed in a cut within the driveway, and pavers were used to fill in the gap.

then either repour the concrete walkway or place pavers there—as if it were designed that way on purpose.

However you dig the tunnel, make sure you are digging in a straight line: It's not a good idea to bend piping too much, especially under a walkway, where cleanout is almost impossible. Once your tunnel surfaces on the opposite side, you should be able to see through it in a fairly straight, gently sloping line.

Overflow

The overflow has to be placed with care as far from the inflow as possible, to maximize the time the water has to infiltrate into the soil. Remember, the elevation of the overflow is the top of the ponding area. The overflow elevation can be adjusted some—things can and usually do look different in the real world than they do on a paper design—but it should be close to the final measures when placed and be situated in relation to the inflow. This means allowing for the 6 inch (15cm) ponding depth while being lower than the inflow and as far from the inflow as possible. Measuring the elevation of the inflow and the elevation of the top of the mulch layer in the ponding area, calculate where the 6- inch ponding depth (or whatever amount you have designated) is and place the overflow. Adjust the ponding depth and the overflow as needed, making sure the inflow is higher than the overflow, because *water flows downhill.*

Overflow pipe with cleanout installed

Cleanout

In this rain garden, designed by a professional, the overflow pipe ends in a rock-lined dry well.

When building the overflow out of pipes, use the same technique you used for the inflow. The pipe should be sloped 2 percent or steeper. If multiple pipe segments are used, you will have to glue them together. Follow the trench outline to where you designed the overflow to be. If the overflow connects back into the original drainage system (often done by reconnecting to the downspout), make sure you follow the specifications of your jurisdiction for the downspout assembly. If the pipe is longer than 40 feet (12.2m) or has a lot of curves to it, consider installing the cleanouts the same way you did for the inflow.

Installing a Vertical Underdrain

To install a vertical underdrain, follow the instructions that come with the design (typically from the conservation district, or other professional designers). If you purchased it at a hardware store, the manual will show you how to assemble it. Vertical underdrain overflow control structures can also be purchased from some of the conservation districts as a kit.

In general this is how a vertical underdrain overflow control structure should be installed if it is made from scratch (meaning you make it from pipes):

1. Purchase an 18-inch (46cm) diameter septic pipe section. These are usually sold in 10-foot (3m) pieces.
2. Cut the pipe to the desired length using a circular saw. It needs to be longer than the depth of the rain garden (see illustration on the following page).

With the grate on top, this vertical underdrain is connection ready.

3. Drill the holes into the pipe as shown.

4. At the farthest place from the inflow, dig deeper down below the bottom of the rain garden. The native soil gives stability to the pipe because it is solid soil and not loose like the rain garden soil mix.

5. Place at least 6 inches (15cm) or so of drain rock in the bottom of the deeper hole you dug for the underdrain.

6. Place the drilled vertical underdrain pipe into the hole, and center it within the excavated area. Using a plumb and a leveling rod, make sure it is vertical and level.

7. Fill around the pipe with more drain rock as you backfill the rest of the rain garden using the rain garden soil mix. The drain rock should surround the big pipe like a blanket.

8. Glue the horizontal PVC or HDPE pipe to the vertical pipe and elbow system (assembly) as shown in the drawing. This will become the overflow pipe, so place it as appropriate for your overflow location. If a shutoff valve is designed into the system, install the valve between the horizontal pipe and the elbow, as shown on the diagram. If a restriction plate (to control even further the residency—the length of time the runoff spends in the rain garden soil mix—of the runoff in the rain garden) is

designed, follow the instructions for the sizing of this orifice.

9. Drill a hole large enough to tightly house the horizontal pipe as it moves the water into the overflow location. Make sure this horizontal exiting pipe is at the elevation needed to connect with the overflow location. The vertical underdrain section will determine the level of the typical ponding. The top will have to be flush with the top of the ponding area.

10. Connect the horizontal pipe assembly to the sidewall of the vertical pipe. Seal this connection with silicone caulk so it holds strongly.

11. Finish off the backfill with the mulch all the way to the pipe, covering the rock blanket as well on the top.

12. Place the lid on the vertical underdrain pipe. If you are afraid that backfill material will collect in the pipe, you can temporarily cover the top with the lid and a piece of fabric or plywood.

ADDING RAIN GARDEN SOIL MIX

Once the inflow and overflow are installed, you need to start refilling the bowl of the rain garden with the rain garden mix. Make sure to backfill only when the weather is dry, even if you are installing the rain garden during the fall/winter

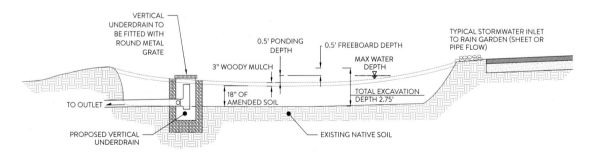

This rain garden cross-section shows how a vertical underdrain would be positioned and connected. (Rendering by Derek Hann, P.E.)

Rain garden soil mix with native soil (Photo by Sindea Kirk)

season. Wait on the soil work for a sunny day—wet soil mix will compact more densely, which often results in really poor infiltration.

If the excavated soil will be used for the refill, it needs to be mixed with the high-quality compost you ordered, as detailed below. (If you ordered pre-engineered rain garden mix, skip down to Fill in the Rain Garden.)

Mix the Soil and Compost

Make a sample batch of rain garden mix in a bucket by thoroughly combining *two parts excavated soil with one part compost*. Keep this bucket nearby as your color reference for the final look of the mixed soil.

Mixing can be done with the help of the excavating machine, but you must know how to work the equipment's finer settings. It also takes a lot of space: You will have to stage the piles close to each other and move the arm back and forth, transferring compost or soil between piles. In tight side yards or backyards where there was only enough room for the excavation in the first

place, mixing like this may not be possible, but if there is enough space, it's a good learning opportunity. *Note, however, that the excavator can be used only to place the soil and compost in the rain garden hole. The actual mixing must be done by hand, using shovels and rakes, in the rain garden bottom.* This ensures that the soil is boot-packed. Boot-packing eliminates any air pockets without damaging the soil. In the end, rain garden soil will need to be loose yet firmly packed. This is easily achieved by walking on it during the refill phase.

One of our clients used a small electric concrete mixer with success. If you do that, you must make sure the rain garden soil is not over-mixed; you do not want to *pulverize* the compost and the soil, just mix them.

The soil and the compost should be fairly dry for this process—not bone dry, but not wet. If they are wet, the material will compact tightly and lack pore space. Even if the base material is almost 100 percent sand, compost should not be handled when wet.

Fill in the Rain Garden

You should still have lots of wooden stakes on hand, and you'll need them for this next step. Plant them securely in the ground at the bottom of the rain garden—enough of them that you can gauge the refilling levels well everywhere, but not so many that moving around the rain garden is impossible without tripping over one. Using the transit or other leveling tool, mark the desired depth of the rain garden soil mix on each stake with ribbon or tape or paint. It is important that you calculate this from the *transit or other tool down* and not from the bottom of the rain garden up.

The marks on your stakes will provide a steady reference point, ensuring that the refill soil ends up at a close-to-even level. For a garden backfilled with 18 inches (46cm) of rain garden mix, and a transit at a zero of 3 feet (91cm), the top of the refill should read 4 feet (1.2m). This is because you'll

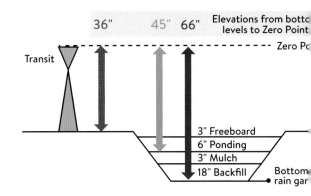

Ensure you're maintaining consistent levels across the bottoms of all the layers.

have, in this example, 3 inches (7.5cm) for woody mulch, 6 inches (15cm) for ponding, and 3 inches (7.5cm) for freeboard above the top of the mix. So, the top of the rain garden mix should be 12 inches (30.5cm) below the original surface of the yard.

Measuring the stakes

Filling (note depth change)

Backfilling and bootpacking

12 inches + 3 feet (36 inches) =
4 feet (48 inches, 1.2m)

Before you start backfilling, double-check that the bottom is scarified, not smooth. As you add the soil mix, gently boot-pack it in layers. It is best to walk on it after each 6-inch (15cm) deep layer is put in place. If you are hand-filling the rain garden, you will already be walking on the soil as you rake it around. This compacts the soil by about 80 percent, so it will remain stable as it fills with runoff and drains out. Without boot-packing, the soil will shrink and fail in spots during the rainy season as the air pockets collapse.

ADDING ARMORING

Once the soil is placed and boot-packed, it's time to add the armoring, the layer of rocks at the inflow and overflow areas that protects the rain garden from erosion.

Place the rocks you ordered—which should be large enough that they do not mix with the soil easily—in a natural, aesthetically pleasing manner. You can also get very creative using pieces of woody debris 3 inches (7.5 cm) in diameter and 3 or so feet (1m) long, placing them so as not to block the flow, but to look as if they were carried in by the water. Art can be used in the inflow and

Armoring can also help direct water away from the inflow toward the overflow.

The armoring is larger than the direct inflow area, wider than just the exact width of the pipe or swale where it connects to the rain garden. Placing the rocks in a bit larger area than the opening of the pipe or the swale allows you to create a natural-looking armoring that adds to the rain garden's beauty and function. (Note the walkway rebuilt over the inflow pipe in this example.)

overflow areas as well: Jumping fish made of metal, wood, or glass are always beautiful!

MULCHING

At this point in the installation phase, you have to make a decision. Do you plant the rain garden now, while the weather is still dry, or do you lay down the woody mulch and wait to plant until the end of the dry season? Remember, the rain garden is still not online, meaning the inflow should not be connected to its source, as it is not ready for runoff processing yet.

If you have been babysitting your plants for a long time already (perhaps you bought them from conservation district sales at the end of winter) and now they are really miserable, you may want to just go ahead and plant them. (If so, read Planting Your Rain Garden, below.) If it is early fall, it is OK to wait a few more weeks to plant until the fall rains begin—but at least talk to the poor souls and tell them you love them!

If you are using burlap bags to control weeds in the new rain garden, place the bags on top of the soil mix now, before you add the mulch layer. Mark the depth of the mulch—3-4 inches (7.5-10cm)—on the stakes the same way you marked them for the soil refill. Load in the woody mulch layer 3-4 inches deep on the bottom and sides of the rain garden and boot-pack it. In our scenario, with a transit zero of 3 feet (91cm), the transit should read 3 feet 9 inches (1.1m) when the mulching is finished. This is because in our example the

Spreading mulch (Photo by Sindea Kirk)

Top layers (Photo by Sindea Kirk)

Pouring mulch (Photo by Sindea Kirk)

zero level is 3 feet. The freeboard is 3 inches and the ponding depth is 6 inches, for a total of 3 feet plus 9 inches to the top of the mulch layer.

If you're mulching after you plant, do the same thing, but create small wells around each plant, leaving room for the bases and stems of the plants.

PLANTING YOUR RAIN GARDEN

Your rain garden is almost ready to go online! The simple summary of this section is to place the plants according to the design and plant. But you will want to approach plants and planting with care, so follow the guidelines laid out in this section to ensure your plants will be happy and thrive in the rain garden.

Handle Plants Carefully

Plants are sometimes awkward to handle. However, they're often easily injured, so it is important to approach them with care.

Avoid dragging plants by their branches or trunks; it pulls on the young and tender wood, creating hairline cracks that can later result in failure. When moved around by their canopy, shrubs can lose branches and their shape is affected. Bark, if pulled on hard or rubbed roughly, can peel off the stem. All of these injuries can lead to diseases and death.

Lift plants by their rootballs, and hold the entire plant by the bottom of the roots (or the container). For heavier plants, use a wheelbarrow or a handcart for easier transportation. If a branch does break, prune the remaining stub off with a sharp pruner disinfected with rubbing alcohol or hydrogen peroxide and wiped with a clean rag.

Young plant roots can be smashed if they are dropped, especially from up high. Plants are particularly susceptible to this type of injury if they are in burlap without a solid container around them. Set them down gently to protect their roots. If you are handling a very heavy plant, have someone help you. Slowly wiggle the rootball along the ground to the hole, and lower it into the hole by holding it at the root ball, not the trunk or branches.

Test the Layout

Distribute the plants around the rain garden based on the design, without planting them, and look at the layout. If you want to move something, this is the time to do so. Just keep in mind each plant's mature size. Plants can easily fool you: Something tall and wide today may not get much bigger over the next five years, while a tiny twig becomes a fifteen-foot-tall tree and the formerly tall plant its understory. Look up and take note of where any overhead wires are. If you need to move a tree from under the wires, this is the time. Keep thinking in four dimensions, including time as a factor in your decisions.

Remove Containers

Once you have shuffled your plants around a little, making final decisions about exactly where everything should go, it's time to get them ready for planting. Remove any container around the plant, even if it's papier-mache or coir (coconut fiber). Containers take time to break down, and plants can get root bound in the meantime. We take these containers off and toss them into the compost pile. Also take off dibble tubes, very small containers that normally house grass and emergent plant starts, when transplanting or planting, as they will not break down.

Some plants come "balled and burlapped" (B&B), and sometimes larger B&B plants are then put into a container—not a good practice for the plants, but it still happens. There may even be several layers of burlap, if roots growing out of the first burlap cover were then covered with a second layer of burlap, and so forth. Always check

Balled and burlapped plant stock

large root balls for hidden burlap layers. If there are multiple ones, you will need to cut the roots to remove all the fabric, but it is better to do this than leave the burlap on. Remove as much twine and burlap as possible.

There is a debate regarding whether *bare rooting*, or washing the soil off of B&B plants, is a good practice or not. We do not recommend it; instead, we do our best to keep the root balls as intact as possible. However, these root balls can introduce a lot of clay-based soils into the rain garden (B&B root balls are typically clay grown because clay will ball into burlap easily), so avoid placing B&B plants within Zones 1 and 2. This makes no real difference in Zone 3, and you can plant trees or larger shrubs that came in burlap as long as you take the burlap off.

Plant

If you already mulched, move the mulch aside from the spot where you will dig each hole—*always plant into the rain garden soil mix, not into the mulch layer*. The mulch layer is not designed to support plants but to keep weeds and other plants from growing; it needs to break down into humuslike material before it can feed plants.

Dig a hole as deep as the rootball or container and twice as wide. Spread the plant's roots out. If they have started to grow in circles, cut through them using that magical hori-hori tool. These roots are still very fine, and they will recover from the pruning. If the plant has a main anchoring root, also called a *taproot*, make sure the hole is deep enough that the taproot can be straight. A bent root will damage the plant over time, as the root system will be malformed.

Center the plant in the hole, and refill the hole with the dug-out rain garden soil mix. Do not add extra amendments! Making the backfill rich in nutrients does not help plants. Of course, as good plant parents, we want to spoil the little critters, but while the plants would love the rich soil and quickly put on lush new growth (and attract lots of pests in the process that want to suck the juices out of the fresh greens), they will be reluctant to extend their roots outside of the sweet spot. Spoiled plants often eventually girdle themselves and die.

Zsofia placing plants after reviewing mature sizes and looking for overhead wires

Loosen roots. (Photo by Sindea Kirk)

Gently press the refilled soil around the roots, ensuring that it touches the root surfaces and holds the plant up. Do not step on it or use a tamper, just use your hands. Press enough to create the soil-root bond, but not enough to crush the roots. Because the soil is already enriched with compost, there is no need to put extra compost as top dressing around the plant.

If there's mulch there, pull it close to the plant but leave a small well around the plant. *Do not cover the stems with mulch*—that will choke the plants to death. Even woody stems can be either burnt by the wood chips as they break down (remember, it is composting at 140+°F, 60+°C!), or the moisture held at the base of the stem by the mulch will rot out the stem.

Spread out the plant's roots. (Photo by Sindea Kirk)

Move mulch aside to plant into soil. (Photo by Sindea Kirk)

Leave a well around the base of the plant.

Stake If Necessary

A plant should be staked only if it really cannot hold itself up, and a stake should never be left in place for longer than a year. Preferably, it will be removed after just a few months. Woody stems, canopy, and root systems grow as a response to prevailing wind forces and other conditions specific to the site. Without that stimulation, the plants will not form roots and branches able to withstand the challenges of the site, and they will fail over time. Stake ties can also damage bark and wood if left on too long or placed too tight.

Use wide plastic ties sold specifically for tree staking, and wrap them with enough "give" that your hand can comfortably fit into the loop along with the stake and the tree. To ensure that the tree can move in the wind, tie the stake to the tree in a figure 8 two-thirds of the way up the trunk. This recommendation is based on the 2014 revised International Society of Arboriculture's specifications; you may find conflicting information in both older and newer sources based on other data.

Staking has been done for a long time, so if you do find different information, it's OK. Whatever instructions you follow, do your best to allow the tree some movement within the staking, protect the bark from damaging ties, and remove the stakes after no more than a year.

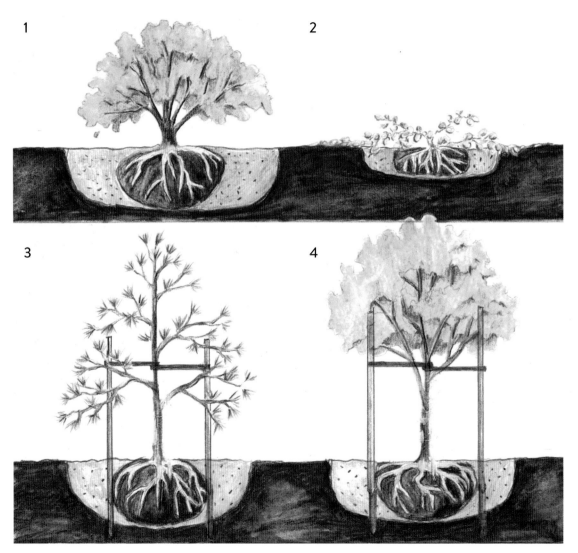

1   2   3   4

Most new plants don't need staking, but for those that do, stake them loosely so they have room to move and grow. Correct planting of 1) shrub; 2) groundcover; 3) evergreen tree; and 4) deciduous tree.

Water

As you put each plant in the ground, water it, getting the soil around it moist; water again after all of the planting is done. When you water after the planting, use a gentle, shower-like spray. Water the plant well enough that the soil around it feels wet—not flooded and not merely moistened, but wet. (Check the next chapter for details on further watering.)

ACTIVATING YOUR RAIN GARDEN

And that brings us to the end of the steps for installing the rain garden. Once everything has been measured and dug and sloped and filled, and the plants and mulch are all in place, the rain garden is completed and it is time to put it online! Connect the inflow to the downspout, remove anything blocking the runoff from the system, and let that stormwater find its way in! If your inflow is via a downspout, simply disassemble the original downspout connection and replace it with a pipe section that connects the downspout pipe to

Connecting downspout to inflow pipe

Some downspout–gutter connections require inspection.

your inflow pipe, as shown in the illustrations. *If disassembling the connection between the gutter and the downspout required a permit, an inspector must look at it before it can be considered done.*

Attach the end of the gutter to the inflow connection as designed, and cap the actual downspout to prevent any critter climbing into it.

Online or not, if it's still the dry season, you'll need to keep watering the plants until the wet season returns. But you can start enjoying the beauty of the rain garden right away. Sit on the bench or rock you placed by it, and celebrate the finish. You've come a long way!

CHAPTER 6

CHAPTER 6

Maintenance and Troubleshooting: Caring for Your New Pride and Joy

Like animal babies, even low-maintenance rain gardens need some care and feeding as they start out, in order to live a full and healthy life. Horticulture professor Walt Bubelis was once asked if a garden design his class was working on would be no-maintenance. He answered, "If you want no-maintenance greenery, you should consider plastic."

Walt is right! Most people equate low maintenance with having to do nothing, but living things need care; that is what makes them beautiful and real. In an urban site, the plants may need very little care, but they will need something—especially while they are little babies! Plus, a rain garden is a wonderful wildlife habitat, and in order for it to provide all the elements animals need to thrive, we have to maintain it using natural gardening principles. This chapter covers maintenance plans for the first three years of your rain garden's life, as well as troubleshooting solutions to common problems.

YEAR 1

Let's start where we ended the installation phase: You have a brand-new rain garden! The soil is new, the mulch is fresh, and the plants are small (compared with what their mature size will be) so they'll need special care.

Monitoring Inflow and Overflow

After your new rain garden is online, stay in town for the first forecasted storm. You must watch the rain garden and make sure the inflow and overflow work as intended. Keep tabs on how fast or slow the rain garden infiltrates, and be ready to make adjustments if necessary. There is nothing worse than sipping a margarita on vacation while reading a text from the neighbor whose front yard is flooded because your overflow malfunctioned.

Inspect the inflow and overflow regularly, and clean them out if sediment or other debris builds

Pest control and weeding should be done by hand, not with chemicals.

Plants will require watering for the first two summers. (Photo by the Hanson Family)

up on top of the armoring or within the structure. Use a hose to wash out the pipes each fall and, if storms blow leaves into the gutters, during the winter too. Rocks may need to be adjusted, added, or rearranged to ensure the water flows unobstructed as planned.

Any and all garbage should be removed from the rain garden regardless of the timing.

Watering

As mentioned in the previous chapters, it's best to build rain gardens during dry weather. By default that means that most rain gardens in our area are built during the summer, so they will need watering in the beginning. We usually recommend watering the rain garden for the first two years, more in the first dry season and less in the second.

How much should you water? Well, you have to ensure that the plants survive, which generally takes about an inch (2.5cm) of water per week. To determine a watering schedule, place an empty tuna can in the rain garden and measure how long it takes to fill with 1 inch of water using your watering method (sprinkler, irrigation spout, etc.). If it takes 30 minutes to fill the can, it means you have to water your rain garden 30 minutes a week to provide 1 inch of water to the plants. This amount can be broken down to either three times per week for 10 minutes or twice per week for 15 minutes. Before watering again, check whether the rain garden soil is moist; the top 10–12 inches (25–30.5cm) should be moist for good plant growth. If the soil is dry, it is time to water.

During very hot and dry periods, like recent summers, we needed to water more than an inch a week. There is no magic formula; each site has different microclimates, sun and wind exposure, and plant material. This means that each rain garden has its own specific water need and drying-out pattern. Just keep touching and feeling the soil to make the decision.

————— • • —————

TIP You can capture rain in cisterns or rain barrels and use it for the rain garden. This not only helps reduce the cost of watering, it also conserves potable water for drinking. (For more on rain barrels, see chapter 7.)

————— • • —————

PLANT DOCTORING

If your plants start to look sparse or off-color or show other signs of trouble, they may need some food; a couple of handfuls of compost can go a long way if applied around the base of a plant. Or you can make the diluted compost mixture, and water with that to provide a faster, more even feeding for each plant. Call a professional to help you identify the problem if you can't figure it out. Ultimately, if a plant is sick and you cannot find a natural solution (please do not use synthetic fertilizers and pesticides in a rain garden), you may have to say goodbye to it.

Weeding

If the rain garden has 3–4 inches (7.5–10cm) of mulch on it (which should be maintained at this depth for the garden's entire lifespan), weeds should not be a big issue. However, this brings up a good question: What is a weed? A weed, by definition, is a plant we do not want. But no plant grows in the wild with an "I am a weed" tag; it is purely what we make of it. Most of us in the Pacific Northwest shiver when we see lush new blackberry stems taking root in the middle of an English ivy–covered corner, yet in Hungary, these two plants are precious collectors' items displayed together at the heart of one of Budapest's oldest botanical gardens. Keep this in mind when thinking about weeds. We are very lazy when it comes to weeding. We prefer to sit in gardens, and we love watching wildlife—we pick our battles.

Every time you enter a rain garden, you compact the ground. The more you disturb the ground, the longer it takes for living organisms to make a home in the soil and for the desired plants to spread and grow. If weeding is necessary in a rain garden, and you need to walk into the bottom area, place a plank across the surface to reduce compaction. Use hand tools, pruners, trowels, or a hori-hori to weed. We love using the hori-hori: You can cut, chop, dig, level any soil, and smash snails and slugs with ease. Do not use a weed whacker in the rain garden, because the plants in it are not suitable for this type of trimming.

TIP Pesticides and fertilizers should never be used in a rain garden. You built the system to filter out these chemicals from the runoff; using pesticides or fertilizer would add it all back into the water. These treatments also often hurt wildlife, especially insects. Remember, without insects to eat, the birds you love so much are affected as well.

We used to tell people to weed during the growing season, but with climate change we no longer say a silly thing like that. You need to weed when you need to weed, which is whenever you can enter the rain garden safely because there is no ponding water in it and the soil is not saturated.

Have you ever seen little fairy armies marching through nature regularly, cleaning up, raking, and pruning? No—it doesn't work that way. Plant debris falls to the ground, builds up the duff layer and eventually the humus layer; humus feeds the forest and the meadow. Play the forest game and help create this layer by deliberately placing some of the debris on the ground on your own. If the mess bothers you, simply toss new wood chips over the debris and make it look orderly again.

Dandelions

Weeds are often allies in our garden. Dandelions grow easily, and can be pulled most of the time with little effort from the loose rain garden soil, or with the help of a small shovel. If the weed is deeply rooted, a weed wrench will pull it and save your back. If you need the services of a weed wrench in the bottom of a rain garden, however, that might be a sign that your soil mix was not up to snuff, or that you did not use enough mulch and weeds were able to take root. Let's hope you do not have to replace the soil mix! Pull the weeds and monitor the site. If drainage seems fine, then those dandelions are not a more serious omen.

If allowed to grow and if mixed with other plants, however, dandelions can serve as good companion plants. This bright plant flowers non-stop from early spring, thus providing food for early pollinators. Its deep roots pull water from deeper soil layers. Once it initiates the capillary action and water starts to move upward, against gravity, it does not use all the water it pulls. There-fore, other, shallower rooted plants can also access water from the ground. The dandelion is a built-in irrigation system!

———— •• ————

TIP If you raise chickens, shear off the green tops and flower buds of dandelions and give them to your feathery girls, who love this treat. They love morning glory, too.

———— •• ————

Buttercup and Horsetail

We have learned to accept these two famous Pacific Northwest weeds with a humble heart whenever we see them in the rain garden. As Northwest gardening expert Ciscoe Morris says, "If you have horsetail in your garden, it means you have bad karma. You should consider moving." He may be right, but our own gardens are some of the sites Ciscoe is talking about, full of buttercup, horsetail, and morning glory . . . and we are not moving. Here's why:

Horsetail is native almost everywhere on earth except in a couple of spots, like New Zealand. It is one of the oldest plants, with origins that go back millions and millions of years. It was tree-sized when the long-necked Brachiosaurus dinosaurs roamed the planet—compared with that, today's versions are skinny little afterthoughts! Many native cultures ate the fresh new shoots as a springtime delicacy. Pulling on the plant triggers the adventitious buds on the deep root system to make the plant grow more vigorously, but you can hide it in a garden fairly well. We recommend you leave horsetail alone and hide it, rather than pulling it out of the rain garden. Slough sedge, for example, will grow tall around it and hide it completely (see slough sedge in Top Plants for Pacific Northwest Rain Gardens).

Buttercup is a very thick groundcover. Once its roots are in the ground, they are always in the

RIGHT-OF WAY CONCERNS

People often tell us horror stories of road maintenance crews simply using a tractor mower to "trim" the plants in right-of-way (ROW) rain gardens. If you are planting a rain garden in the ROW, you need to think about this very likely future for the plants. This is why we recommend using emergents and tough woody plants such as red or yellow twig dogwoods for these sites (see Top Plants for Pacific Northwest Rain Gardens). These plants can take mowing and regrow just fine.

Buttercup—at least it's a pretty weed! (Photo by Holli Margell)

Lawn

Sometimes lawn grass will creep into the rain garden from the nearby lawn. This will quickly grow wild if not pulled right away—a well-matted clump can be hard to remove. Use a digging fork for this work. Do not be shy, just dig it out and replace the soil with compost if you do not have access to rain garden soil mix. *Lawn grass, crabgrass, and other invasive grasses, if allowed to grow and spread, will destroy the rain garden quickly.* They can reduce the infiltrating capacity of the soil by not allowing the water to penetrate into the ground. Off with their heads!

Invasive Plants

Himalayan blackberry, English ivy, English holly, English laurel, Japanese knotweed, and Scotch broom must go as well. Pull these invasive noxious weeds, and if you have to, dig them out, rain garden soil mix or not. You can always replace the soil mix, but these weeds have no place in your

Himalayan blackberry (*Rubus armeniacus*), a common invasive plant (Photo by Holli Margell)

ground. It is sometimes referred to as a "weed of concern," which means it should not be sold or planted on purpose, should be controlled if possible (when the plants are newly emerging and easy to pull), and is considered invasive.

As anyone who has tried to eliminate buttercup without poisoning the environment knows, it's close to impossible, unless it can be pulled out while very small, before it starts rooting. We actually don't mind it, and we'll pull just enough so that smaller, more desirable plants are visible. Buttercup leaves are evergreen and beautifully ruffled, while the yellow flowers signal the return of spring. Buttercup in Zone 1 even reduces phosphorus leaching, tying up phosphorus by flowering for most of the growing season, from early spring to late fall.

Please do not plant buttercup on purpose, however! We are not here to market it, or to persuade people to let it spread. If you can't control it, though, it's OK—it doesn't mean you failed as a gardener! Buttercup is tough to fight.

garden. They are often useful and even edible plants, and they are great in their natural environment, but in our region they get out of hand quickly and kill other plants by not allowing them to grow. These plants do not play nice at all!

Winter Maintenance

Once again, we encourage everyone to lazily enjoy their gardens. Leave seed heads and dry foliage standing; these add "winter interest" and are precious food and nesting sources in the winter for birds. Grasses also use their own foliage as a shield against too much wet rain and snow. The grass blades bend on each other, creating a tent over the base of the plant that repels water and snow and protects it from excess moisture. If perennial grasses are cut down in the fall, they can easily rot or freeze out during the winter.

Once the new growth emerges in the spring, these dry leftovers can be removed easily. In nature, they fall away and get pushed to the ground once the new leaves emerge in the spring; the grass regrows larger and more beautiful than the year before. You cannot only allow some of

the dry plant debris to fall to the bottom of the rain garden, but should also place some there as a mulch.

Snow

If your area receives snow, and the rain garden collects runoff from the driveway, walkway, or a nearby road, you will end up with lots of snowmelt in the rain garden, as you will be the one shoveling it aside and into the rain garden contributing area. While the use of deicing chemicals and salts should be minimized, sometimes that is beyond your control. If you designed your system well and chose plants that can tolerate the salty runoff, your plants will be OK. During snowmelts, make sure to allow water to enter the rain garden and dilute

A "rain chain" bides its time during snowy weather. (Photo by the Hanson Family)

Ninebark in winter

Mahonia in winter

the salt levels. If a plant wears out from these seasonal elevated salt levels, replace it with another species growing in your rain garden that shows no sign of stress.

Pruning

A well-designed rain garden does not need much pruning, unless you used larger plants (such as the full-size red osier dogwood) on purpose with the idea of pruning them.

———— • • ————

TIP You can find very good information about pruning practices at Plant Amnesty (www.plantamnesty .org). Their website, classes, and training events are worth checking out. If you want to learn as much as possible about pruning, try signing up for a class at a local community college. Your extension office probably has pruning information, and you can find great books on pruning as well (see Resources). If you want to maintain the health of your plants by pruning the right way, investing in these resources is wise.

———— • • ————

When pruning, always use a sharp pruner. Disinfect it between plants by spraying rubbing alcohol or hydrogen peroxide on the blades; this prevents the spread of diseases. Remember, pruning is essentially wounding the plants; it's just like surgery. Think about the pruning, and only make cuts if there are good reasons for it. This will ensure that the plants are not butchered but rather gently cared for.

Consider these questions when figuring out why, what, when, and whether to prune:

- What is the plant?
- How sensitive is it to injury?
- How does this species usually respond to pruning?
- What is your goal? Do you want to control growth and size? Or are you pruning to enhance the color of new shoots?
- Are you pruning to restore a plant?
- Are you taking out dead or diseased parts?

Time your pruning to prevent diseases from spreading. Plants pruned at the wrong time can be more susceptible to certain diseases—understanding this can save you lots of headaches. For example, if the plant has dead or diseased sections, those can be removed at any time. However, some species and even varieties and cultivars are more prone to certain infections than others, so pruning them at a time when diseases are rampant, such as humid rainy weather, can easily expose them to infection.

If your goal is to control size and growth, prune in late summer or fall, before the freezing weather sets in. Plants go into dormancy late in the summer and start to pull food and nutrients into their root system. Because the hormone triggering new growth is no longer concentrated in the branch endings, a plant pruned at this time of the year will typically not respond with regrowth right away. The plant will preserve the new shape longer, so the size can be influenced more easily.

———— • • ————

TIP If you find that the plant layout or placement in your rain garden is not working out, you can move things around as long as the soil is not overly wet and you use planks to walk on. Make sure to fill in the gaps you create with rain garden soil mix or, if it is not too big a gap, just compost; do *not* use regular nursery soil or potting soil. Place wood chips as needed to maintain or redo the 3-inch (7.5cm) minimum layer.

———— • • ————

If you want to see bright new colorful shoots, then you want to prune to trigger new growth. Pruning in the late winter or early spring, right before the buds break, will encourage plants to grow vigorously. For example, cutting up to one-third of the old canes out of the red and yellow twig dogwood (or any other cane grower shrub) will provide plenty of strong new shoots without damaging the plant.

Pruning by cutting branches in half at random places between buds, called *heading cuts*, causes the plant to regrow quickly in the spring. The shoots are ready to stretch out and push new leaves into the world, with hormones in abundance in each branch tip, so the plant will sense the pruned tips and quickly replace them. BUT it won't replace them with just one new branch each—it will do its best to ensure the branch stays there by growing two, three, or even more new branches there! This is what causes a tree or shrub to look like a broom after a bad pruning.

A different method, *selective thinning*, cuts out entire branches instead of just shortening them. These cuts remove branches that are clogging up

airflow within the shrub and do not usually trigger such strong regrowth on most plants. But again, pruning lightly is a better practice: Once a branch is cut, it cannot be glued back on, and pruning influences plants for a long time to come.

We strongly recommend allowing shrubs to grow in a natural shape when you prune them. Lollipopping trees and shrubs weakens their immune system and shortens their life. If you desire rounds and mounds in the landscape, consider planting trees and shrubs that naturally grow in very compact globe and mound shapes. Your local nursery can advise you about what plants fit these categories. Use the growing habit of plants to shape them, rather than the pruning shears.

Mulching

The mulch layer should be maintained at 3–4 inches (7.5–10cm) deep for the life of the rain garden, so replenish it late in the spring and, if needed, in the fall too, or as the weather and the garden dry out.

Maintain a robust mulch layer.

YEAR 2

The second year, the rain garden still needs a little help. Maintain the same practices as in the first year. Fortunately, as the rain garden plants grow, shrinking space around them will allow fewer weeds to grow! Cut back on the irrigation, and water 1 inch (2.5cm) or less per week if the weather is really hot, and less when it is cooler.

———————••———————

TIP Do not rake the rain garden as part of regular maintenance! If you need to get the leaves off the lawn, use a mulching mower. You can clean your walkways and put the leaves you gathered from the hard surfaces into the landscape beds and the rain garden. Leaves are great mulch and will break down into wonderful humus.

———————••———————

YEAR 3 AND BEYOND

Celebration time! In the third year, you will generally cut off the rain garden from irrigation. However, with climate change, we must be flexible: Support your site with whatever it needs to survive. During a long summer, watering two or three times is plenty. Do not start up a weekly watering regime for mature sites.

Sometimes, happy plants take off fast in the third year and get too big in Year 4. This little rhyme says it all: "The first year they sleep, the second year they creep, and the third year they leap." It's true! If something gets too big for the site, it's OK to divide it and share it with others—or even switch out with another plant. But two things are key:

- Don't mix too much of another type of soil (especially clay and nursery potting soil)

into the rain garden from the new plant's root ball.
- Do this work during the dry season, when the rain garden soil can easily be worked with and will not get damaged.

TROUBLESHOOTING

Rain gardens can have problems, despite all due diligence. Some of them are easy to fix and others can be a pain in the runoff. This section will help you identify the issues and determine solutions. Whatever your problem might be, do not let mistakes scare you too much.

Also keep in mind that, at some point, hiring a professional to evaluate the situation and offer solutions may become necessary. If all else fails—and we mean *all* else—try turning the rain garden into a simple garden bed with lots of natives, especially with a tree or two to soak up as much of the water as possible.

The only failure is doing nothing because we are afraid to make a mistake. Let's keep that rain garden working!

The Rain Garden Does Not Drain

We'll begin with the chief problem a rain garden can have, namely, that it doesn't do what it is supposed to do—it doesn't drain. There can be many reasons for this, and finding a solution may require some detective work on your part.

First, be sure that drainage is actually a problem. Remember, during continuous storms, rain can pond in the garden for a longer time. When was the last rainfall? If it rained less than three days ago, wait longer before worrying. If the rain garden is still full of water four days after the last rainfall, however, it is not draining well. A five- to six-day draining speed means you have an infiltrating bog garden (or boggy rain garden) rather

Stagnant water may be a sign your rain garden isn't draining well.

than a true rain garden. A rain garden that ponds for longer than six days is considered a bog or artificial wetland, and we need to investigate!

To investigate, divert the inflow away from the rain garden so you can access it if needed. Connect a pipe to the downspout or other inflow area that will temporarily move the water directly to the overflow area, bypassing the rain garden.

Simple Solutions

Let's start with the rain-garden equivalent of checking that we're not just out of gas or the toaster isn't plugged in.

First, check the overflow. Is it clogged? If so, clean it out! Run a hose through the system and wash the pipes clean. Clean any sediment-catching box or catch basin, if you have any. Move the armoring around so no rocks are blocking the pipe.

Second, check the inflow. Is it clogged? Just as with the overflow, clean out the inflow and adjust the armoring so the flow is not blocked. Clean the gutter and downspout.

Third, look at the bottom of the garden, aiming a flashlight into the water to look for the following conditions:

- A large piece of trash on the bottom. If you find one, remove it and monitor the drainage.
- A heaping pile of mulch somewhere in the bottom or any other depressions or high points. If you find this, level it out using a rake, then monitor the drainage.

TOO MUCH OF A GOOD THING

At one of the rain gardens we built, the ponding area was always full during the first month. It took us a while to find the cause. A golf course nearby opened up a berm along the property line not long after we finished the rain garden. They also were testing their irrigation system for winterizing and repairs. Every time it rained and every time they turned on their irrigation, the runoff was inundating our little rain garden, which was not designed for the golf course runoff! Closing off the gap in the berm solved the problem.

Further Investigation

If those three investigations didn't turn up any easy fixes, and the garden truly does not drain, it typically means that your soil is clogged. So what could be the cause? Here are some possibilities:

- The soil test was not done right. Did you run all the soil tests and correctly determine your soil type?
- The infiltration testing wasn't done right. Did you use a pipe and only measure the vertical gravitational flow? Did you fill the hole with water three times before starting the tests? Did you run three tests and calculate the average of the three for infiltration?
- The existing water table is too high in the area, and that was not discovered during the assessment.

- There is an undetected hardpan layer below the rain garden.
- The design was too optimistic, resulting in a rain garden that is too small (shallow and/or not wide enough) to compensate for the amount of runoff or the soil conditions.
- The actual contributing area is larger than was measured.
- The design was good, but the rain garden was not built correctly to scale and is not large, deep, or wide enough.
- The bottom is not level.
- The bottom was not scarified.
- The bioretention soil mix is not right (this could be a supplier problem).
- The native soil was simply refilled without compost added.
- The soil has too much compost content (compost holds water very well, and if too much compost is in the system, it can hold back the water).
- The native soil has high clay content and simple sand was mixed in with it, thus forming a crust at the bottom.
- The soil was compacted during the installation, planting, or maintenance work.

The vast majority of these problems can be solved and still result in a functioning rain garden. Others will require a more creative approach. The following suggestions may help you find a solution.

Water Table

Another possible reason your garden isn't draining might be caused by the water table. To find out if the water table is too high or to verify that the soil test was correct, dig another test hole near the rain garden. If the water in the rain garden is the same depth as in the test hole, you have a water table challenge. Your easiest solution? Turn the rain garden into a "bog garden." If the ponding bothers you, however, raise the level of the overall garden by taking out the plants, adding more soil, mulching again, and replanting with slightly different material to fit the wetter conditions better. If the existing plants show no signs of stress, and they are suited for more flooded conditions, just plant them back into the new more boggy space. In any case, you have a bog and you should embrace it as such!

If you do not see the high water table in the new test hole, test the soil again using the various soil tests described in chapter 3. Redo all the tests. It's true that soils can vary greatly just a few feet apart, but the retesting will still be worthwhile. If you kept good, detailed records of the data collected originally, you can check the new tests against the old ones.

If the results are near the same as before and the original design matches the actual installed rain garden, there may be some deeper problems. Here is a list of what those deeper problems might be:

Soil Mix

Test the added rain garden soil. Does it feel like loose, sandy loam with organic matter all the way through? If instead it feels compacted and dense, do a jar test to see what is in it and where it fits on the Soil Triangle. If it is dense and clayey rather than loamy, you need to break it up. Try to auger two or three holes and see if it helps. If not, you may have to dig it all out and replace it with a good soil mix. Digging it all out is a big job, so do try augering first.

Bottom Problems

If the rain garden soil is high quality, the problem may be that the bottom is not level or is too smooth (not scarified). You can only go back and level or scarify the bottom if you dig out the soil completely to the original excavation line. That is a lot of work, and, as in the previous item, augering a few holes in the bottom of the rain garden may get the job done faster and more easily, even if you need professional help with it, so try that first. The goal is to auger into the soil below the rain garden's bottom, as deep as possible. Just like removing the drain plug in a bathtub, this opens up the bottom. Once the runoff filters back into the system, monitor the drainage to see if the augering helped or not. The augered holes should fill as soil falls into them, but if you need to add soil to replenish the fallen material, you can do so as needed, as you monitor the system. It is OK even if mulch falls in. Add what you need from the top and leave the holes in permanently.

A Problem of Size

Another potential cause of poor drainage is that the rain garden is undersized for the runoff amount. Here, you have a few options. First, you can divide the runoff and build another rain garden for the overflow coming from this first one, as long as the site conditions (soils, water table, etc.) allow it. Or, you can also reduce the contributing area by eliminating some of the inflow areas and excluding them from the rain garden.

Last, if the plants are too small or are not working well for the rain garden, plant larger ones or plant a tree to help with taking up the excess runoff.

Erosion

But maybe poor drainage is not your garden's problem. Erosion is another area of concern.

Exposed, Eroding Soil on the Bottom

If your garden's soil is exposed on the bottom, it is likely that the mulch either was not thick enough or was the wrong kind, such as bark, and it washed away. Replenish the mulch, making sure the plants are not buried in it, and keep an eye on the new mulch to see how it works.

Eroded Soil near the Inflow and/or Overflow Area

In this case, there is likely not enough armoring, or the rocks may be too small. This is actually a common challenge, particularly when, for various reasons, people decide to use pea gravel rather than large drain rocks or cobblestones in the armoring area. Pea gravel washes away easily and behaves as an aggregate rather than a rock. It mixes with the mulch and the soil mix, and within days of installation it essentially stops providing protection against erosion. The solution is to use large enough rocks, and place them deep enough and wide enough into the inflow and overflow areas to cover the soil beyond the flow of the water.

Other Rain Garden Problems

Following are some other issues you may encounter, and how to remedy them.

Sediment Buildup on the Armoring near the Inflow

Sediment builds up on the armoring if the inflow has no chance to be filtered before entering the rain garden. Add larger armoring material, and create a longer run for the water over the armoring to help reduce this problem. The inflow in these locations will need a cleanout at least once a month.

Bottom erosion is a sign that too little or the wrong kind of mulch was applied.

Avoid inflow erosion and soil collapse by using larger rocks and placing them deep enough into the soil.

Sediment buildup like this indicates the inflow needs more filtration.

Plants Are Too Small, Young, and Undeveloped

The newly planted plants are spaced well, according to their mature size, but they are too little now and are being overwhelmed. The ponding water covers them all the way and may even drown them. These small plants don't have a chance. Replace them with taller plants that won't be completely submerged and larger plants with more developed root structures that will allow them to get established.

Weeds Everywhere

If your rain garden is overrun by weeds, probably not enough mulch was placed during planting. You need at least 3–4 inches (7.5–10cm) of wood chips or hog fuel for weed control (see Mulch in chapter 4).

Plants Not Thriving

If your plants look unhealthy, straggly, or vulnerable to insect damage, perhaps they were planted in the wrong zone. Plants will struggle in zones that are inappropriate for them, such as sedges in Zone 3 or dwarf mugo pine in Zone 1. It is important that zones be clearly marked on the design and that the people doing the planting understand what the marks mean. The solution is simply to switch the plants around.

Collapsing Soil

When the soil is placed, especially if by a machine, it is important to place it in layers. While installing each layer, walk around in the rain garden basin and boot-pack the soil to eliminate large air pockets. If the soil is collapsing, boot-pack it and bring in more soil to return it to the correct depth. The plants will need to be lifted and the rain garden finished with woody mulch.

Too-small plants may be overwhelmed by ponding.

Too many weeds may mean too little mulch was placed.

These plants aren't thriving because they were planted in the wrong zone.

Blooming Algae

If you see algae in your rain garden, it is likely receiving excess fertilizer from somewhere. This happened to the rain garden we built on a property neighboring a golf course (see earlier sidebar). The golf course decided to remove a berm separating the two properties, and this allowed their runoff to wash over into the rain garden site. The runoff contained lots of fertilizer, which triggered an algae bloom. Once we realized what was happening, we were able to discuss the problem with the golf course management, and as a result, the golf course rebuilt the berm and altered how they fertilize their grass, including no longer applying chemicals in cold temperatures. (Fertilizers, organic or not, need at least 55°F, 13°C, temperature to work. If the weather is colder, the chemicals just sit in the landscape and leach away with every rainfall.) If you get algae, check what is happening on neighboring properties and in your landscape; whatever its source, try to get the amount of fertilizer reduced, and get it applied at the right time.

Plants Are Too Big

In small rain gardens and right-of-way plantings, plants can quickly outgrow the space. Replace them with plants that are more suitable for the site and will fit well even when mature. Pruning can offer temporary peace of mind, but in the long run it will be a struggle if the plants are simply too big for the garden.

MOSQUITOES AND RAIN GARDENS

"If you think you're too small to make a difference, try sleeping in a closed room with a mosquito."
    —*African proverb*

Often people ask, "What about mosquitoes in rain gardens, huh? Aren't rain gardens basically mosquito motels?" But while mosquitoes get excited when they first smell a rain garden, this landscaping style is not for them!

Mosquitoes are annoying, everywhere, and carriers of diseases such as malaria and West Nile virus. They belong to the fly family—mosquito means "little fly" in Spanish—and there are more than 3,500 species of them around the world! The itchy bump at the bite site is caused by their saliva, which keeps the blood flowing but also irritates our skin. A typical female mosquito can drink up to three times its own body weight in blood. Imagine . . . aren't you glad they're tiny?

They have specific habitat needs for their life cycle. If those needs aren't met, mosquitoes don't breed.

Generally, a female mosquito can lay eggs three times before it dies. Each time, it lays an average of about 300 eggs into at least an inch of water. The eggs hatch between five and seven days later, and the larvae will turn into mosquitoes after three to five days. So, typically, mosquitoes need standing water for eight to ten days to multiply, *and* they need no predators hunting them during this time!

This means that rain gardens are not good habitat for mosquitoes because, when properly designed, they infiltrate too fast—in a matter of a few days—to provide the standing water these insects need for their eggs. On the flip side, slower-draining rain gardens, ponds, or bogs are generally such healthy habitats that dragonflies, newts, and occasional frogs help control any mosquitoes.

If you notice mosquitoes in *other* parts of your garden, however, here are some tips for controlling them:

Avoid pesticides. Even organic pesticides are "broadband mechanisms" and do not recognize the difference between mosquitoes and other

Remove plants that have outgrown the space.

IT'S ALIVE! AND LIFE IS MESSY! BUT GREAT FUN, TOO!

A rain garden is a complex *living* ecosystem. Plants, microorganisms, wildlife, and people all interact within it—and you just built one! Like a brand-new parent's first baby, a new rain garden requires patience and care. If you see a problem, and it is not an emergency, such as a clogged overflow pipe causing flooding outside the rain garden or a lack of mulch with weeds growing everywhere, take time and observe before doing something about it.

We sometimes think we have a problem, when in reality it is nothing more than the in-between time as an ecosystem gets established. Rain gardens improve over time: They drain better and function better as the plants mature, the soil biology builds up, and the symbiotic connections develop. In the majority of cases, it is just a matter of time before your new rain garden starts working as you planned.

beneficial insect buddies. Many of our pollinators are also members of the fly family, more than 95 percent of which are beneficial! By killing all fly family insects with pesticides, we create severe imbalances in our ecosystem and jeopardize our plant pollination. (Even the donut-shaped "mosquito dunks" for use in water, which may be safe for some wildlife, kill *all* of the fly family insects.) Even organic sprays can encourage resistance in pest populations, so avoid all!

Add moving water. Because female mosquitoes want standing water, a small pump with a fountainhead can turn any little pond from a nesting ground to a healthy habitat for other wildlife critters. You only need a little movement for this purpose; large waterfalls imitating the Niagara are not necessary or attractive to beneficial insects, birds, or even frogs, and they use a lot of power to run. So choose a pump that will provide just a gentle and continuous movement and enough sound to be audible when you are outside, and use very little electricity. (Remember: Rain gardens are not "water features"

A small fountain is enough to deter mosquitoes in a bog garden or small wildlife pond.

and should never have circulating pumps—because they shouldn't have standing water in them for long enough!)

Create natural habitat. Any yard can serve as wonderful habitat for mosquitoes if people leave containers and tarps lying around. It takes only an inch of water in place for eight to ten days to allow them to multiply! Keep your gardens (and your skin!) safe by checking on where hospitable pockets of standing water can collect and eliminate them, or instead create places—like a rain garden!—where the frogs, newts, dragonflies, birds, and bats that eat the mosquitoes and their larvae can thrive.

CHAPTER 7

JILL NUNEMAKER

Smarter Gardening with Other LID Techniques: All Roads Lead to Rome

Rain gardens are one tool in the Low Impact Development (LID) toolbox for restoring hydrological function to developed areas. But there are many tried-and-true solutions, and if a rain garden is not a good fit for a certain site, have no fear—there are other LID options for managing your stormwater, whether it be as simple as a rain garden planter that functions as a mini-rain garden in a box, or as complex as a green roof that filters precipitation even before it's had a chance to turn into runoff!

Stream ecosystem within the inlet

Puget Sound inlet in Olympia, Washington

Or perhaps you're interested in layering your rain garden with other LID techniques. Installing rain barrels or cisterns and allowing their overflow to run into the rain garden is a simple but elegant pairing of systems that increases the overall impact of LID in your own yard.

This chapter provides a general overview of the many Low Impact Development options, their aims, their best uses, and how to combine them within a site. In the end, there's an LID tool for every challenge and every site; you just have to find the best one for your situation. We can make a difference in our developed environment, and we can have fun doing it. Innovation is a big part of this; if you are serious about using LID, always check for new ideas and solutions, because they are emerging worldwide as we speak.

BOG GARDENS

Bog gardens are close relatives of rain gardens. In a bog garden, the soil has a drainage rate of 0.1 inch (2mm) or less per hour—very slow. To avoid

A bog garden was created as a solution to the runoff from a big box store's parking lot.

LID AND NEW DEVELOPMENT

LID techniques are not meant to offer impunity for new development that isn't environmentally sound. Moreover, they will not preserve a site as it originally functioned. There is much more to ecosystems than just hydrology. In fact, we understand very little about ecosystems, even with all the research going on—the more we know, the more we realize how little we know. In our opinion, the only sustainable development today is *re*development of already developed and underutilized sites. We have no excuse for disturbing one more untouched site, for cutting one more old growth tree in a still-standing forest. LID is a powerful tool for retrofitting and restoring our urban environment. That is what it was intended for.

constant overflow, the ponding area is sometimes deepened to 9 inches (23cm), and because these systems can have standing water long after the rains stop—attracting kids and critters to play in—we typically do not recommend making it deeper than that.

Bog gardens contain plants that love being flooded and do well with saturated, very wet soil conditions over long periods. Bogs do a great job at filtering runoff, but flow control can be difficult because, unless they are built 50 percent of the size of the contributing area, they overflow more often than a rain garden would.

The best way to build a bog garden is to plan on creating diverse habitat for host predators, who will prevent mosquitoes (see the sidebar on mosquitoes in chapter 6).

Rain barrels line the side of this house.

RAIN BARRELS AND CISTERNS

A rain barrel or cistern system captures and holds rainwater from your rooftop. Not only does it reduce the amount of stormwater immediately pouring into the urban drainage system, it stores water for dry season irrigation as well. On a larger scale, for commercial buildings, roof rainwater harvesting can create resilience by increasing on-hand water supplies and reducing the impact of increased winter rainfall. A rain barrel holds less than 300 gallons (1136L) in volume, a cistern normally more.

Calculating Your Needed Volume

What type of barrel and how many of them you should use depends on what you are planning to water. You will need to do a water audit, measuring the inches of rain needed each week to keep each area watered during the dry season, then calculating the overall volume of that water. Finally, you have to project how many weeks you plan on using the rainwater.

ECOSYSTEMS AT WORK

Ecosystem services are the benefits people obtain from ecosystems. These include provisioning services such as food and water; regulating services such as flood and disease control; cultural services such as spiritual and recreational benefits; and supporting services, such as nutrient cycling, that maintain the conditions for life on Earth.

Rain barrels cost less, but cisterns take up less space.

Rain barrel collecting water from a downspout; the top is covered with a screen for filtration of large debris.

Let's say you have a 100-square-foot (9.3m²) veggie garden and another 100-square-foot landscape bed with perennial flowers. You want to be able to water them for 12 weeks during the dry and warm summer, so you need to save the rain for it. Perennials are fine with just 1 inch (2.5cm) a week, but tomatoes need up to 2+ inches (5+cm) a week! So, for a 100-square-foot veggie garden, multiply 2 inches (5cm) of water by your square footage to come up with your weekly total of 28,800 cubic inches, 124 gallons (469L) of water. For the perennial bed, 1 inch a week adds up to 14,400 cubic inches, 62 gallons (235L) of water.

Add both garden beds together to get a total of 186 gallons (704L) per week. You want to water for 12 weeks, so you will need a total of 2232 gallons (8449L) of water. To hold that much water, you would need about ten 225-gallon rain barrels or five 450-gallon cisterns. The cost for this much storage capacity, based on 2015 average prices, would run about US$3000 for the rain barrels and US$3500 for cisterns. Depending on what

type of rain barrels or cisterns you are using, this much collected rainwater can take up anywhere from 90 to 250 square feet (8.4–23.2m²). (If narrow and tall barrels or cisterns are used, they take up less space.) And this is for two small garden beds only.

––––––– • • –––––––

TIP Regardless of where you source your water (rain or tap), reduce your need for irrigation! We usually only water our annual veggies, not the lawn or well-established plants. We also mix annuals and plant very intensively so that exposed soil is minimized.

––––––– • • –––––––

If you have the space and means for storing water on that scale, go for it! Even if you can't source all of your irrigation from a cistern system, however, collecting some of the rainwater is still a very good thing, as it helps to reduce the use of potable water for gardening. Rain barrels and cisterns can overflow into a rain garden, an excellent treatment-train solution by which the runoff is moved through several different solution stations before it is allowed to infiltrate into the ground or overflow into the traditional drainage system. Combinations may include several rain barrels or cisterns, an infiltration swale, and a rain garden.

If you plan to store rainwater, have a Plan B in case you run out of it during the dry season. Either use multiple cisterns or rain barrel systems, maybe from multiple roofs, or be prepared to tap from your main water source toward the end of the dry season.

Using Rainwater Safely

Not all roofs are made of the same material, but some roofing materials are actually toxic and in general roofs are not clean—bird droppings contain salmonella and *E. coli*, among other bacteria. We strongly recommend against using unfiltered roof runoff to water leafy greens, because of the infection risk if you do not wash them thoroughly or forget and stuff them in your mouth. Water greens with drinking water, and if you plan on watering vegetables with captured runoff, use a filter that can clean the water to potable quality. Always clean your veggies before eating them. You can, however, use the rainwater for your ornamental plants without worries about filtration—really, watering ornamental plants with potable water is a waste.

There are commercial products and systems for turning rainwater into potable water. Some methods are easy to use and work very well, but consult a professional before you create such a filtration system. The product you use should come with warranties and replacement parts. Remember, this is not a small thing: If you drink water that is not clean enough, you can get very sick; young children and older people can even die from pathogens or pollution in unclean water.

This is a gravity-based heavy debris fallout system with an easy-to-remove cleanout at the bottom.

Connecting the Cistern to an Irrigation System

To connect the cistern to your irrigation system, you will need a pump and additional filters. Use a pump that can sit outside the cistern—this will be easier to maintain and repair. At a minimum, you need one screen filter to catch the sediment and large particles, such as leaves and various leftover squirrel treasures hidden in the gutter. This should be installed to filter the water before it reaches the cistern. Finer mesh filters can be placed at the intake of the cistern (after the coarse filter) and at the outflow toward the pump.

If you decide to use drip irrigation, you can add one more screen filter, even finer, before the water goes into any drip lines. You can never have too many filters, but you do not want to go bankrupt over the cost, either. Some pumps actually have a filter built into their intake pipe, so in that case you can skip this step. But remember, *these are all mechanical filters, and none of them will turn runoff into potable water.*

A CISTERN CASE STUDY

The Community of Hope Church, located in West Seattle, is typical of many urban houses of worship. Its footprint includes an 11,400 square foot (1059m²) asphalt parking lot and an 8,340 square foot (775m²) roof, impervious surfaces that contribute about 336,000 gallons (1.27 million liters) each year to an already overloaded sewer and stormwater system.

LID advocate and business Rain Dog Designs contacted the church pastor and proposed to build a RainWise project featuring a series of rain tanks, or cisterns, at the rear of the church and two rain gardens in the front. But during project planning, everyone realized there was just not enough room in the front of the church for rain gardens to safely infiltrate the expected volume of rainfall. So Rain Dog and the church took a more cautious approach, replacing the rain gardens with cisterns that overflow safely away from the church, into gravel dispersion trenches, and then across the sidewalk to the street.

The system is now in place, and during the winter months, rainfall continuously releases from the cistern systems, reducing peak flow, and is stored for irrigation in the drier months of summer. The installation made the church property eligible for as much as a 25 percent reduction in annual stormwater fees, which are increasing in the Seattle area at a rate of 10 percent per year. The Community of Hope Church's project reflects its name, reducing stormwater impact, creating irrigation storage, and providing long-term stormwater fee reduction—with 142,000 gallons (538,000L) of rainfall captured and now *slowly* released into the combined stormwater system each year.

DURASOXX

Another LID solution for your yard, especially if your site is sloped steeply and a rain garden installation isn't possible, is DuraSoxx (see Resources). Planting native vegetation on these slopes will help reduce erosion and prevent a landslide, and the Soxx form a pocket for easier and faster plant establishment, just like logs do in nature. Unlike logs, the Soxx do not break down as long as the plants protect them from UV. If you just want to create a native habitat or otherwise planted area on a slope, you can safely use DuraSoxx and plant away with very little effort. However, consult a professional before you start any restoration or stabilization work on a critical slope area; regardless of your intent, you can cause more problems if you do not know the best approach and technique.

For a detailed description of how to use Soxx, see chapter 4.

DuraSoxx planted with kinnikinnick to reduce UV exposure

GREEN ROOF FILTERING CREATES SAFE EDIBLE GARDENS

The Campus Community Farm at Edmonds Community College in Washington State is a great example of combining many LID practices in a treatment train. First, a green roof captures and filters the rain. This overflows partially into a large 3,000-gallon cistern and partially, along with the overflow from the cistern, into a rain garden that grows lots of edible plants, such as rhubarb, salmonberry, strawberry, blueberry, and currant. Because the green roof ensures that the runoff is filtered, it is safe to grow food plants in the rain garden.

GREEN ROOFS

Green roofs capture the rain right where it falls. They help to mitigate the *heat island effect*, reducing the cooling and heating costs of the building, cleaning the air, and improving the mood of everyone who looks at them.

Green roofs are more than just soil and plants placed on a roof: The structure below the roof must meet many specific requirements. For example, the building must be able to support the weight of the roof with saturated soil and plants. Furthermore, the surface of a green roof has many layers without which the plants will die, grow right into the building, or slip off entirely! If you want to build a green roof, even if it's just on your toolshed, you must talk to a professional. If nothing else, you at least need to find out whether the building can handle the added weight. Consulting with an expert can save you lots of money and headaches.

Extensive vs. Intensive

Normally, green roofs are categorized as either *extensive* or *intensive* systems. The choice depends on the overall goals for the project (such as site access) and specific conditions.

*Ex*tensive roofs have a shallow soil layer, so they support only shallow-rooted plants, often stonecrops or sedums only, that are drought tolerant and need minimal care. Extensive roofs can be used on single-family homes, but they can also be appropriate on large flat roofs where weight makes a big difference. The parking garage near the Gates Foundation headquarters in Seattle has an extensive roof system with a variety of sedums growing on it.

*In*tensive green roofs have deep soil, 10 inches (25cm) or deeper, that can support a wider variety of plants. An intensive roof can become a park of sorts, growing shrubs and small trees, maybe even a small orchard or berry patch. It might also accommodate a relaxing patio or seating area. But remember, intensive roofs are heavier than extensive ones and require much sturdier buildings to support them than regular roofs.

Soil is a relative term here: Green roof "soil" is a lightweight engineered medium, yet it is able to hold roots, store nutrients, and of course absorb rain and drain well! Not too much to ask for from "soil," right?

Are Green Roofs Green?

A green roof may or may not be a truly green solution for a site. That's because these roofs come with lots of "baggage," normally in the form of plastic materials. The layers under the soil typically include a moisture barrier, waterproofing membrane, insulation, root barrier, root barrier protection membrane, drainage mat, filter mat (for sediment control), and irrigation mat. Only after these are all securely in place are the growing

Sedum green roof on the "Going Green at the Beach" demonstration home in Snohomish County

medium and plants brought in. That is a lot of additional stuff that uses resources and energy to produce and, in the end, will be disposed of when and if the building is, or when the occupants lose interest in their green roof.

To make a green roof truly green, have it serve more purposes than just stormwater management. It should also add to the green space in the developed area, providing heating and cooling mitigation. And of course, to help make up for all the materials used, it should remain in place for decades.

A DIY Green Roof

If you just want to have fun and build a risk-free green roof, try your hand at creating one for your chicken coop or garden shed. (Still, if people will be inside the structure at all, ask a professional to review your ideas and plans before you go through with it.)

For a chicken coop, use treated plywood for the roof, attach a shallow rim around the edges of the roof, and cover it with felt and pond liner. Fill planting trays with a lightweight green-roof mix or a mix of compost and coir you can make yourself. Plant the trays with sedums and stonecrops that fit the site's light conditions, and place the planting trays on the roof

GREEN WALLS

Green (or "living") walls do not capture rain runoff directly. However, they are still considered an LID solution because they are often irrigated with captured rainwater and they provide additional valuable ecosystem services.

Living walls can be simple modules attached to a building and containing growing medium and plants. Or they can be complex systems not only providing beauty and temperature control but also working as retaining wall structures. Concrete retaining walls provide one and only one function: holding back the soil. Living walls that are engineered to act as retaining structures, yet contain soil and vegetation, offer additional ecosystem services: They bring nature into a developed environment, become habitat for birds, insects, frogs, and lizards, and so much more. They absorb and filter runoff, are great to look at, change with the season, and calm the mind. They help improve air quality, and they instantly reduce the heat island effect.

You will want to choose your specific vertical planting technology based on site size and conditions, access, budget, and the overall goals of your project. Below is a list of living wall materials of various types. All of them offer the same strength and capacity as the traditional Keystone or similar concrete blocks do. Most of them are manufactured and distributed by Filtrexx. This is currently the only company worldwide providing comprehensive design and engineering support as well as research data and variety of applications.

The Trinity Living Wall system here helps support a highway ramp. It's planted with native grass and does not require mowing. (Photo courtesy of Filtrexx)

- **EnviroBloxx,** by Filtrexx, are fantastic and easily doable for a DIY project. Made of recycled plastic, they weigh about 3 pounds (1.4kg) and can easily stack with DuraSoxx in between to hold the soil mix in place and allow the plants to take root. The plants will eventually grow into the soil behind the wall. These walls are good to use up to a height of 5 feet (1.5m), although most jurisdictions might require a permit for a project of such height. The blocks can be lit up using LED lights, and you can run drip irrigation lines through them to water the plants if needed.
- **EarthBloxx,** EnviroBloxx's much heavier relative, are concrete blocks combined with DuraSoxx. They weigh 80 pounds (36kg) each, the same as Keystone blocks, but can be used for very tall retaining wall structures. So if you feel up to using concrete blocks for retaining walls in your DIY project, these blocks will work well instead, and you can plant them!
- The **Trinity LivingWall** system uses interlocking metal cages to hold the planted Soxx in place. These cages are anchored into the fill material and the native soil behind the system for stability.
- **GreenLoxx** walls are also secured into the native soil and held in place firmly, but they are made of DuraSoxx entirely.

The EnviroBloxx system is used in St. Louis to create a rain garden. (Photos courtesy of Filtrexx)

There are other modular living wall systems that are also DIY friendly. Before you invest money in them however, check their specifications, what support the company provides, the warranty conditions, the ease of maintenance, and their expected lifespan.

Many companies are currently innovating in technologies and solutions for living walls. It is worth checking out online and in local stores for what is new and what is regularly available. We recommend working with modules that are self-contained, meaning they have irrigation channels, drainage channels, root barriers, and clamps or other attaching accessories all within the modules.

See Resources for further information on living walls.

PERVIOUS HARD SURFACES

Pervious pavement is a hard surface that allows rain to infiltrate into the ground below. We sometimes joke that pervious pavement is a rain garden with pavers on top. While that is a stretch, the concept of infiltration is the same. Pervious pavement needs reservoirs below it so the runoff can be collected and then infiltrated into the deeper soil. These reservoir courses must include an overflow, just like a rain garden, because if they are full, the runoff has to flow somewhere instead of just flooding the pavement.

Not all design standards for pervious pavement are the same; it depends on the actual pavement material. Generally, if a reservoir is a requirement, a designed, excavated basin is filled in with large drain rocks, round and minimum 2 inches (5cm) or larger. (The usual requirement is that the rocks have a minimum of 50 percent void space.) These rocks are covered with a layer of smaller rocks that will not fit into the void spaces; this is called a *choker course*. On top of this layer lies an even smaller rock layer, or large, aggregate free-draining sand, which holds the pervious pavers. The uncompacted subgrade soil underneath all this rock infiltrates the water, and the reservoir is often as deep as a rain garden would be.

You can find many pervious options, such as concrete, asphalt, and pavers that are pervious themselves (meaning the material they are made of allows water to penetrate it), or pavers that are pervious only because of their shape, such as solid concrete blocks with ribs or other bump-outs on their edges. You can create a pervious flagstone patio with a rain catchment system beneath it. Or you can simply use round pea gravel for your walkways and allow the rain to be absorbed into the ground. Each solution has pros and cons.

If you want to build a pervious paver patio, walkway, or parking space, you need to decide what matters most for you regarding this area, then assess your site conditions and limitations. Choose the materials you think best, based on those factors (and make sure to follow the manufacturer's instructions). Following are some particulars.

Pervious Pavers

Pavers that are themselves pervious often consist of small pebbles glued together using a two-part epoxy or similar adhesive, and formed in molds into consistent sizes, shapes and even colors. These pavers are very showy, because the pebbles

Pervious pavers are worked into this decorative installation.

One drawback is that weeds grow in pervious pavers.

are nice and colorful, and the glue also makes them shiny. But they are often hard to maintain because weed and grass seeds can easily take root in the pores. They are firm but still easily broken, so use a vacuum, not a pressure washer, to keep the pores clean. The pavers can support foot traffic and, if used as inserts on stronger pavement—such as a strip in a concrete driveway—lightweight vehicles. They cannot support trucks and heavy loads.

Another type of pervious paver is solid concrete made with bumps of various sizes on its edges, which create gaps that rain can flow into. These are usable on any main road or street because they can withstand any vehicle, just like regular concrete pavers. The drawback to using them is weeds: The gaps between them can harbor dandelions and moss if the pavers are not used regularly. The gaps need to be maintained, or the pavement will become slippery from the smooshed vegetation. Areas of heavy traffic do not end up with lots of weeds, because the constant traffic takes care of any sprouts.

Turf Blocks

Turf Blocks are concrete lattices with diamond-shaped openings designed to hold sandy loam and growing grass. In the Northwest, grass does not grow very well, so here these spaces usually end up harboring moss and clover. You can plant herbs such as thyme in the gaps and fill the blocks with strong, tough plants that will elbow out weeds. Turf Blocks are good for a driveway or extra parking (for an RV or trailer space), but not for access roads if the grade is steeper than 2 percent. One downside of Turf Blocks is that the smooshed vegetation can become very slippery, creating a great challenge for anyone navigating the road in a car and for people with canes and walkers or in high heels.

Pervious Concrete

Pervious concrete looks like Rice Krispies in stone. It offers the best of all worlds: It is easy to clean using a pressure washer or vacuum, it does not grow weeds, it performs just like any other concrete road, and it can be installed fairly fast in large sections. Add decorative elements during installation, just like conventional concrete, or paint it after the installation if you'd like.

The trick to pervious concrete is the installation. It has no "fines" such as dust and sand, which form impervious layers in concrete. It has only aggregate, various sizes of pebbles and rocks, and cement. However, since rocks are always dusty even after multiple washings, the pervious concrete must be installed differently than regular concrete. Rocks have fines around and between them; even after washing, some small amounts will remain. The concrete is poured into place, quickly raked around, and then rolled with a heavy roller, never agitated with tools. The roller compression must be limited, to keep the fines from coming to the surface and forming a layer on top. Once the rolling is done, the concrete must be covered with plastic for the curing period, so that there is no interference with the surface hardening and fines are minimized.

Pervious concrete looks like Rice Krispies to us!

Maintaining the pores of pervious concrete should be a major concern if the surface is used for storage of landscape or building materials. Any fine materials—sand, compost, bark, etc.—dumped on the surface can clog the pores. These need to be vacuumed out as soon as possible. The best approach is to prevent such damage by storing these materials on another surface, or covering the pervious concrete with an impervious tarp or barrier.

Pervious concrete, if installed correctly with adequate reservoir space below, can infiltrate a tremendous amount of water, often 1,000 or more gallons (3785L) per hour as industrial testing has shown. In the tests, water was applied directly onto the concrete with a firehose, and the surface just kept swallowing up the water! (If we ever have a storm dumping this much rain, we all need to get to the nearest ark, because bad times are coming!) Even if the surface is 90 percent clogged, these pavements usually perform well, but clogged pores can and do grow small weeds or grass. Not only do they look terrible when that happens, but the vegetation will damage the surface, cause cracks, and lead to potholes. So it is important to vacuum the concrete if the surface is not a high-traffic area and fine particles start clogging the pores.

A pervious walkway

TIP Roads paved with pervious asphalt or pervious concrete should never be sanded for traction in ice and snow. Sand will clog the pores. Actually, ice will not form on these types of pavement anyway, because it can't sit on top of them. So these surfaces help reduce the negative effects of winter road maintenance and deicing—they simply need none of it. If sanding happens accidentally, a vacuuming is in order.

Pervious Asphalt

Pervious asphalt looks just like regular asphalt. It is very hard to tell the difference unless it's raining—water will not stand on pervious asphalt like it does on impervious. Road repair crews often place a layer of pervious asphalt over old asphalt, not because that will make it pervious but because the pores in the surface absorb sound and help reduce noise pollution.

Pervious asphalt is cost effective and easy to install using the same techniques as for regular asphalt. The only challenge is the maintenance! Pervious asphalt should be vacuumed and never swept. It also should be maintained during snow events with a rubber-bladed plow, because the regular metal blade will scratch it and fill the pores with scraped-off asphalt dust.

Flagstones

Flagstones placed on top of a reservoir basin can double as a patio or walkway *and* a rain collection system. Place plants between the flagstones to help with rain absorption if the choker course (the layer below the flagstones) allows it. Flagstones should never be used for vehicle traffic. They can be challenging for wheelchair and walker navigation, depending on the installation.

Gravel

There are many ways to use gravel for walkways and even driveways. Crushed rock usually compacts under traffic. Plastic grid systems are available that help prevent such compaction and

A flagstone patio

allow infiltration. Consult a professional if you are planning to use these grids, because they have very specific requirements if they are to work as intended. In the Northwest, especially west of the Cascades, where moss and algae grow readily on you if you stand in one place long enough, these grid systems tend to become a weedy mess after just a few seasons. They are almost impossible to weed.

Round pebbles, such as pea gravel, will not compact. But it is difficult to hurry on a pea gravel path, and they are terrible for vehicles, wheelbarrows, and anyone in a wheelchair or with a walker.

Wood Chips

Wood chip paths also allow for infiltration. They're great to walk on—although not ADA (Americans with Disabilities Act) accessible—but they break down in just a few years, so replacement is part of the maintenance.

RAIN GARDEN PLANTERS

Rain garden planters are containers filled with rain garden soil mix and planted with Zone 1 plants. An inflow allows rain into them (usually from roofs) and the rain flows out, filtered, into a safe overflow. You can create rain garden planters using large containers such as horse troughs, for example. In areas where infiltration is not a good solution, these container rain gardens can still help filter pollution.

Another option is Splash Boxx (see sidebar), a rain garden planter pre-engineered based on the size of the contributing impervious surface. Advantages include aboveground installation (no excavation or permits required), a small footprint, and easy relocation or replacement. They are also scalable: You can connect them in series for large area treatment. Splash Boxx is established as an approved best-management tool in Washington State.

SPLASH BOXX

Splash Boxx is the brand name of an innovative stormwater system developed by Rain Dog Design of Gig Harbor, Washington, that features a large (12 foot x 8 foot; 3.6m x 2.4m) bio-retention planter box constructed of steel and coated with nontoxic paint. The inside of the box is layered with aggregate, an underdrain, bioretention soil, vegetation, and storage to promote retention and filtration of stormwater runoff. It's essentially a rain garden on wheels, and it is especially useful for places where soils may be contaminated.

The Port of Seattle is using two Splash Boxxes at its Terminal 91 in a "Moving Green Infrastructure Forward Project" that will comparatively evaluate two bioretention soil mix designs, one with conventional sand and compost, the other with volcanic sand (from a local source) and compost. Hypothesis? Volcanic sand will reduce pollutants in water more effectively. Pier 91 is an ideal testing site: The roof of a derelict building sheds galvanized metal and also features city air pollution, soil contamination, and bacteria from resident seagulls.

The water entering and leaving the boxes will be tested once a month during the rainy season for phosphorus, nitrogen, bacteria, zinc, and copper. Soil monitors will also measure moisture, to reveal how the water moves through the two different soils and how much water is available to plants. Preliminary research has shown that volcanic sand is significantly better at keeping water available to plants—important for plant survival in metal boxes during the regional droughts.

CHAPTER 8

Case Studies:
Rain Garden Successes

This chapter details case studies that represent the variety of yard sizes, home styles, and family needs that rain gardens can be adapted to. We're sure that among these stories you'll meet someone you can relate to, whether they learned about and got their gardens through a municipal program, or have had long relationships with environmental sustainability and wanted to contribute even more to their goal of conservation. What all these rain garden friends do share is their enthusiasm for the multiple ways their rain gardens have positively contributed to their quality of life.

HANSON HOME, SEATTLE, WASHINGTON

The Hanson family lives in a mid-20th-century rambler in a north Seattle community called Bitter Lake. They live at the bottom of a blocks-long slope to the east; to the west, a bluff drops into Elliott Bay in Puget Sound.

Their front yard formerly consisted mainly of grass, overgrown rhododendrons, and an unwanted rose garden. Because of their location at the base of the slope and a high water table, they and their neighbors frequently had saturated yards and damp basements. Overall, the yard was uninviting and underused. The Hansons explain, "We never knew what was happening in the neighborhood, because there's no window from the main part of the house onto that area, and we'd focus our outside time on the backyard."

In 2013 the family decided to get rid of the grass (which had taken time and energy to maintain but offered little in return) and replace it with an environmentally friendly option. Their search for that option led them to the website of Seattle Public Utilities' RainWise program (see Resources for details), where they discovered rain gardens. They eventually contracted with Zsofia Pasztor to develop a rain garden and overall front yard design for their property.

The Rain Garden Design

One of the first challenges was siting the rain garden between a gas line to the north and a sewer line to the south. The Hansons decided on an oval-shaped rain garden to fit between the two, and they hand-dug it to reduce cost and the risk of accidentally digging into a pipeline.

Their excavated soil became the rain garden's berm, which they then covered with sandy loam and finally burlap coffee bean bags, which they sourced locally ("We'd go to the coffee shop and one of us would get coffee while the other got bags—it was a win-win!"). Once the height of the berm was established, they refilled the rain garden with compost-amended soil mix and mulched with hog fuel, creating Zone 1 and Zone 2. They

The oval shape of the Hanson rain garden fit between two utility lines and created a large planting area.

After just a couple of years, the plants filled in and reduced weed growth. (Photo by the Hanson Family)

This is the view the Hansons now enjoy when they open their front door.

worked with Zsofia to select multiseason, zone-appropriate plants, including some edibles such as blueberries for Zone 3.

Half of the Hansons' rooftop's runoff is delivered to the garden via an overhead "aqueduct" built off of the home's rooftop drain. (Because of their location, they were not connected to the sewer and didn't need a disconnect permit.) The runoff is directed down a rain chain—an alternative to typical gutter downspouts that guides the runoff visibly down chains or a series of ornamental cups from the roof to the ground—onto a homemade splash guard and into a concrete trough that empties into the west end of the garden.

The overflow pipe is also located at the west end of the garden, but because the garden is somewhat oversized for the amount of runoff (due to the high water table), at the time of this writing the overflow pipe had yet to be used! When and if the overflow gets used, water will be directed toward the backyard, 15 feet (4.6m) from the basement.

The Results
As of this writing, with the rain garden installed

Hanson rain garden in 2015

several wet Puget Sound seasons ago, the Hanson yard has not been saturated and the basement has remained dry. The family has performed maintenance including watering in the plants for the first year and then watering the plants approximately every six weeks during the third year (which happened to be a drought summer). They refresh the mulch annually to keep it at 3 inches (7.5cm), and they try to stay ahead of the (nonnative) edible strawberries planted on the berm that would willingly take over the entire yard!

Most important, the Hansons now go outside and enjoy their front yard. The kids pick the edible fruit that grows on the berm and check the rain gauge to monitor what the rain garden is capturing and filtering ("Even when it's raining!"). "We'll take some hot tea and sit on our new patio to watch birds, and watch the kids play in the neighborhood. Installing the rain garden has decreased the amount of maintenance we have to do out front, but at the same time it has increased our connection to our neighbors."

REINA HOME, PORTLAND, OREGON

When the Reinas moved from Atlanta, Georgia, to their new home in Portland thirteen years ago, they put all new sod in their yard and then went about their lives. Unfortunately, it being Portland and not Atlanta, the new sod quickly turned to soggy moss, leading them into a search for a more native-based and sustainable landscaping approach.

A community- and environmentally focused household, the Reinas were early adopters of the rain garden lifestyle. They had one installed by 2009, but because the practice was still somewhat new and recommended plants were still being studied, they ended up with monster grasses that quickly took over the small rain garden and completely hid the two-foot-square piece of granite with a carved bird basin meant to be one of the focal points of the landscape.

The Rain Garden Design

Fast-forward to October 2014, and the inception of Portland's stormwater mitigation programs. The Reinas received a Willamette Watershed letter containing information about rain gardens and offering homeowners free installations. Thinking, "There's gotta be a catch—nothing's completely free," they sent an email of interest to program director Josh Robben, who "got back to us within the hour!"

Replanted in 2015, the Reina garden features smaller, lower plants in order to focus on the granite bird basin and added sculptural pieces. (Photo by the Reina Family)

Plants chosen for year-round interest continue to delight with changing fall colors.

After doing a thorough assessment of the yard and calculating the rooftop's potential contribution amount, the city's designers, along with the Reinas, decided to install two rain gardens—one in the western-facing front and one on the southern side of the house (replacing the original rain garden with one deeper and wider). As the installation progressed, the designers showed the Reinas how the stormwater runoff would be controlled: Their downspouts would be disconnected and rerouted underground as inflow pipes, overflow would be directed to the front walkway, and a weir made from a juniper log would be placed in the front garden to slow the water's journey toward the overflow, giving it more time to seep in. "The log is a beautiful element," adds Sandy Reina. "We love it."

The homeowners had a lot of input in terms of the garden design and plant selections. The design reused materials and rock already in the yard, supplemented with rock provided by the city to re-create the look of dry streambeds that the Reinas love. They worked with the city to select smaller, slower-growing plants that would stand out individually and provide year-round interest but still maintain views to other focal points in the garden, such as the birdbath and the creative art pieces that blend harmoniously into the landscape. Much of the art was given to them by metalworking artist friends who get to enjoy the coming together of their hand-wrought beauty and nature in the yard.

The Results

Installation took place in 2015, and part of the agreement with the city for receiving a rain garden is that it needs to be managed and maintained for at least two years. This won't be a problem for the Reinas, who are so thrilled with the idea of rain gardens that, just by extolling their virtues to neighbors, they persuaded three other homeowners to install them in their own yards through the same program.

The Reinas say they are "over the moon" about their rain gardens! The gardens are generally low maintenance with some weeding, and the owners enjoy watching the southern garden fill up like a pond, while raindrops create ripples on the surface of the water. Sandy adds, "We love the combination of form and function that comes with a rain garden, and we are really proud of it!"

Inflow pipe surrounded by rocks of many sizes for armoring and visual interest

SEAVIEW NEIGHBORHOOD, EDMONDS, WASHINGTON

The Seaview Neighborhood in Edmonds, Washington, north of Seattle, is a typical midcentury Northwest development featuring ranch-style and split-level homes with the usual selection of rhododendrons and conifers fronted by wide expanses of lawn. The neighborhood was built on a slight slope running east to west, and much of the runoff from the area ultimately drained into nearby Perrinville Creek.

The creek, a tributary of Puget Sound, supports a cutthroat trout population throughout its length and coho salmon at its lower end. Stormwater pollution from this watershed area threatens these fish populations as well as the water's ultimate destination, Puget Sound.

The Rain Garden Design

Because rain gardens have been found to be most effective clustered within a neighborhood, the city of Edmonds partnered with the Snohomish Conservation District and Washington State University's Snohomish County Extension Master Gardeners in 2015 to install a series of rain gardens in Seaview to promote their use in the city of Edmonds.

Half a dozen homeowners on either side of a city block participated in the project, with rain garden sizes ranging from 130 square feet (12.1m²) to 240 square feet (22.3m²). The rain garden plant designs were done by WSU Snohomish County Master Gardener rain garden mentors, working closely with the homeowners to match their existing garden styles. Snohomish Conservation

The new rain gardens are attracting a wider variety of birds to the area.

Prep work for Seaview sites was done with the help of Earthcorps volunteers. Note the white outline on the lawn to guide the digging.

District installed the gardens with the help of EarthCorps volunteers. City of Edmonds Public Works crew conducted the initial excavation.

The Results

By the beginning of 2016, based upon the size of the rain gardens and the contributing roof surfaces' sizes, it is estimated that these gardens will be treating close to 150,000 gallons (568000L) of stormwater per year. If you're wondering how much water that is, a 150,000-gallon water storage tank is 33 feet (10m) wide and 24 feet (7.3m) tall!

As of this writing, the participating Seaview residents were very pleased with their new landscape enhancement, as evidenced by an email from one of the homeowners: "I just thought that you would like to know that the rain garden has been wonderful for our birds! We have seen numerous black-capped chickadees, several red-breasted nuthatches, Steller's jays, juncos, and the odd rufous-sided towhee! Also crows!! It has been a delight to see them rustle around the rain garden."

The residents reported quite a buzz of interest throughout the neighborhood after the installation of the rain gardens and are considering creating a neighborhood garden club.

A rock-lined swale intersects with this rain garden. (Photo by Cynthia LaBlue)

RAIN GARDEN AND STAGE SET, SEATTLE, WASHINGTON

The yard in Lorrie's newly purchased home was a blank canvas: a 1,500 square foot (139m²) lawn that sloped slightly away from the house, anchored by a single hawthorn tree. She knew it could be much more and envisioned a healthy eco-system that was welcoming for the neighborhood and included a rain garden, a bench, and some educational signage.

Because Lorrie didn't have the resources to implement the project, she contacted Aaron Clark at Stewardship Partners in Seattle (home of the "12,000 Rain Gardens" campaign—see Resources for further details) for some brainstorming around funding. Aaron Clark writes, "I had already explained that we didn't have funding for a project like that but that I wanted to help any way I could, so I brought a copy of the *Rain Garden Handbook* and a bunch of pictures to share for design ideas. As I left I promised that I'd keep her in mind if any funding opportunities came up and hoped we could keep in touch."

Several months later, Stewardship Partners started considering creating a miniature Puget Sound in rain garden form for a promotional video. "The vision," Aaron explains, "was that the viewer was looking at a downspout during a rainstorm, but as the camera zooms out you realize that it is literally pouring straight into Puget Sound. . . . Puget Sound literally starts in their front yard. My boss was hooked, but I was skeptical about the message and the ability to create this vista. I asked 'How much money do we have to spend on this video project? You under-stand that a rain garden doesn't really hold water in it for more than a few hours after a rain event, and it is supposed to be full of plants, right?' After working out some details, we had to determine where on earth we could build this Puget Sound Rain Garden."

Aaron remembered Lorrie and called her up the same day with the proposal: "We want to build the mother of all rain gardens in your front yard and make a video about it, and we will pay for everything out of our video production budget." Of course she said yes!

What Puget Sound looks like when reduced to fit in your front yard

The Rain Garden Design

Stewardship Partners hired Zsofia Pasztor for this unique project. "You can't make a rain garden look anything close enough to Puget Sound," she told them. "And even if you did, no one would recognize it. I can design something beautiful and functional that approximates the shape of Puget Sound, but you will have to do some kind of special effects to make anyone realize that it is Puget Sound."

Eventually they figured out they would need to build two totally different things: first a miniature movie set that looked exactly like Puget Sound, then a rain garden where the movie set had once been. Zsofia created a beautiful and functional design for the rain garden, and the Stewardship Partners crew set about tearing up Lorrie's entire

Detail of Puget Sound "stage set" (Photos on this page courtesy of Stewardship Partners)

front lawn in a brutal approximation of the shape of Puget Sound.

The movie set was built entirely by trial and error: Rocks and broken concrete created shapes and elevations, hundreds of square feet of moss from a tree farm on (the real) Hood Canal made the set instantaneously green and vegetated. They lined "Puget Sound" with plastic so it would actually hold water, and planted hundreds of tiny evergreen tree seedlings that would later be transplanted to other restoration projects in the Snoqualmie Valley.

Piles of soil and rock made Mount Rainier, Mount Baker, and the Cascade and Olympic ranges. Bob Berger, a model railroad professional, arrived with an Airstream trailer full of models to make the movie set complete: suspension bridge, Space Needle, airport, model ferries, Peace Arch, orcas, and more. Twenty pounds of white flour created snow atop the peaks.

The Results

In the fall, once the film shoot was over, the movie set was converted into a rain garden and zero-lawn landscape, including native and ornamental trees, shrubs, and groundcovers. The rain garden now captures and filters stormwater from 1,200 square feet (111m²) of roof and driveway contribution areas, and Lorrie continues to this day to evangelize everyone she knows about rain gardens.

BEFORE: This Seattle yard was transformed into a miniature Puget Sound before becoming a rain garden.

AFTER: Finally, a healthy, inspiring rain garden (Photos on this page courtesy of Stewardship Partners)

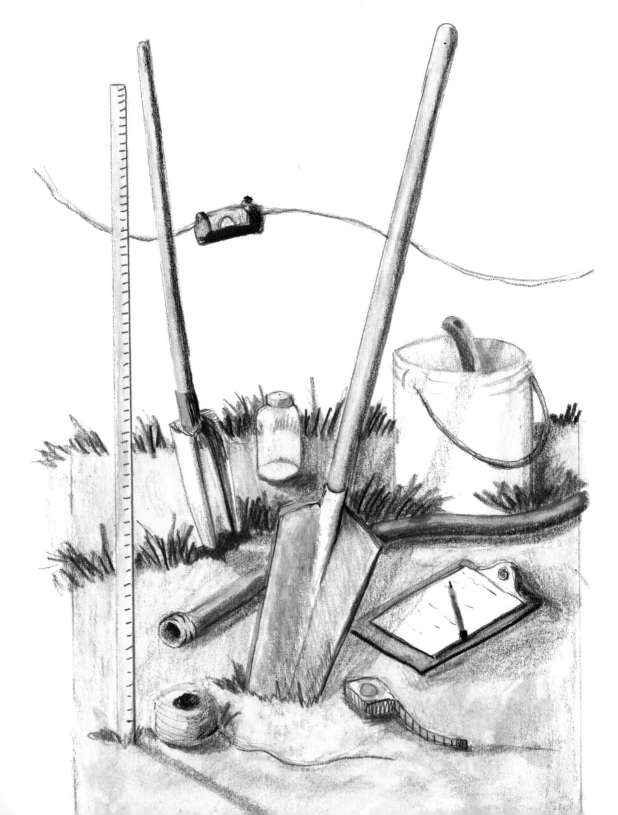

Last Words:
Welcome to the Rain Garden Club

We certainly love rain gardens for what they do, how they look, and how they feel. We love walking down streets where rain gardens are built on every lot, and we enjoy urban spaces that feature these great planted drainage facilities rather than boring lawns.

For us, however, the greatest fun comes from being able to design and build them in the Pacific Northwest. Rain gardens are not simple and often not easy to design and build in our part of the world, but they are *so* worth it. You will get decades of joy from watching yours grow and mature over the years.

We've just taken you on a long and winding road through various regions of our beautiful Pacific Northwest, thinking about both mountain peaks and itty-bitty plant treasures. We've sent you to talk with your neighbors. We've made you dig holes, touch and smell soil, look for water and play with it if you found it. We've asked you to draw maps, filling the page with plants, circles, and lines. And finally we dispatched you into the thick of it with tools and plans and made you build a rain garden—and you did it! Celebrate and be proud of your work. Congratulations, and welcome to the club, Fellow Rain Gardener!

Top Plants for Pacific Northwest Rain Gardens

This appendix provides specific details about plants to consider using in your rain garden. The listings include each plant's hardiness and size, the size of rain garden it is suitable for and the appropriate zone of that garden, what area(s) of the Pacific Northwest it will thrive in (these follow the same system we used in the soil and hydrology chapters), and additional information. Some plants can be used in more than one part of the region, while others will thrive only in a specific area.

The plants listed here make up only a sampler of the many available to you. We chose them for a variety of reasons, not least of which is that we really love using them. They are fairly easy to maintain, they are interesting plants providing for creative combinations, wildlife loves them and will be attracted by them, they live fairly long plant lives, they are reliable, and they are not too difficult to acquire. Talk to your local nursery, botanical garden, university extension, and garden club to get more ideas for awesome plants you can use. If you are using this book for a rain garden outside of the Pacific Northwest, you should check whether any of the plants recommended here are considered noxious invasive weeds in your area—a plant that is wonderful in one region can mean devastation for another.

RAIN GARDEN SIZE

For the purposes of this list, a *small* rain garden is one that needs less than 10 square feet (0.9m²)

of ponding area. A *medium-size* rain garden has between 10 and 50 square feet (0.9–4.6m²) of ponding area, and a *large* rain garden has 50 square feet (4.6m²) or more.

LIGHT REQUIREMENTS

Some plants grow in deep shade in their natural habitat, others thrive in the blasting sun. These conditions are what they evolved with and therefore will determine their preference for light conditions; however, most plants can grow successfully even in less than ideal conditions, and thus can tolerate a wider range of light scenarios than are found in their natural habitat. In the world of horticulture, plants are grouped into light preference categories so we can predict how they will do in certain situations, and choose plants for success in every kind of light condition.

In our plant list we use these standard categories:

☼ Direct sunlight for 6+ hours per day, including some or all of the afternoon hours

◐ 4–6 hours of direct sunlight daily, regardless of time of day

◑ < 4 hours of direct morning sunlight or filtered light throughout the day; no intense midday sun

● No direct sunlight; some bright indirect light

Opposite: Let your creativity lead you down a path of beautiful plant and material combinations.

PLANTS FOR ZONE 1

In Zone 1 (the ponding area), water will collect, stand for some time, flood the plants, and infiltrate into the soil. Plants for this zone need to be able to tolerate, or even love, being flooded periodically and completely drying out periodically.

TREES

We usually recommend that you do not plant trees in Zone 1 in a small rain garden (see Calculating Rain Garden Volume in chapter 4, Design and Planning). But, if you are building a medium-to-large rain garden, you can definitely think of using at least one tree in Zone 1, sized to fit the space well as it matures.

Betula nigra

River birch

HARDY TO: −30°F (−34°C)

SIZE: 50–70 ft. (17–21.5m) tall x 50–70 ft. (17–21.5m) wide

REGION(S): all

RAIN GARDEN SIZE: large

☼/☀/☀/●

The river birch is a fantastic tree. We especially love using this species as multitrunk trees with 3–4 trunks in clusters. Its bark is gorgeous, especially in the winter. It can take very wet conditions easily in a rain garden, and during the spring snowmelt it can absorb most of the runoff by itself in a rain garden. It also tolerates hot weather and drought conditions.

Betula papyrifera

Paper birch

HARDY TO: −75°F (−59°C)

SIZE: 60 ft. (18m) tall x 45 ft. (13.7m) wide

REGION(S): all

RAIN GARDEN SIZE: large

☼/☀/☀

The paper birch's white bark can be a showstopper all year. Other colorful bark or foliage placed near this tree will highlight its color. It is one of the most cold-tolerant trees in our area and has no problem in sizzling heat, either, as long as it has access to moisture in the ground. It is also very nice in multitrunk cluster form.

Fraxinus latifolia

Oregon ash

HARDY TO: 0°F (−18°C)

SIZE: 60 ft. (18m) tall x 60 ft. (18m) wide

REGION(S): mild climate regions, sometimes mountains to 5,000 ft. (1524m)

RAIN GARDEN SIZE: large

☼/☀

This tree is native to the southwest Washington and western Oregon areas, but it is not a good plant east of the Cascades, as it freezes out in very cold areas. Really warm temperatures are fine as long as it can reach moisture in the ground. It will grow roots deep below the rain garden and find the water it needs. Note that Oregon ash takes a long time to reach full size.

Fraxinus latifolia (Photo by Roseann Barnhill)

Malus fusca

Swamp crabapple, Oregon crabapple, Pacific crabapple

HARDY TO: –10°F (–23°C)

SIZE: 35 ft. (10.5m) tall x 17.5 ft. (5.5m) wide

REGION(S): coastal forests, Puget Sound

RAIN GARDEN SIZE: medium to large

☼/◑/◐/●

The swamp crabapple needs moisture in the ground to thrive, and it is not able to tolerate drought for long periods. This tree is great for slower-draining soils; it is also a good tree for wet areas if you cannot build a rain garden. The fruit is small and the wood is thorny, but it provides excellent wildlife habitat. It can also sucker and look more like a shrub than a tree. If it's protected from cold, dry winds, it can tolerate slightly colder temperatures once established.

Picea sitchensis

Sitka spruce

HARDY TO: –10°F (–23°C)

SIZE: 90 ft. (27.4m) tall x 30 ft. (9.1m) wide

REGION(S): west of the Cascades, and western slopes

RAIN GARDEN SIZE: large

☼/◑/◐

A wonderful tree found in the coastal forests of the Northwest, the Sitka spruce can tolerate occasional hot weather as long as its roots have ample moisture; it does not like long stretches of hot and dry weather. It will be fine if it grows in salt spray area or with some salt water mixed with fresh in boggy conditions, in just about all soil conditions. It will survive long periods of flooding but won't get as large as it would under better conditions.

Quercus palustris

Pin oak, swamp oak

HARDY TO: –30°F (–34°C)

SIZE: 60 ft. (18m) tall x 25 ft. (7.6m) wide

REGION(S): all

RAIN GARDEN SIZE: medium to large

☼/◑/◐

The leaves of the swamp oak are pointed and lobed, turn a great red color in fall, and cling to the tree all winter. This Pacific Northwest native tolerates salt spray, salt from ice prevention (as long as it is followed by snowmelt or rain to dilute), snow, and floods from time to time. It will live a long life, if allowed, and bear its first real acorn crop in 20–25 years.

Salix discolor Muhl.

Pussy willow

HARDY TO: –30°F (–34°C)

SIZE: (tree): 20 ft. (6m) tall x 15 ft. (4.6m) wide

SIZE: (wide shrub): 6–8 ft. (1.8–2.4m) tall x 6–8 ft. (1.8–2.4m) wide

REGION(S): all except desert

RAIN GARDEN SIZE: medium to large

☼/◐/☾

A very nice ornamental plant with fuzzy and large catkins in the spring, the pussy willow can handle drying out in the summer so long as it receives winter or spring moisture. You can prune it to be a tree or a multitrunk shrub with showy branches that can be utilized in flower arrangements more easily in the spring. It tolerates flooding, snow, and even some salt. Not a desert plant, it will die if exposed to lasting drought.

Salix sitchensis

Sitka willow

HARDY TO: –35°F (–37°C)

SIZE: Up to 25 ft. (7.6m) tall, width varies

REGION(S): all

RAIN GARDEN SIZE: large

☼/◐/☾

A very resilient plant, the Sitka willow is not as showy as some other plants. It has a mounded shape and bright green leaves with 2- to 3-inch (5–7.5cm) catkins. It can become a small tree or a large shrub just like pussy willow can and is similar in its tolerance and needs. We usually recommend using it in very large rain gardens and as a backdrop to other showy plants.

SHRUBS

Cornus sericea cultivars (also *Cornus stolonifera*)

Red, red osier, yellow, and other colorful twig dogwoods

HARDY TO: –30°F (–34°C)

SIZE: 6–8 ft. (1.8–2.4m) tall x 6–8 ft. (1.8–2.4m) wide

REGION(S): all

RAIN GARDEN SIZE: medium to large

☼/◐/☾/●

These cane-growing shrub dogwoods grow small, sweet flowers followed by beautiful berries that are important food for birds. The twigs provide good hiding spots for our feathery friends, and sometimes you will find small birds nesting among them. The leaves can be green or variegated, and they often turn great color in the fall. Once the foliage drops in the winter, the bark on the stems shines bright and colorful—black, red, yellow, or orange depending on the cultivar—showstoppers if placed well. Use several in a larger space; in a smaller space, one carefully pruned shrub can do great work.

Cornus sericea (Photo by Stacey Sowers)

Cornus sericea "Kelsyi," a dwarf red osier dogwood
(Photo by Stacey Sowers)

The strong roots can grow into clay and hardpan with persistence, creating small cracks that water enters. Eventually this collaboration of plants and elements will improve the soil deep below the surface of the rain garden.

Choose varieties with the brightest bark colors you can find and, if it fits the design, complement them with variegated foliage. While they need regular pruning to keep their bright color and desired size, their resilience to most diseases and ability to recover from injuries makes them a good choice even in places where hedging or mowing all plants is common practice, such as right-of-way rain gardens. They will work in all zones of a rain garden.

Dwarf twig dogwoods: The dwarf forms of twig dogwoods, typically red, grow only 24–30 in. (61–76cm) tall and should be used with caution: If mixed into Zone 1, they may be lost among larger plants. These plants are not as robust in color as their relatives, and their berries are also much smaller. However, they look great in very small rain gardens if the other plants are also small, or you are planting a rain garden in a box. These dwarf forms are good for all regions in this book and handle full shade to full sun, though the bark is brighter if it gets more light.

Myrica californica (also *Morella californica*)

Pacific wax myrtle

HARDY TO: 0°F (−18°C)

SIZE: 30 ft. (9.1m) tall x 20 ft. (6m) wide

REGION(S): west of the Cascades

RAIN GARDEN SIZE: large

☼ / ◑ / ◐ / ●

An evergreen native shrub, the Pacific wax myrtle can be used in larger rain gardens near sea beaches and if the native soil is rocky and poor in nutrients. As it fixes nitrogen and tolerates high salt levels, it can grow in soils typically not suitable for plants and can put up with being flooded for longer periods as well as being very dry. If you prune it, reduce the number of canes near the base of the plants rather than shortening branches. The berries smell fragrant when crushed and can be used in home crafts, such as soap and candle making. A much smaller deciduous relative of this plant, *Myrica gale*, or bog myrtle, can be used in smaller spaces, but it is not evergreen.

Physocarpus spp.

Ninebark

HARDY TO: −30°F (−34°C)

SIZE: 15 ft. (4.6m) tall x 15 ft. (4.6m) wide

REGION(S): all

RAIN GARDEN SIZE: medium to large

☼ / ◑ / ◐ / ●

The original native *Physocarpus capitatus*, native to the West Coast, is a huge plant; the right species, hybrids, or cultivars can be fabulous for all zones of a rain garden. This is a very important wildlife plant: The flowers serve as nectar sources, the shrubs themselves are great to nest in, and the peeling bark

Physocarpus "Diablo" in autumn (Photo by Cynthia LaBlue)

of older canes is good nest-building material. The colorful foliage of the cultivars and hybrids looks brighter the more sun it gets.

The shrub can be hedged well, although that will shorten its lifespan and rob the plant of its wonderful natural structure. If left to grow naturally, the canes will arch gracefully in the landscape, adding a nice form to the winter garden.

Ninebark is resistant to diseases, pests, and environmental challenges. Many shades of red and gold foliage, a variety of mature sizes, and even a range of flower colors from creamy white to pink are available. Look at the tags and research the specific variety or cultivar before you buy. Because the plants are constantly being developed, newer and newer selections will be available each year.

Rhododendron groenlandicum
(also Ledum groenlandicum)

Labrador tea

HARDY TO: −45°F (−43°C)

SIZE: 3 ft. (91cm) tall x 4 ft. (1.2m) wide

REGION(S): all

RAIN GARDEN SIZE: all

☼/◑/◐/●

This cool-weather evergreen shrub is good for rain gardens on native soils with higher clay content. In its natural habitat it grows in swamps, cold soils, and rocky areas that receive a lot of snow and have a short growing season. The flowers are white and showy. It will tolerate the cold as long as the plant was very wet before the soil froze, and it prefers dappled light.

Rosa pisocarpa

Clustered wild rose, cluster rose

HARDY TO: 0°F (−18°C)

SIZE: 7 ft. (2.1m) tall x 6 ft. (1.8m) wide

REGION(S): west of the Cascades

RAIN GARDEN SIZE: medium to large

☼/◑/◐

This beautiful flowering rose grows along the coast from BC to California. As long as it has access to some moisture periodically during the year, it will tolerate up to 100°F (38°C). Salt spray, flooding, and dry conditions are fine.

Salix lucida

Shining willow, Pacific willow

HARDY TO: –50°F (–46°C)

SIZE: 6–10 ft. (1.8–3m) tall x 6–10 ft. (1.8–3m) wide

REGION(S): all except desert

RAIN GARDEN SIZE: medium to large

☼ / ☀ / ☀

The shiny leaf willow is one tough plant: It tolerates salt, snow, ice, fairly hot and dry periods, flooded conditions, just about anything we can throw at it besides desert conditions. It needs to have wet feet periodically. While native to the Midwest and East Coast, it's a great plant for tough urban rain garden locations.

Salix purpurea and *S. purpurea* "Nana"

Dwarf blue arctic willow

HARDY TO: –30°F (–34°C)

SIZE (full size): 6–10 ft. (1.8–3m) tall x at least 6–10 ft. (1.8–3m) wide

SIZE (dwarf): 3–4 ft. (1–1.2m) tall x at least 3–4 ft. (1–1.2m) wide

REGION(S): all except desert

RAIN GARDEN SIZE: medium to large

☼ / ☀ / ☀

Similarly tough and versatile as *S. lucida*, this plant has foliage that is a nice blue instead of bright green and much finer, smaller leaves. The stems take on a reddish-purple hue during the spring. People often prune this shrub the same way they prune red osier dogwood, so the new shoots can provide great winter interest with their bright color. Its color is best in sun.

Spiraea betulifolia

Birchleaf spirea

HARDY TO: –30°F (–34°C)

SIZE: 3 ft. (91cm) tall x 3 ft. (91cm) wide

REGION(S): all

RAIN GARDEN SIZE: small

☼ / ☀ / ☀

Most people do not know about this wonderful, virtually indestructible plant, whose size makes it perfect for an urban rain garden. It can live in flooded conditions or complete drought, clay or sand, heat or cold. It blooms in late spring with clusters of pink flowers and turns red in the fall for a lasting show of stunning color. Its roots will grow deep into the ground and well below the amended soil, helping to increase infiltration over time and connect the rain garden to the deep groundwater. The variety "Lucida" is especially beautiful.

EMERGENTS

Acorus gramineus "Ogon"

Grassy-leaved sweetflag

HARDY TO: –20°F (–29°C)

SIZE: 1 ft. (30.5cm) tall x 2 ft. (61cm) wide

REGION(S): Coastal Forest, Salish Sea, Willamette Valley

RAIN GARDEN SIZE: all

☼/☼/●

The great golden color of this semi-evergreen is a very nice addition to shady spots. As it needs to have wet feet periodically, it will tolerate hot weather only as long as it is in shade and has access to moisture.

Acorus gramineus "Ogon"

Carex buchananii

Leatherleaf sedge

HARDY TO: 0°F (–18°C)

SIZE: 2 ft. (61cm) tall, spreading clumps

REGION(S): Coastal Forest, Salish Sea, Willamette Valley, West Coast regions

RAIN GARDEN SIZE: all

☼/☼/☼

This really interesting sedge comes all the way from New Zealand. It is excellent for our Coastal Forest, Salish Sea, and Willamette Valley regions, along the West Coast, and it loves well-draining rain gardens but usually freezes out east of the Cascades. Slow spreading, and much smaller than the native emergents listed above, it needs to be maintained with gentleness; pruning and rough pulling on its leaves can damage the crown and the plant may die. Note that this plant is brown by nature and not dead! One client's family once surprised her by cleaning up her yard on her birthday, and when she came out to see the result, she was shocked to find her brown grasses and sedges missing because her family had pulled the "dead stuff."

Carex elata "Aurea"

Bowles golden sedge

HARDY TO: –20°F (–29°C)

SIZE: 2 ft. (61cm) tall, slightly wider

REGION(S): all

RAIN GARDEN SIZE: all

☼/☼/☼

Bowles golden sedge is semi-evergreen, meaning it may lose its yellow leaves if the weather gets too cold for its liking, or if it is covered with deep snow. It does well in dry, warm summer weather as long as it gets wet periodically. The yellow foliage stands out

Carex elata "Aurea"

and brightens the area well, so it is a nice addition to Zone 1 or the lower edges of Zone 2.

Carex obnupta

Slough sedge

HARDY TO: 0°F (−18°C)

SIZE: 4 ft. (1.2m) tall x 4 ft. (1.2m) wide

REGION(S): west of the Cascades

RAIN GARDEN SIZE: all

☼/☼/☼/●

Because this species can be mowed, chopped, chewed, trampled, chilled, shaded, flooded, salted, dried, and heated yet will still look bright, it's a go-to plant for many municipal rain garden projects and right-of-way designs. In warmer winters semi-evergreen and tall, it spreads fast, growing to full size in just one season—even if you plant it from a dibble tube or a 4-inch container! So be careful: Do not mix this guy with small dwarf plants in Zone 1, because you will end up with nothing but this plant. However, it is great under full-sized dogwood shrubs and ninebark plants.

Carex stipata

Sawbeak sedge

HARDY TO: −40°F (−40°C)

SIZE: 2–3 ft. (60–91cm) tall x 2–3 ft. (60–91cm) wide

REGION(S): all

RAIN GARDEN SIZE: all

☼/☼/☼/●

Sawbeak sedge is another tall sedge, but slower growing than *C. obnupta*. Since it's tough and deciduous, it can take extreme cold. Its salt tolerance makes it a great plant for rain gardens in areas where icy roads are salted in the winter.

Carex testacea

Orange sedge

HARDY TO: −5°F (−21°C)

SIZE: 16–24 in. (41–61cm) tall x 16–24 in. (41–61cm) wide

REGION(S): Coastal Forest, Salish Sea, Willamette Valley

RAIN GARDEN SIZE: all

☼/☼/☼

Another nice sedge also from New Zealand, and similar to leatherleaf sedge in its preferences and size, orange sedge mixes well with leatherleaf sedge; the two will provide a swaying carpet at the rain garden bottom.

Juncus effusus

Common rush

HARDY TO: −30°F (−34°C)

SIZE: 3 ft. (91cm) tall, spreading clumps

REGION(S): all

RAIN GARDEN SIZE: large

☼/◑/●

Native to most of the globe, including New Zealand, this is a plant you probably see on a daily basis if you live west of the Cascades, and weekly east of them where the soil gets seasonally wet. It will lose its leaves if packed into snow in very cold temperatures, but it can stay green even under snow if the temperature is mild. While excellent for right-of-way sites or where a tough Zone 1 plant is needed, this plant does not work well for typical small home-scale gardens because it spreads aggressively and can seed outside the rain garden as well. It can grow in lawns and landscape beds that are wet at times, so most people end up fighting it in a very small space. If you use it, you will not need any other emergent in the rain garden.

Juncus effusus (Photo by Stacey Sowers)

Juncus ensifolius

Daggerleaf rush, swordleaf rush

HARDY TO: −40°F (−40°C)

SIZE: 2 ft. (61cm) tall, spreading clumps

REGION(S): all

RAIN GARDEN SIZE: all

☼/◑/◐/●

A hardy plant that is similar to the common rush, daggerleaf rush can put up with cold as well as very hot summer weather. It spreads much less aggressively, can grow well in typical-size urban rain gardens, and tolerates salt spray. It plays nicely with other plants.

Scirpus acutus (also *Schoenoplectus acutus*)

Hardstem bulrush

HARDY TO: −40°F (−40°C)

SIZE: 7–10 ft. (2.1–3m); very tall, spreading clumps

REGION(S): all

RAIN GARDEN SIZE: medium to large

☼/◑/◐/●

This tough giant is an important food plant for Native Americans and grows *huge*! It is a really fun plant. If you want this in your rain garden, install only one in Zones 1 or 2—no need to plant other shrubs or other emergents, because this big, awesome plant will choke them out. It tolerates salt if it is diluted with freshwater periodically. It can withstand heat well past 100°F (38°C) and prefers sun. It spreads at a steady pace, doubling its size each year. It does not like being cut down to the ground regularly, however, so it's not a good right-of-way plant. But since it can be flooded all the way to 5 ft. (1.5m) deep, it can absolutely take the ponding depth of a rain garden. The question is, can your rain garden take this plant?

Scirpus microcarpus

Small-fruited bulrush, panicled bulrush

HARDY TO: −40°F (−40°C)

SIZE: 18 in. (46cm) tall, spreading clumps

REGION(S): all

RAIN GARDEN SIZE: all

☼/◑/◐

Refined, with small blossoms and brown seeds, this very hardy plant often stays evergreen even under snow. It will be lost if planted with larger emergents, so use it only with similar-size sedges and rushes. It tolerates salt spray, salty runoff if it is diluted with snowmelt periodically, and heat past 100°F (38°C).

Scirpus microcarpus

PERENNIALS

Caltha palustris

Marsh marigold

HARDY TO: −50°F (−46°C)

SIZE: 2 ft. (61cm) tall x 2 ft. (61cm) wide

REGION(S): all except desert

RAIN GARDEN SIZE: all

☼/◑/◐/●

The hardy and beautiful marsh marigold is good for rain gardens that pond and drain in 3–4 days after the rain stops, but not for those that drain fast and rarely pond. Since it usually goes dormant by mid-summer, it tolerates dry conditions and heat as long as it also has periodic flooding, so it also works in Zone 2. It has large leaves and large yellow flowers—a real gem in spring, when it comes back strong as the snow melts. It can tolerate some salt runoff as long as melting snow or rain dilutes it.

Iris sibirica

Siberian iris

HARDY TO: −40°F (−40°C)

SIZE: 18 in. (46cm) tall x 18 in. (46cm) wide

REGION(S): all

RAIN GARDEN SIZE: all

☼/◑/◐

The hardy Siberian iris tolerates periodic flooding, hot and dry conditions, even periodic drought. It spreads and multiplies through rhizomes.

Iris tenax (Photo by Roseann Barnhill)

Iris tenax

Coastal iris

HARDY TO: 0°F (–18°C)

SIZE: 18 in. (46cm) tall x 18 in. (46cm) wide

REGION(S): west of the Cascades

RAIN GARDEN SIZE: all

☼/◑/◐

This beautiful yet tender plant is suitable for regions west of the Cascades, as long as the local winter microclimate is on the milder side—it does not tolerate prolonged freezing weather. The rain garden should be well draining, as coastal iris does not tolerate flooding for long periods.

Lobelia cardinalis

Cardinal flower

HARDY TO: –40°F (–40°C)

SIZE: 2–4 ft. (61cm–1.2m) tall x 2 ft. (61cm) wide

REGION(S): all

RAIN GARDEN SIZE: all

☼/◑/◐

This tough perennial loves full sun and moist soil, but will tolerate partial shade and very dry conditions as long as it is periodically wet during the rainy season. The long-lasting flowers attract many beneficial pollinators such as butterflies and hummingbirds.

Lysichiton americanus

Western skunk cabbage

HARDY TO: –10°F (–23°C)

SIZE: 5 ft. (1.5m) tall x 2 ft. (61cm) wide

REGION(S): west of the Cascades

RAIN GARDEN SIZE: medium to large

◑/◐/●

This stunningly beautiful plant usually has little smell unless the leaves or stem are crushed. As the flower is growing, two large leaves—up to 3 ft. (91cm) long—emerge next to it, eventually allowing other foliage to unfurl. The plant can tolerate really warm summers as long as it is shaded, but is not drought tolerant and prefers rain gardens that drain slowly (3–4 days) and clay rather than sandy soils.

Mimulus guttatus

Seep-spring monkey flower

HARDY TO: –30°F (–34°C)

SIZE: 18 in. (46cm) tall x 18 in. (46cm) wide

REGION(S): all

RAIN GARDEN SIZE: all

◐

A very tough little plant with yellow summer flowers, the seep-spring monkey flower loves wet and moist soil as long as it is not in standing water for too long. It tolerates seasonal dryness as well, and can grow even in wet ponds within desert environments if shaded. It grows as a native in every region in our book and is great for attracting native insects if it's part of a healthy habitat.

Mimulus guttatus (Photo by Roseann Barnhill)

Typha latifolia

Cattail

Typha minima

Dwarf cattail

HARDY TO: −30°F (−34°C)

SIZE: (full size): 3 ft. (91cm) tall x 4–6 ft. (1.2–1.8m) wide

SIZE: (dwarf): 1.5 ft. (46cm) tall x 2–3 ft. (61–91 cm) wide

REGION(S): all, with added moisture

RAIN GARDEN SIZE: medium to large

☼/◐/☾

These well-known deciduous marshland plants have traditionally provided food, building materials, and other useful raw materials in many parts of the world. Heat tolerant, they will spread extensively all the way into Zone 2 if the rain garden is slow draining. In mostly sandy and very well-draining soils, cattails can be kept at bay to a degree if dried out completely during the dry season. Try planting them in large containers with the bottom cut out: This way they are still part of the rain garden but are kept in check by a root barrier. They are a favorite food source for blackbirds. Even though it is a perennial and not an emergent, if you use this plant it will spread as an emergent, and you will likely not need many emergent plant species for the bottom.

GROUNDCOVERS

Vaccinium macrocarpon

American cranberry

HARDY TO: −50°F (−46°C)

SIZE: 6 in. (15cm) tall, with indefinite spread

REGION(S): all except deserts

RAIN GARDEN SIZE: all

☼/◐/☾

The American bog cranberry is an important agricultural crop that grows in bogs and very wet areas and produces tart red berries: Yes, it's what you make your cranberry sauce from. In a rain garden, however, you are not going to grow it for the berries, but the birds will sure appreciate them. It tolerates summer weather as long as it is in moist, acidic soil that floods periodically. A deciduous plant, it comes back well each spring as the snow melts. It does not tolerate salty runoff well.

Vaccinium vitis-idaea

Lingonberry

HARDY TO: −50°F (−46°C)

SIZE: 6 in. (15cm) tall, with indefinite spread

REGION(S): all except desert

RAIN GARDEN SIZE: all

☼/◐/☾

A low-growing and slow-creeping groundcover, the lingonberry is a close relative of the cranberry and similar in its needs and tolerance levels, except that this plant tolerates dry summer conditions (not drought!) and is evergreen. Birds will keep an eye out for the ripe berries.

PLANTS FOR ZONE 2

Because of the hydrology within the rain garden, sometimes Zone 2—the sloped sides—is very small. If the garden ponds frequently because the underlying soil is poorly draining, Zone 2 can be as little as the distance between the top of the ponding area and the top of the slope. If the garden drains well and the water level fluctuates often within the system, Zone 2 can be the entire sloped area.

Many Zone 1 plants work well in the lower sections of Zone 2, where the soil will be moist longer than in the upper section. Zone 1 plants that need more moisture, however, should not be used in Zone 2.

TREES

Acer circinatum

Vine maple

HARDY TO: -20°F (-29°C)

SIZE: 20 ft. (6m) tall x 20 ft. (6m) wide

REGION(S): all except desert

RAIN GARDEN SIZE: medium to large

☀/◑/☀

Native from southern BC to Northern California, this is commonly found along the coastline, streambanks, moist woods, and lower elevations of the Cascades. The multitrunked tree can tolerate warm, dry conditions as long as it gets moisture periodically during the year—drought stresses it. It is used in urban development because of its tolerance to pollution and even some salt runoff, as long as it is diluted by melting snow and rain. The leaves are almost round yet deeply lobed. Vine maple has several cultivars that are stunning ornamentals, such as "Pacific Fire," which has bright red bark. Others are miniature and grow as shrubs but have differently colored and shaped leaves. It grows well under large conifers or other deciduous trees, but the fall colors are best in sunny spots.

Acer circinatum

Amelanchier alnifolia

Serviceberry, juneberry, Saskatoon berry

HARDY TO: −40°F (−40°C)

SIZE: 20 ft. (6m) tall x 10 ft. (3m) wide

REGION(S): coastal areas, prairies, Columbia Plateau

RAIN GARDEN SIZE: medium to large

☼ / ◑ / ●

The hardy serviceberry, another smaller tree or large shrub, loves sun, tolerates salt spray and cold, and grows well in most forests as well as in drought conditions. In sun the leaves are bluish; flowers form in early spring and berries in June. The berries are very tasty and have long been a staple for Native Americans.

Amelanchier alnifolia (Photo by Roseann Barnhill)

Frangula purshiana (Rhamnus purshiana)

Cascara tree

HARDY TO: −40°F (−40°C)

SIZE: 25 ft. (7.6m) tall x 15 ft. (4.6m) wide

REGION(S): all except desert

RAIN GARDEN SIZE: large

☼ / ◑ / ●

A great wildlife habitat tree and a sturdy understory in Pacific Northwest forests, the cascara tree withstands hot, dry weather as long as it has periodic access to moisture. It often grows alongside red osier dogwood shrubs in its natural habitat. The more sun it gets, the nicer fall color it displays. Birds flock to the ripening berries.

Frangula purshiana (Photo by Roseann Barnhill)

Magnolia virginiana

Swamp magnolia, sweetbay magnolia

HARDY TO: −20°F (−29°C)

SIZE: 30 ft. (9.1m) tall x 30 ft. (9.1m) wide

REGION(S): all except desert

RAIN GARDEN SIZE: medium to large

☼/◐/●

This beautiful tree is native to the eastern United States yet perfect for rain gardens in our area. It has large, fragrant, whitish flowers from midspring to early summer followed by showy fruits. It loves moist soils, but will tolerate dry and warm periods as long as it is followed by some rain eventually. If there is space, plant one with 3–4 trunks, as these create an instant focal point in the garden.

Thuja plicata

Western red cedar

HARDY TO: −20°F (−29°C)

SIZE: 200 ft. (61m) tall x 30 ft. (9.1m) wide

REGION(S): Coastal Forest, Salish Sea, Willamette Valley, and the Cascades

RAIN GARDEN SIZE: large

☼/◐/●

The western red cedar is a *big* tree: Use it only in large rain gardens and large sites. One healthy red cedar can actually perform the work of a small rain garden with ease. It tolerates snow and salt spray and warm, dry summer weather, but drought stresses it. In bogs, where it is flooded all the time, it grows much slower than in well-draining moist soils. It can live for thousands of years.

Xanthocyparis nootkatensis

Alaska yellow cedar

HARDY TO: −30°F (−34°C)

SIZE: 100+ ft. (30+m) tall x 60 ft. (18m) wide

REGION(S): Coastal Forest, Salish Sea, Willamette Valley, and the Cascades

RAIN GARDEN SIZE: medium (narrow form)/ large (regular form)

☼/◐/●

The Alaska yellow cedar is normally very large but has a weeping and narrow form that is widely used in urban landscapes. Some people call it the Dr. Seuss tree because of its fascinating shape. The narrow form grows somewhat shorter and much slimmer than the regular form, which is similar to the western red cedar but shaggier. Both forms can tolerate snow, flood conditions, salt spray, and varying temperatures. The tree is found in bogs, at the water's edge, and in moist forests along the West Coast from Alaska to Northern California. It tolerates dry conditions, but drought will stress it; flooded conditions will stunt it. It is not uncommon to find 1,500-year-old Alaska yellow cedars in older forests. Place the regular form in very large rain gardens on large sites. The narrow form, however, can be planted easily in medium-size rain gardens. Use the "Green Arrow" cultivar as a cluster of 3–5 trees in regular urban-size yards; each tree will get only about 2–3 ft. (60–91cm) wide over a very long time.

SHRUBS

Corylus cornuta and cultivars

Beaked hazel, Western hazelnut

HARDY TO: −30°F (−34°C)

SIZE: 6–9 ft. (1.8–2.7m) tall x 6–9 ft. (1.8–2.7m) wide

REGION(S): all

RAIN GARDEN SIZE: medium to large

☼/◑/☾

Some cultivars of this hardy shrub are curly, red leaved, or golden leaved; some are more compact than the native species, but all have flat, fuzzy green, red, or yellow leaves. The shrub tolerates salt spray and snow, even colder temperatures than −30°F (−34°C) if it has enough moisture before the deep freezing weather arrives, moist and dry conditions, and even periodic drought. You will need two different plants for good pollination, and you also had better love squirrels, because as soon as the nuts form, the squirrels will be checking in daily and harvesting them for you. Beaked hazel can be used as a very large hedgerow and will form thickets if allowed, but it is deciduous. We also want to make sure that the "cousins" are mentioned: Curly and twisted forms of hazel as well as red-leaved cultivars are fun plants and can add great focal points to rain gardens. A couple of them—Harry Lauder's walking stick and red majestic hazel—are specifically interesting plants.

Gaultheria shallon

Salal

HARDY TO: −10°F (−23°C)

SIZE: 5 ft. (1.5m) tall, with indefinite spread

REGION(S): coastal areas and the Cascades

RAIN GARDEN SIZE: medium to large

☼/◑/☾/●

Salal will grow as a sturdy evergreen groundcover or shrub once it is established. It does not mind salt spray and will be all right in moist soils if it is sunny, or dry soils if it is shaded; lasting drought stresses the plant, however. An evergreen with leaves resembling leather or sandpaper, it has small edible flowers that last for weeks and attract wildlife. It takes time and patience to establish because the roots are sensitive to the ecosystem within the soil and need symbiotic partners to succeed. Once the site takes, salal will grow and spread nicely. Maintenance is easy, and it tolerates pruning or even mowing.

Gaultheria shallon (Photo by Holli Margell)

Hydrangea cultivars

Hydrangea

HARDY TO: −20°F (−29°C)

SIZE: 30 ft. (9.1m) tall x 30 ft. (9.1m) wide

REGION(S): all except desert

RAIN GARDEN SIZE: medium to large

☼/☀/☀/●

While not native to the Pacific Northwest, these shrubs are wonderful for our area. The genus offers many species and cultivars of countless shapes, colors, and sizes; all are wonderful, as they can tolerate wet to dry conditions and very acidic to very alkaline soil. They stay denser, bloom better, and have stronger fall color in full sun, but they will do OK in shade. Blooms of the *H. macrophylla* species will be pink in alkaline soils and blue in acidic conditions. The *H. paniculata* form species and cultivars have elongated, cone-shaped flowers. Another group of hydrangeas, oakleaf, have leaves resembling oaks, hence their name. Flowers last till late fall, and the foliage keeps until severe freezing weather sets in—plant at least one of these beauties in a rain garden setting, if you have the space.

Hydrangea

Lonicera involucrata

Twinberry

HARDY TO: −30°F (−34°C)

SIZE: 7–10 ft. (2.1–3m) tall x 7–10 ft. (2.1–3m) wide

REGION(S): all except desert

RAIN GARDEN SIZE: medium to large

☼/☀/☀/●

While twinberry does not look like much in the winter, it has nice yellow flowers that come in pairs, attract hummingbirds, and turn into jewellike fruits. These edible berries are sweet on some bushes but bitter on others, so not everyone likes them. The shrub can be pruned and even divided but will regrow in a few years. It can put up with very warm summer weather as well as periodic drought.

Lonicera involucrata (Photo by Vicki Demetre)

Mahonia spp.

Oregon grape

HARDY TO: –20°F (–29°C)

SIZE: Varies by species; the low groundcovers usually stay under 1.5 feet (46cm) and spread indefinitely, the taller one reaches 5–10 feet (1.5–3m) or taller over time, and gets similarly wide

REGION(S): all except desert

RAIN GARDEN SIZE: all

☼/☀/☀/●

The Oregon grape comes in many species and cultivars. The *Mahonias* from China and Japan are stunning and large and offer a tropical feel few other plants can provide. *Mahonias* can be groundcovers, low shrubs, fairly large shrubs, and even tree-shaped—there is a *Mahonia* for every site. They produce large yellow flower clusters that are a food source for birds, especially hummingbirds, and insects. The leaves form miniature cups that collect the dew, supplying water to small wildlife. The foliage, whether low or tall, is very prickly and evergreen. Because of all these qualities, *Mahonia* makes great hummingbird condos, where the birds can nest, eat, drink, and hang out protected by spiky leaves. Dry and hot summer weather, even periodic drought, salt spray, and snow and salt runoff from urban deicing (as long as it is diluted by snowmelt or rain) are all fine for this plant.

Oemleria cerasiformis

Indian plum

HARDY TO: –30°F (–34°C)

SIZE: 6–9 ft. (1.8–2.7m) tall x 6–9 ft. (1.8–2.7m) wide

REGION(S): all

RAIN GARDEN SIZE: medium to large

☼/☀/☀/●

Indian plum can take hot and dry weather; it will grow in moist soils and put up with salt spray. The berries are a wonderful wildlife attraction, but you have to get both the male and female plants if you want them. They are edible when ripe, although the seeds are large and some of the fruit can be bitter. The flowers are among the first to come out, usually as early as late January or early February. The greenish clusters are fragrant and important food for hummingbirds and insects.

Mahonia (Photo by Vicki Demetre)

Oemleria cerasiformis (Photo by Roseann Barnhill)

Philadelphus spp.

Mock orange

HARDY TO: −30°F (−34°C)

SIZE: 6–9 ft. (1.8–2.7m) tall x 6–9 ft. (1.8–2.7m) wide

REGION(S): all

RAIN GARDEN SIZE: medium to large

☼/☽/◑

When it is in bloom, this plant is drop-dead gorgeous: The flowers are large, white, and fragrant, and are sometimes used in perfumes—make sure you can enjoy the late spring and early summer blooms! Some varieties have double flowers and really large, showy blooms; just check that the particular variety is fragrant, as not all hybrids are. The soft yellow fall color is not stunning but not bad. Mock orange tolerates salt spray and occasional moist soil conditions, and can live well on very dry slopes and rocky soils.

Ribes sanguineum

Red-flowering currant

HARDY TO: −10°F (−23°C)

SIZE: 6–9 ft. (1.8–2.7m) tall x 6–9 ft. (1.8–2.7m) wide

REGION(S): all except desert

RAIN GARDEN SIZE: medium to large

☼/☽/◑

An ornamental shrub, the red-flowering currant tolerates salt spray, snow, and dry—even periodic drought—conditions. It can take heat, especially if it is shaded and has access to moisture. The edible dark pink to red flowers appear early in the spring and stay for weeks. Hummingbirds flock to this shrub while it is in bloom. Its great red fall color becomes more enhanced with the more sun it gets. The maple-shaped leaves are similar to ninebark and high bush cranberry leaves; make sure you do not repeat the same leaf shape too much in the garden.

Ribes sanguineum (Photo by Roseann Barnhill)

A well-designed site can benefit from all of these plants, but they need to be spaced apart, with some contrast between them. Can be used as the focal point in a small rain garden, if in these cases it is the only medium-size shrub planted.

Rosa rugosa

Rugosa rose

HARDY TO: −50°F (−46°C)

SIZE: 6 ft. (1.8m) tall x 6 ft. (1.8m) wide

REGION(S): all

RAIN GARDEN SIZE: medium to large

☼/☽/◑

A very nice, large flowering rose, Rugosa tolerates salt spray, salty runoff, heat and hot weather, dry conditions, and drought. It can be pruned and maintained as a graceful rosebush, or allowed to sprawl and become a thicket. Birds love it too.

Rubus parviflorus

Thimbleberry

HARDY TO: −30°F (−34°C)

SIZE: 3–6 ft. (91cm–1.8m) tall, with indefinite spread

REGION(S): all except desert

RAIN GARDEN SIZE: medium to large

☼/◐/◑/●

Another raspberry relative, thimbleberry is thornless and has large leaves. It tolerates warm and dry weather, periodic drought, salt spray, snow, and urban salt runoff after snowmelt. While it will grow well in just about any light conditions, it prefers shade, drier soils, and periodic access to moisture in full, hot sun. The flowers are white and turn into one red berry.

Rubus spectabilis

Salmonberry

HARDY TO: −30°F (−34°C)

SIZE: 5–6 ft. (1.5–1.8m) tall x 5–6 ft. (1.5–1.8m) wide

REGION(S): all except desert

RAIN GARDEN SIZE: medium to large

☼/◐/◑

A raspberry relative, salmonberry has similar foliage, leaves, and even berries, but it is a much less aggressive and less thorny shrub. It grows usually on the edges of bogs and ponds, riverbanks, and other periodically moist-then-dry areas. It does not tolerate drought but can handle some flooding and salt spray well. The spring flowers are hot pink and followed by orange-red berries early summer. The berries are delicious for people, but wildlife loves them just as much.

Sambucus nigra "Eva" and "Gerda"

Black Lace elderberry, Black Beauty elderberry

HARDY TO: 30°F (−34°C)

SIZE: 20 ft. (6m) tall x 20 ft. (6m) wide

REGION(S): all

RAIN GARDEN SIZE: medium to large

☼/◐/◑/●

Elderberry can be nice ornamentals, large graceful shrubs, or small trees, depending on how you train them. A cane grower, elderberry produces flowers followed by berries, which are an important agricultural product. It tolerates wet and dry conditions and can tolerate drought and salt spray. It produces best in partial to full sun. The black cultivars have stunning dark red foliage during the growing season, then pink flower clusters followed by deep-blue berries. Flowers and berries of the S. nigra cultivars can be used raw or cooked in syrups and other dishes.

Sambucus nigra (Photo by Holli Margell)

Symphoricarpos albus

Snowberry

HARDY TO: −45°F (−43°C)

SIZE: 3–4 ft. (1–1.2m) tall x 3–4 ft. (1–1.2m) wide

REGION(S): all

RAIN GARDEN SIZE: medium to large

☼/◑/◐/●

This tough, thicket-forming shrub can tolerate 100+°F (38+°C) heat, both moist and dry soils, salt spray, snow and salt runoff in winter, air and soil pollution—you name it, this little guy will not disappoint! It is an excellent wildlife plant; birds can easily nest in it, and the flowering lasts from spring to midsummer, feeding hummingbirds and insects alike. The white berries ripen by fall and in winter seem to be floating above ground on delicately thin stems. The berries are not a favorite with birds, but they will eat them once everything else runs out and the berries start to ferment a little at the end of winter. If you need a plant you can prune, hedge, and mow, this is it.

Symphoricarpos albus (Photo by Holli Margell)

Vaccinium ovatum

Evergreen huckleberry

HARDY TO: −10°F (−23°C)

SIZE: 6–7 ft. (1.8–2.1m) tall, and a little less wide

REGION(S): Cascades and west of the Cascades

RAIN GARDEN SIZE: medium to large

☼/◑/◐/●

Evergreen huckleberry is a much easier plant to grow than its red relative. It can tolerate salt spray, moist to dry soils, and even occasional drought periods. It can be hedged well.

Vaccinium parvifolium

Red huckleberry

HARDY TO: −10°F (−23°C)

SIZE: 9–10 ft. (2.7–3m) tall x 4–5 ft. (1.2–1.5m) wide

REGION(S): Cascades and west of the Cascades

RAIN GARDEN SIZE: medium to large

☼/◑/◐

Red huckleberry is a finicky deciduous plant but worth the effort, and with care and patience you can get it growing. It's not drought tolerant but can take periodic dry weather and full sun as long as it has enough moisture. It grows best on cedar chips or shavings, in old cedar logs, and near salal.

EMERGENTS

In Zone 2, it's best to use the emergents of Zone 1, as long as they do not require very wet conditions. If the conditions suit them they will likely spread into Zone 2 from Zone 1 on their own. Plant them in Zone 1 and let them spread into Zone 2 over time.

PERENNIALS

Anemone spp.

Anemone, windflower

HARDY TO: –25°F (–32°C)

SIZE: (spring flowering): 6–12 in. (15–30.5cm) tall

SIZE: (fall flowering): 2 ft. (61cm) tall

REGION(S): all

RAIN GARDEN SIZE: all

☼/●

Japanese windflowers are native to Asia. The flowers of the fall-flowering (*Anemone hupehensis* and *Anemone* x *hybrida*) variety look like they are floating because the stems are thin and the blooms large. Plant with bleeding heart for perfect flower succession. The flowers of anemones last for weeks and are a great addition to rain gardens. They tolerate snow, light salt spray, and periodic dry and even drought conditions as long as they are not permanent.

Aruncus dioicus

Goatsbeard

HARDY TO: –30°F (–34°C)

SIZE: 5–6 ft. (1.5–1.8m) tall x 2.5–3 ft. (77–91cm) wide

REGION(S): all except deserts

RAIN GARDEN SIZE: medium to large

☼/☀/☀

A hardy and beautiful native flower, cream-colored goatsbeard brightens the shady rain garden. It does not tolerate drought; as long as it has enough moisture it can put up with dry and warm—but not hot—summer weather.

Camassia spp.

Camas

HARDY TO: –20°F (–29°C)

SIZE: 2 ft. (61cm) tall x 9–12 in. (23–30.5cm) wide

REGION(S): all

RAIN GARDEN SIZE: all

☼/☀/☀

This lily is a bulbous plant, growing and flowering usually blue or white in the spring, then going dormant for the rest of the year; by summer, you won't even know it was there. It spreads slowly and does not like to be disturbed, so leave it alone for a few years before dividing it. Camas tolerates snow, but not much salt. It can die in prolonged drought, as it needs springtime moisture for strong growth each year. It thrives in meadows and prairies, and even withstands desert conditions as long as it rains some in the spring.

Camassia (Photo by Roseann Barnhill)

Dicentra spp.

Bleeding heart

HARDY TO: −35°F (−37°C)

SIZE: 16–24 in. (41–61cm) tall, with slow, indefinite spread

REGION(S): all

RAIN GARDEN SIZE: all

☼/☀/●

Bleeding heart (some also called *Lamprocapnos*) is perfect for a rain garden. Both the native, *D. formosa*, and the Japanese *D. spectabilis* are very hardy in cold, very dry areas with enough moisture in the spring, and even drought conditions. They grow in early spring and flower early as well. By midsummer they are dormant, so plant them near perennials that flower in late summer. The flowers resemble tiny, waxlike hearts.

Dicentra (Photo by Roseann Barnhill)

Hemerocallis spp.

Daylily

HARDY TO: -40°F (-40°C); some species up to -50°F (-46°C)

SIZE: 12 in. (30.5cm) tall and wide to 3 ft. (91cm) tall and wide

REGION(S): all

RAIN GARDEN SIZE: all

☼/☀/☀

Not only beautiful, with often fragrant flowers, daylily is also versatile and hardy. The tens of thousands of available cultivars come in multitudes of colors, sizes, even shapes, as hobby hybridizers and collectors have focused on the species for a long time. Some bloom all summer, each bloom lasting for a day or so, while others bloom into the fall. Not all species and cultivars are fragrant, so check with your nursery before you buy. Daylilies can tolerate moist, even wet conditions to very hot and dry weather, periodic drought, and salt runoff as long as the runoff is diluted by snowmelt or rain. The plants disappear during the winter and are dormant under the ice and snow, ready to grow again as the soil warms. They are easy to divide and transplant.

Hosta spp.

Hosta, plaintain lily

HARDY TO: -35°F (-37°C); some species up to -40°F (-40°C)

SIZE: a few inches tall to 6 ft. (1.8m) wide, depending on what species and cultivar are used

REGION(S): all

RAIN GARDEN SIZE: all

☼/☀/☀

While this is a well-known and very much loved hardy perennial, it's often misunderstood. People think this plant is delicate and fussy—that couldn't be further from the truth! Hostas are tough as nails and put up with very difficult conditions elegantly. Granted, they come in so many species and thousands of cultivars that some are less hardy. Generally speaking however, there is a hosta for every garden! They vary in size from a few inches to 6 ft. (1.8m) in diameter. They tolerate warm, dry summers, snow all winter, and even some salty urban deicing runoff. Once the spring rains start, so does the hosta. Hostas tolerate full shade but flower better and color more strongly in more light, as long as they have access to some moisture periodically. In shade they can tolerate dry conditions easier, and they can be divided easily. Go forth and find your favorite!

Maianthemum racemosum (Photo by Vicki Demetre)

Maianthemum racemosum (also *Smilacina racemosa*)

False Solomon's seal

Polygonatum biflorum

Great Solomon's seal

HARDY TO: −40°F (−40°C)

SIZE: 2–3 ft. (60–91cm) tall, with spreading clumps

REGION(S): west of the Cascades

RAIN GARDEN SIZE: all

☼/☼/●

Both false Solomon's seal and great Solomon's seal belong to the same family, but they are different genuses and species. Both are native to North America, with false Solomon's seal native to the Pacific Northwest. They both take wet and dry conditions, occasional drought once established, snow, and even light salt spray. *Maianthemum racemosum* is fragrant and produces red berries, and the foliage turns yellow in the fall. *Polygonatum biflorum* produces blue berries in the fall and also turns yellow. Use them together if you have the space, each in its own cluster in different spots in the rain garden so people have to take a second look, as the similar plants are very different.

Trillium ovatum

Coast trillium, western trillium

HARDY TO: −20°F (−29°C)

SIZE: 12–18 in. (30.5–46cm) tall, with slow, indefinite spread

REGION(S): all except desert

RAIN GARDEN SIZE: all

☼/☼/●

This tough little plant comes up early in the year, and by midsummer it is usually dormant. It does not tolerate hot, dry conditions very well without shade; if the rhizome in the ground is exposed to very hot weather and drought, it can dry up and not come back the next spring. It naturalizes slowly, and plant collectors treasure their specimens if they start to spread and eventually form larger clusters.

FERNS

Ferns, a large group of plants with countless genuses, species, and cultivars, are grouped together here because they are found together in nurseries and often thought of as one plant group. While they look and often are delicate, they are essential in a forest ecosystem as well as in shrubby meadows, and are important for wildlife habitat. Many ferns are native to the West Coast forest regions, in the Cascades, and some in the wooded areas of the Columbia Plateau. These ferns can put up with snow, cold, and moderately warm summer weather as long as they have enough moisture; they normally prefer full to partial shade. They propagate through spores and have no true flowers. Some of them are deciduous and others are evergreen (which do drop their leaves but only after the new foliage emerges). Leave the old ferns, rather than cutting them off, for wildlife. They are best used in Zone 2 and, if shaded, in Zone 3 in the rain garden.

These are the four best ferns for your rain garden:

Blechnum spicant

Deer fern

HARDY TO: –10°F (–23°C)

SIZE: 12 in. (30.5cm) tall x 12 in. (30.5cm) wide

REGION(S): Cascades and west of the Cascades

RAIN GARDEN SIZE: all

☼/☼/●

This smaller native fern has shiny black stems. The narrow, fertile fronds grow upright, and the sterile fronds stretch out flat below.

Blechnum spicant (Photo by Heidi Koonz)

Dryopteris erythrosora

Autumn fern

HARDY TO: –10°F (–23°C)

SIZE: 18–24 in. (46–61cm) tall x 18–24 in. (46–61cm) wide

REGION(S): all

RAIN GARDEN SIZE: all

☼/☼/●

Native to Japan, the autumn fern gets its name from its coppery color: The new shoots emerge a fantastic orange in the spring and turn light green over the summer, so for the early part of the year these ferns look like it is autumn in the woods. It spreads slowly over time. It is fine being dry or even in periodic drought, as long as it is in a shady spot. It can take full sun with moist soil conditions unless the site gets very dry.

Polystichum munitum

Western sword fern

HARDY TO: −20°F (−29°C)

SIZE: 2 ft. (61cm) tall x 2 ft. (61cm) or wider

REGION(S): all except desert

RAIN GARDEN SIZE: all

☼/☀/☀/●

This large native fern will spread over time to cover large parts of the garden as it multiplies through rhizomes. While it loves partial shade and moist, well-draining soil, it will put up with anything from full shade to full sun and wet to periodically dry conditions, even occasional drought.

Polystichum munitum (Photo by Stacey Sowers)

Polystichum polyblepharum

Tassel fern

HARDY TO: −10°F (−23°C)

SIZE: 2 ft. (61cm) tall x 2 ft. (61cm) wide

REGION(S): Cascades and west of the Cascades

RAIN GARDEN SIZE: all

☀/☀/●

The tassel fern is a close relative of the sword fern from Asia and similar to the sword fern in its needs.

SAXIFRAGES

As plants from the *Saxifraga* genus love moist soil in their native, typically mountain valley, habitat in many parts of the world, they are perfect for Zone 2 in a rain garden. Saxifrages are another very large group of plants; the three highlighted here, our favorites, are similar in their preferences and even in their appearance. In medium to large rain gardens, we normally cluster two to three of each together and enjoy when people try to figure out why these similar-looking plants are so different when seen close up. Saxifrages can take snow and salt spray and tolerate periodic dry conditions, but not drought. Not as delicate as they look, they will spread over time in the garden.

Consider these three saxifrages for your rain garden's Zone 2:

Tellima grandiflora

Fringecup

HARDY TO: –10°F (–23°C)

SIZE: 12 in. (30.5cm) tall, with spreading clumps

REGION(S): all except desert

RAIN GARDEN SIZE: all

☼ / ◑ / ◐

Fringecup sometimes tolerates much colder temperatures and deeper freezes than foam flower and piggyback plant. Because of its cold tolerance and even occasional drought tolerance, it can be used in a fairly wide range in the Pacific Northwest.

Tellima grandiflora (Photo by Roseann Barnhill)

Tiarella trifoliata

Foam flower

HARDY TO: –10°F (–23°C)

SIZE: 12 in. (30.5cm) tall, with spreading clumps

REGION(S): all except desert

RAIN GARDEN SIZE: all

☼ / ◑ / ◐

One of the three saxifrages that grow naturally in the widest range of the Pacific Northwest, foam flower is found in the drier forests east of the Cascades as well.

Tiarella trifoliata

Tolmiea menziesii

Piggyback plant

HARDY TO: −10°F (−23°C)

SIZE: 12 in. (30.5cm) tall, with spreading clumps

REGION(S): all except desert

RAIN GARDEN SIZE: all

☼/☼/☼/●

Piggyback plant gets its name from the shape of its new plantlets, which look like they are getting a ride from the larger ones. It is a native in the Cascades and west of them, but will work well for the entire Pacific Northwest as long as there is moisture and partial to full shade.

GROUNDCOVERS

Asarum caudatum

Wild ginger

HARDY TO: −10°F (−23°C)

SIZE: 6 in. (15cm) tall, with spreading clumps

REGION(S): Cascade lower slopes, west of the Cascades

RAIN GARDEN SIZE: all

☼/☼/●

An evergreen, wild ginger grows very low and slowly spreads under other vegetation. It flowers, but the leaves often hide the interesting bloom.

Asarum caudatum (Photo by Vicki Demetre)

Convallaria majalis

Lily of the valley

HARDY TO: −40°F (−40°C)

SIZE: 6 in. (15cm) tall, with indefinite spread

REGION(S): all

RAIN GARDEN SIZE: all

☼/◐/◑/●

A great perennial spring groundcover, lily of the valley has fragrant flowers that are wonderful inside in a vase—a few can fill the whole house with fragrance. The plant goes into dormancy during the summer, so combine it with another plant that fills the space during the later part of the growing season, such as hosta. It takes snow and ice valiantly and can handle dry, warmer weather in the summer as well, and drought to a degree. The warmer the summer, the more shade it needs.

Gaultheria procumbens

Wintergreen

HARDY TO: −40°F (−40°C)

SIZE: 6 in. (15cm) tall, with indefinite spread

REGION(S): all

RAIN GARDEN SIZE: all

◐/◑/●

This creeping evergreen plant gives us the red berries used in many products, such as toothpaste. It tolerates dry shade but thrives if it has moisture periodically. A great wildlife plant, since the flowers attract pollinators and larger critters like eating the berries.

Mahonia nervosa

Cascade Oregon grape

Mahonia repens

Low Oregon grape, creeping Oregon grape

HARDY TO: −20°F (−29°C)

SIZE: 6–18 in. (15–46cm) tall x 6–18 in. (15–46cm) wide

REGION(S): all except desert

RAIN GARDEN SIZE: all

☼/◐/◑

These two low-growing species of the *Mahonia* genus tolerate snow and salty deicing runoff after snowmelt, as well as dry and hot summer weather and even periodic drought and salt spray. They will also deal with shade.

Maianthemum dilatatum

False lily of the valley

HARDY TO: −40°F (−40°C)

SIZE: 6 in. (15cm) tall (or less), with indefinite spread

REGION(S): all

RAIN GARDEN SIZE: all

☼/◐/◑/●

A close relative of false Solomon's Seal, this deciduous perennial groundcover has a very nice fragrant flower followed by red berries. It tolerates salt spray and moist or periodically dry soil, but not drought. Normally it is found with Sitka spruce trees, huckleberries, and sword ferns. It's an especially great choice for the Cascades and west of them.

Oxalis oregana

Wood sorrel

HARDY TO: –10°F (–23°C)

SIZE: 12 in. (30.5cm) tall, with indefinite spread

REGION(S): Cascades and west of the Cascades

RAIN GARDEN SIZE: all

☼/◐/◑/●

This low perennial spreads steadily but not aggressively and prefers partial shade. It withstands dry soil conditions and occasional drought as well as snow, salt spray, and salty runoff after snowmelt as long as it is diluted by melting snow or rain. The bright green foliage shows off the white flowers.

Oxalis oregana

PLANTS FOR ZONE 3

For Zone 3, anything goes: This is the top edge, where you integrate the rain garden into the rest of the landscape. Some of the plants from Zone 2 will grow into Zone 3, and many of the Zone 2 plants will actually work well here, especially if they do not need periodic wet soil. Choose plants based on your typical landscaping needs and requirements, rather than the wetness of the soil during the rainy season. If you have a well-draining site, alpine plants work very well and offer a unique feel when planted so close to emergents.

TREES

Abies koreana "Horstmann's Silberlocke"

Silberlocke Korean fir, Horstmann's Silberlocke fir

HARDY TO: 20°F (–29°C)

SIZE: 25 ft. (7.6m) tall x 12 ft. (3.7m) wide

REGION(S): all

RAIN GARDEN SIZE: medium to large

☼

This slow-growing tree tolerates snow as well as dry, warm summers, and occasional droughts once it is established.

Abies koreana

Arbutus unedo

Strawberry tree

HARDY TO: 0°F (−18°C)

SIZE: (full size): 25 ft. (7.6m) tall x 10 ft. (3m) wide

SIZE: (dwarf): 13 ft. (4m) tall x 5 ft. (1.5m) wide

REGION(S): west of the Cascades

RAIN GARDEN SIZE: large

☼

The evergreen strawberry tree has full-size and dwarf forms, both wonderful. The full size is hardier, especially in winter exposure. A nonnative yet very close relative of the native Pacific madrona, it serves similar ecosystem functions as the Pacific madrona but can be transplanted. (Pacific madrona is not listed here, because transplanting one larger than a few inches is very difficult and the survival rate is less than 25 percent. It is an important habitat tree, however, and planting its relative helps the ecosystem greatly.) Its bark is orange and peeling, offering great interest. The flowers are showy and the berries usually many colors, from light yellow to orange or dark red—and all on the same tree at the same time! It tolerates dry and warm weather well, even drought and salt spray once it is established, but not snow and cold.

Calocedrus decurrens

Incense cedar

HARDY TO: −20°F (−29°C)

SIZE: 120 ft. (37m) tall x 45 ft. (13.7m) wide

REGION(S): all except desert

RAIN GARDEN SIZE: large

☼

Native to the Pacific Northwest, this evergreen tolerates snow, salt spray, and periodic dry and warm conditions, and loves sun. In drier regions, it will grow more slowly and not reach its full size. Because of its size, it is hard to shade it! It feels substantial even at a young age, sort of like a Great Dane puppy, so use in large gardens only.

Arbutus unedo (Photo by Holli Margell)

Cotinus coggygria

Smoke tree

HARDY TO: –25°F (–32°C)

SIZE: 15 ft. (4.6m) tall x 9 ft. (2.7m) wide

REGION(S): all

RAIN GARDEN SIZE: medium to large

☼ / ◖ / ●

The smoke tree can be a small tree or a larger shrub, whichever you prefer. A versatile tree with several cultivars and hybrids available, it can have dark red, reddish-green, or even golden yellow foliage. The clustered flowers look like smoke puffs floating in the air just above the branches. Fall colors are nice and pronounced, especially in sun. Pollard (a pruning method) the tree to produce larger leaves and a shrub-size plant, or train it into a tree of 1–3 trunks. It tolerates snow, salt spray, and very warm dry weather and drought as well.

Cotinus coggygria (Photo by Holli Margell)

Juniperus scopulorum

Rocky Mountain juniper

HARDY TO: –40°F (–40°C)

SIZE: 30 ft. (9.1m) tall x 15 ft. (4.6m) wide

REGION(S): all

RAIN GARDEN SIZE: large

☼ / ◖ / ●

This evergreen is native to the Rocky Mountains but is also found sometimes in the Pacific Northwest. It can deal with salt spray, snow, dry heat, and even drought, and prefers full sun.

Pinus ponderosa

Ponderosa pine

HARDY TO: –30°F (–34°C)

SIZE: 100 ft. (30m) tall x 25 ft. (7.6m) wide

REGION(S): all

RAIN GARDEN SIZE: large

☼

Another very large tree, the ponderosa pine is suitable only for large spaces and large rain gardens. It can handle heavy snowpack, icy conditions, salt spray, and very hot and dry summers, even occasional drought, but will not tolerate standing water or shady moist sites. It has large needles and cones. This is another very large "puppy" intended for large gardens only. Use it with caution—you are getting a big plant!

Quercus garryana

Garry oak

HARDY TO: –10°F (–23°C)

SIZE: 40 ft. (12.2m) tall x 40 ft. (12.2m) wide

REGION(S): all

RAIN GARDEN SIZE: large

☼

This slow-growing native white oak, with round-lobed leaves, is an especially good choice for meadows, prairies, coastal dry highlands, and dry slopes. It can also be used in eastern regions as long as the winters are not too cold. It is easy to grow, tolerant of dry hot summers and even drought. It needs sun and dry conditions to be happy.

Tsuga mertensiana

Mountain hemlock

HARDY TO: –25°F (–32°C)

SIZE: 90 ft. (27.4m) tall x 15–45 ft. (4.6–13.7m) wide

REGION(S): all except desert

RAIN GARDEN SIZE: large

☼/◑/◐/●

This relatively slow-growing evergreen conifer is native to our area and generally grows on well-draining soils with rocky grounds and exposed or higher-elevation locations. Over time it will get big, but because it grows slowly it can be used in the urban landscape, if you understand the potential long-term size. The short needles grow in a whorl pattern; keep the tree's natural shape by not pruning the lower limbs for an especially nice form. It can take snow loads and seasonal dry weather, and prefers cooler summers and moist air. It can't handle standing water or flood, and definitely not drought.

If you are interested in a full-size evergreen tree and did not plant one in Zone 1 or 2, this may be a good tree for you. Keep in mind, however, that if you have a small rain garden, large plants can overpower it or even hide it from view in the long run.

DWARF CONIFERS

Dwarf conifers come in dozens of genuses, hundreds of species, and even more cultivars, all with their own specific tolerances and preferences. But let's talk about this big group of plants as one group for a second: They offer the same great evergreen characteristics as their full-size counterparts, but you can have more of them and not worry about the trees taking over the yard! You can also mix and match these easily to your very specific regional needs, even the Arctic and the tropics, so you can find one for your rain garden regardless of where you are in the Pacific Northwest.

Cedrus deodara "Snow Sprite"

Snow Sprite Deodar cedar

HARDY TO: 0°F (–18°C)

SIZE: 4 ft. (1.2m) tall x 6 ft. (1.8m) wide

REGION(S): west of the Cascades

RAIN GARDEN SIZE: medium to large

◐

This wonderful small tree, while not very cold hardy, grows well in dry soil, even with occasional drought conditions. If it is protected from wind, it can brighten up shady corners with its silvery white foliage that ages to a soft yellow. It needs some light and does not tolerate full shade.

Chamaecyparis pisifera "Filifera Aurea Nana"

Dwarf golden thread cypress

HARDY TO: –40°F (–40°C)

SIZE: 6 ft. (1.8m) tall x 6 ft. (1.8m) wide

REGION(S): All

RAIN GARDEN SIZE: medium to large

☼ / ◑ / ☾

This is not a true dwarf and not true gold either; the foliage is green with lighter green segments that give it a glow. It is a great brighter-foliage plant that tolerates snow, salt spray, dry and warm temperatures, and occasional drought well.

Chamaecyparis pisifera

Microbiota decussata

Siberian cypress

HARDY TO: –40°F (–40°C)

SIZE: 24 in. (61cm) tall, and 3 times wider over time

REGION(S): all

RAIN GARDEN SIZE: all

☼ / ◑ / ☾

This low-growing conifer shrub turns a dark brownish color during the cold weather, so do not panic: It is not dead, just changing its color for the winter. It loves dry and drought conditions and takes snow, salt spray, and salty snowmelt.

Microbiota decussata in winter color

Picea glauca "Conica"

Dwarf Alberta spruce, white spruce

HARDY TO: −75°F (−59°C)

SIZE: 9 ft. (2.7m) tall x 5 ft. (1.5m) wide

REGION(S): all

RAIN GARDEN SIZE: medium to large

☼/◐/◑

This tough little guy, native to the Rocky Mountains, has a very distinct conical shape. It tolerates snow, snowmelt, and salt spray, salty runoff, dry and hot summers, and even drought.

Pinus mugo var. *pumilio*

Pinus mugo var. *pumilio*

Dwarf mugo pine

HARDY TO: −50°F (−46°C)

SIZE: 4 ft. (1.2m) tall x 4 ft. (1.2m) wide

REGION(S): all

RAIN GARDEN SIZE: all

☼

Dwarf mugo pines are rounded small conifers, slow growing and spreading only a few inches each year. They are great in Zone 3 because their form is unique, the dark green foliage can enhance other colors in the garden, and birds love to perch and even nest in them. This dwarf pine tree tolerates snow loads, salt spray, and salty runoff after snowmelt, dry hot temperatures, and even drought.

Thujopsis dolabrata "Nana"

Dwarf false Hiba cedar

HARDY TO: −20°F (−29°C)

SIZE: 3 ft. (91cm) tall x 4 ft. (1.2m) wide

REGION(S): all except desert

RAIN GARDEN SIZE: all

◑

Do not watch this tree grow, because you will age fast: It takes many, many years to reach full size. It is sometimes so low that it becomes a groundcover. It offers very nice evergreen foliage and can take snow, dry conditions, even occasional drought.

SHRUBS

Ceanothus spp.
California lilac

HARDY TO: 0°F (−18°C)

SIZE: 6–12 ft. (1.8–3.7m) tall x 6–12 ft. (1.8–3.7m) wide

REGION(S): west of the Cascades, Coastal Forest, Salish Sea, Willamette Valley, and Savanna Prairie

RAIN GARDEN SIZE: medium to large

☼

This evergreen shrub blooms for weeks and weeks in the summer, and bees love it! It prefers no snow loads but tolerates salt spray. If an established one does freeze out for some reason, cut it back to the ground to rejuvenate it. It loves sun and dry conditions, even drought, but definitely not wet feet.

Ceanothus (Photo by Roseann Barnhill)

Fuchsia magellanica
Hardy fuchsia

HARDY TO: −10°F (−23°C)

SIZE: 6–10 ft. (1.8–3m) tall x 6–10 ft. (1.8–3m) wide

REGION(S): all except desert and cold plateau

RAIN GARDEN SIZE: medium to large

☼/◑/◐/●

While hardy fuchsia is not a native, maybe hummingbirds think so—they love it! And with good reason: It is beautiful, tolerates some snow, dry warm summer weather, and even occasional drought once it is established. It is deciduous and flowers from spring until frost. If allowed to grow naturally, it has a very nice arching shape and will be loaded with blooms each year. If it freezes back, prune it to live wood and start over.

Hamamelis spp.
Witch hazel

HARDY TO: −40°F (−40°C)

SIZE: Varies by species, 6–10 ft. (1.8–3m) tall x 12–15 ft. (3.7–4.6m) wide

REGION(S): all except desert

RAIN GARDEN SIZE: medium to large

☼/◑/◐

Witch hazel species and cultivars (some are native to North America) grow wider than they do tall and bloom very early in the year (usually February at the latest), with flowers that are yellow to red in color and varying in fragrance depending on the species. The fairly large leaves come out after the flowers and turn a brilliant range of red tones in fall, stronger if in full sun. If allowed to grow naturally, this vase-shaped plant can gracefully arch over other plants in the garden. It tolerates some snow and likes to have periodic moisture alternating with dry periods, but can tolerate occasional drought.

Holodiscus discolor

Oceanspray

HARDY TO: –30°F (–34°C)

SIZE: 9 ft. (2.7m) tall x 9 ft. (2.7m) wide

REGION(S): all

RAIN GARDEN SIZE: medium to large

☼ / ◐ / ◑

This native shrub tolerates snow, salt spray, salty runoff from snowmelt, dry and even drought conditions, and hot weather. The new neon-green leaves come out in early spring, and the flowers look like ocean foam, hence the name. The seed heads are an important food source for birds in winter but not a very pretty sight, so make it a background plant.

Holodiscus discolor (Photo by Stacey Sowers)

Potentilla gracilis

Graceful cinquefoil

HARDY TO: –40°F (–40°C)

SIZE: 2 ft. (61cm) tall x 2 ft. (61cm) wide

REGION(S): all

RAIN GARDEN SIZE: all

☼ / ◐ / ◑

A cold-hardy, deciduous native shrub, graceful cinquefoil offers important habitat for birds and insects and has bright yellow flowers; cultivars offer orange, red, and even pink flowers. It loves dry conditions and takes hot summers well too. Drought does not faze it, but high humidity, especially warm and humid climates, does bother it.

GRASSES

Grasses need lots of caution when planted in a garden because many can become invasive. Look for nonaggressive, native, or more delicate species when shopping, because if the nonnative grass is happy and aggressive, it will spread everywhere in your neighborhood and beyond. In the Northwest, pampas grass in particular gets very large, spreads aggressively, and is very difficult to maintain because of its sharp foliage: You need a chainsaw and very heavy clothing to cope with it. In our opinion, the best management for this grass in the Northwest is removal. However, the following grasses add lovely color and interest to Northwest rain gardens and will not become unmanageable if planted in the right region. One sure way to kill a grass is by flooding it or saturating its roots, so they are only good to use in Zone 3 and are not recommended for the other zones.

Elymus glaucus

Blue wildrye

HARDY TO: −40°F (−40°C)

SIZE: 5 ft. (1.5m) tall x 5 ft. (1.5m) wide

REGION(S): east of the Cascades, desert

RAIN GARDEN SIZE: medium to large

☼

Blue wildrye, a native, is widely used in restoration plantings but can be used in urban rain gardens as well, and in any zone as long as the rain garden drains very well. It tolerates snow and salt spray, yet also takes very hot and dry summer weather and drought well. A great plant for wildlife, especially if you leave the seed heads on in winter.

Festuca glauca

Blue fescue

HARDY TO: −35°F (−37°C)

SIZE: 12 in. (30.5cm) tall x 12 in. (30.5cm) wide

REGION(S): all

RAIN GARDEN SIZE: all

☼

Small but showy, blue fescue adds stunning blue color, and the seed heads, if left on, add great winter interest and bird habitat. It tolerates salt spray and salty runoff from snowmelt, even deep snow cover, but stays evergreen if there is no snow. It loves hot, dry summers and periodic drought.

Helictotrichon sempervirens

Blue oat grass

HARDY TO: −30°F (−34°C)

SIZE: 2.5 ft. (77cm) tall x 2.5 ft. (77cm) wide

REGION(S): all

RAIN GARDEN SIZE: all

☼/◑/◐

Also a blue-colored grass, this elegant plant is not too large and not too small, and is similar in its needs and tolerance to blue fescue—but much larger.

Miscanthus sinensis "Morning Light"

Morning Light maiden grass

HARDY TO: −10°F (−23°C)

SIZE: 6 ft. (1.8m) tall x 6 ft. (1.8m) wide

REGION(S): west of the Cascades

RAIN GARDEN SIZE: medium to large

☼

This tall grass grows wonderful cream- to coppery-colored flowers that turn into great seed heads for year-round interest and bird food. It tolerates some snow, salt spray, dry and hot summers, and even periodic drought.

PERENNIALS

Aquilegia formosa
Western columbine

HARDY TO: −40°F (−40°C)

SIZE: 2 ft. (61cm) tall x 2 ft. (61cm) wide

REGION(S): all

RAIN GARDEN SIZE: all

☼/◐/◑/●

A hummingbird magnet, this reliable perennial rocks and is not an aggressive player in the garden. When happy, it will self-seed; it blooms in early summer, seeds in early fall. It tolerates salt spray, salty runoff, wet and dry soil conditions, hot and dry summers, and even drought. If you are really about hummers, plant this with hardy fuchsias, red-flowering currants, mahonias, lobelias, and kinnikinnick for a nonstop hummingbird paradise.

Aquilegia (Photo by Roseann Barnhill)

Crocosmia "Lucifer"
Crocosmia Lucifer

HARDY TO: −20°F (−29°C)

SIZE: 2.5 ft. (77cm) tall, with slow, indefinite spread

REGION(S): west of the Cascades, milder eastern regions

RAIN GARDEN SIZE: large

☼

Showy *Crocosmia* blooms red and attracts insects, pollinators, and especially hummingbirds! It tolerates snow, salt spray, real summer heat, and dry conditions. In drought the bulb remains alive but the plant dries up above the ground. It does not, however, handle prolonged drought.

Echinacea purpurea
Purple coneflower

HARDY TO: −40°F (−40°C)

SIZE: Up to 5 ft. (1.5m) tall x 2 ft. (61cm) wide

REGION(S): all

RAIN GARDEN SIZE: all

☼

A close relative of black-eyed Susan, purple coneflower grows about the same size and flowers all summer, late into the fall. *Echinacea* comes in many color cultivars. If you have room to grow more, it is worth it to use cultivars that complement or contrast nicely in color.

Heuchera spp. and cultivars

Alumroot, coral bells

HARDY TO: −5°F (−21°C)

SIZE: 12 in. (30.5cm) tall x 12 in. (30.5cm) wide

REGION(S): west of the Cascades, east of the Cascades if milder winter microclimate

RAIN GARDEN SIZE: all

☼/◐/◑

It's worth taking the time to select a heuchera from the many available varieties, with new ones available every year. They come in an almost endless color palette, but not all of them are tough; wait a few years to see if a new variety is as good as promised. Our favorites are "Mocha," "Obsidian," "Palace Purple," "Crimson Curls," "Green Spice," "Lime Marmalade," "Plum Pudding," and "Chocolate Ruffles." They all tolerate some snow and warm and dry summers, but not drought. The tall flower spikes rise above the foliage seasonally. Great plant for insects and pollinators.

Heuchera spp.

Kirengeshoma palmata

Yellow waxbell

HARDY TO: −20°F (−29°C)

SIZE: 3 ft. (91cm) tall x 3 ft. (91cm) wide

REGION(S): all except desert

RAIN GARDEN SIZE: all

◐/◑/●

This native Korean hydrangea relative might as well be native in the Northwest! What a great addition to the garden. It has interesting lobed leaves that color up nicely in the fall, and blooms late in the summer. It takes snowpack and dry summer conditions, as long as it is not in full sun; ongoing drought stresses it. A great choice for a shady site.

Lupinus polyphyllus

Large-leaved lupine, bigleaf lupine

HARDY TO: −35°F (−37°C)

SIZE: Up to 5 ft. (1.5m) tall x 5 ft. (1.5m) wide

REGION(S): all

RAIN GARDEN SIZE: all

☼/◐/◑

This beautiful, self-seeding flowering plant is a nitrogen fixer, so it can be planted in very poor soils. It spreads in the natural environment, but in urban areas it does not always come back well from one year to the next. It needs good drainage, and while it tolerates wet soil conditions, it does not like clayey soil or being flooded. While it is drought tolerant to a degree, years of drought will kill it.

Lupinus polyphyllus (Photo by Vicki Demetre)

Rudbeckia fulgida

Black-eyed Susan, orange coneflower

HARDY TO: −40°F (−40°C)

SIZE: 2 ft. (61cm) tall x 2 ft. (61cm) wide

REGION(S): all

RAIN GARDEN SIZE: all

☼

Easy to grow, black-eyed Susan loves dry, even droughty conditions and takes heat too. Its large golden flowers attract pollinators, and the seed heads, if left on for the winter, are an important food source for birds.

Rudbekia fulgida (Photo by Vicki Demetre)

Salvia officinalis

Sage

HARDY TO: −35°F (−37°C)

SIZE: 2 ft. (61cm) tall and twice as wide

REGION(S): all

RAIN GARDEN SIZE: all

☼/◑/◐

Not just a fine herb, sage is also a very hardy flowering, often woody, perennial. It is native to North Africa and to the Balkans, but it is not invasive in our area. It tolerates snow, salt spray, and very dry, even drought conditions. In shade, it sprawls instead of growing upright shoots, and it does not tolerate wet feet.

GROUNDCOVERS

Arctostaphylos uva-ursi
Kinnikinnick (also bearberry)

HARDY TO: −50°F (−46°C)

SIZE: 6 in. (15cm) tall, with indefinite spread

REGION(S): all

RAIN GARDEN SIZE: all

☼/◐/◑

Because kinnikinnick is actually called *bearberry* in many languages (Latin included), it should be no surprise that bears really do munch on it. This plant is very hardy; it tolerates very dry and hot summer weather once it is established. It stays low and covers the ground well, preventing erosion. It grows in infertile soil, exposed sites, and well-draining soil. It does not tolerate flooding and standing water.

Arcostaphylos uva-ursi (Photo by Holli Margell)

Galium odoratum
Sweet woodruff

HARDY TO: −35°F (−37°C)

SIZE: 6 in. (15cm) tall x 16 in. (41cm) wide

REGION(S): all except desert

RAIN GARDEN SIZE: all

◐/◑/●

Do not be fooled by this delicate-looking groundcover with its dainty white flowers and refined appearance! This plant can take harsh conditions in stride, including deep snow, salty runoff, and salt spray, mowing a few times a year, wet soil conditions, and warm dry summers (as long as it is in shade). If it is in full sun, however, it will go dormant by midsummer.

Galium odoratum

Lewisia columbiana

Columbian lewisia, Columbian bitterroot

HARDY TO: −45°F (−43°C)

SIZE: 6 in. (15cm) tall x at least 6 in. (15cm) wide

REGION(S): all except coastal forests

RAIN GARDEN SIZE: all

☼/☀

The flowers on this beautiful native grow on long stems and hover over the foliage. It takes everything but humidity and wet soil; it survives deep snow cover, loves poor rocky soils that are dry, and considers drought its best friend. Occasional rains are fine, as long as it drains away almost instantly—do not ever irrigate this plant! Try placing some in a gravel-filled pot on the edge of the rain garden to enjoy the flowers.

Viola glabella

Evergreen violet

HARDY TO: −40°F (−40°C)

SIZE: 3 in. (7.5cm) tall, with spreading clumps

REGION(S): west of the Cascades, east if in shade

RAIN GARDEN SIZE: all

☼

This little treasure of a native plant, though not very well known, spreads each year and has very showy, heart-shaped evergreen leaves. If it is exposed to drought it goes dormant, and eventually, if the drought is prolonged over multiple years, it dies. It can handle deep snow, and as soon as the snow is gone the evergreen foliage bounces back and brightens the day. We love this little plant and strongly recommend it for all of your gardening needs.

Viola glabella (Photo by Vicki Demetre)

Rain Garden Planting Design Templates

To get started dreaming of planting your own rain garden, we have included four sample planting plans. A planting plan shows you which plants will be included in each zone. Because we have diverse climate and sun/shade conditions in our region, our sample plans address four distinct yet typical conditions:

- West of Cascades, sunny location
- West of Cascades, shade/part shade
- East of Cascades, sunny location
- East of Cascades, shade/part shade

These plans are suggestions to help you, but are adaptable. To get more ideas, use the plant lists that we have provided. Make sure to pay close attention to a plant's sun/shade and water requirements as well as its hardiness before swapping it in.

HOW TO READ A PLANTING PLAN

A planting plan is like a map that shows where each plant should be located. It is drawn as if looking down on the garden from above (plan view). As you can see, each rain garden zone is indicated on the plan, as is where each plant is located *within* those zones. Each plant has its own symbol, which can be found in the plant key. Plants are indicated on the plan to scale as their mature size. It is very important to know what the ultimate size of a plant will be to ensure adequate room for growth. Note the scale, which is indicated on the plan, and measure accordingly for plant placement.

SOME DESIGN TIPS

A good design is both functional and beautiful. It can be like creating a 3-D sculpture, but with the added 4th dimension of time and season.

1. Make sure to consider the ultimate size (both height and width) of each plant.
2. Include a variety of colors, textures, sizes, shapes, and contrast.
3. The plants you choose should provide interest in all seasons. Use a mix of evergreen, deciduous, and herbaceous plants. Ask yourself, what does the winter picture look like? Does it include evergreen plants or plants with colored bark or seed pods or berries which also feed birds?
4. A focal point with a bold plant or tree anchors the garden and gives it a sense of order.

WEST OF THE CASCADES, FULL SUN EXPOSURE

This rain garden planting plan for a sunny location on the west side of the Cascades includes all-season interest. In spring the huge leaves and flowers of the skunk cabbage emerge in Zone 1. (Skunk cabbage is called swamp lantern on the East Coast, which we think is a much nicer name!) Flowering currant, Oregon grape, and evergreen huckleberry are also harbingers of spring. Then come the wild roses and daylilies and the oakleaf hydrangea blossoms. Late summer into fall the fruit of the strawberry tree turns shades of yellow, orange, and red, while simultaneously blooming with white flowers. The golden smoke tree, flowering currant, and oakleaf hydrangea provide a beautiful display of fall color. In winter the colorful bark of the twig dogwoods brightens the rainy days, while seeds and berries attract birds for your entertainment. The strawberry tree and the golden smoke tree are the focal points that anchor each end of the garden. The dark leaves of the Center Glow ninebark provide a great contrast to the golden leaves of the smoke tree.

 Arbutus unedo 'Compacta'
Dwarf Strawberry Tree

 Carex elata 'Aurea'
Bowles Golden Sedge

 Carex testacea
Orange Sedge

 Cornus sanguinea 'Midwinter Fire'
Midwinter Fire Dogwood

 Cornus sericea
Red Osier Dogwood

 Cotinus coggygria 'Golden Spirit'
Golden Smoke Tree

 Festuca glauca
Blue Fescue

 Gaultheria shallon
Salal

 Hemerocallis 'Yellow Lollipop'
Yellow Lollipop Daylily

 Heuchera micrantha 'Palace Purple'
Palace Purple Coral Bell

 Hydrangea quercifolia 'Ruby Slippers'
Red Flower Oakleaf Hydrangea

 Lysichiton americanus
Western Skunk Cabbage

 Mahonia nervosa
Low Oregon Grape

 Physocarpus opulus 'Center Glow'
Center Glow Ninebark

 Ribes sanguineum
Red-Flowering Currant

 Rosa rugosa
Rugosa Rose

 Vaccinium ovatum
Evergreen Huckleberry

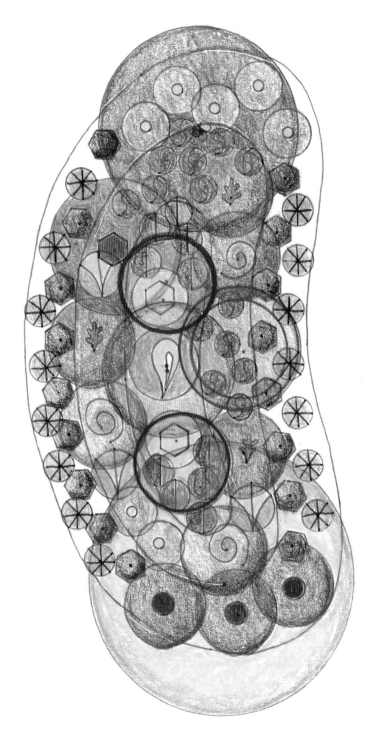

This plan for a shade to part shade location also includes interest in all seasons. Some of the same plants that are found in the previous plan are also found here because of their adaptability. There are plants that bloom from early spring and into the fall. Bleeding hearts and marsh marigolds and Solomon's seal begin the spring show. Siberian iris and hardy fuchsias start to bloom as the early flowers fade. The hardy fuchsias bloom from late spring until the frost kills them in late fall. Hummingbirds love fuchsias! The birch displays beautiful golden fall color. In winter, once again the twig dogwoods provide winter interest, along with the grassy-leaved sweetflag, Oregon grape, salal, evergreen huckleberry, and tassel fern. The wintergreen is sprinkled with red berries. The birch tree establishes the focal point with its delicate swaying leaves.

 Acorus gramineus 'Ogon'
Grassy-Leaved Sweetflag

 Betula pendula 'Youngii'
Weeping European Birch

 Caltha palustris
Marsh Marigold

 Cornus sanguinea 'Midwinter Fire'
Midwinter Fire Dogwood

 Cornus sericea
Red Osier Dogwood

 Dicentra spectabilis
Bleeding Heart

 Fuchsia magellanica
Hardy Fuchsia

 Gaultheria procumbens
Wintergreen

 Hosta

 Iris sibirica
Siberian Iris

 Mahonia nervosa
Low Oregon Grape

 Physocarpus opulus 'Diablo'
Diablo Ninebark

 Polygonatum biflorum
Solomon's Seal

 Polystichum polyblepharum
Tassel Fern

 Ribes sanguineum
Red-Flowering Currant

 Vaccinium ovatum
Evergreen Huckleberry

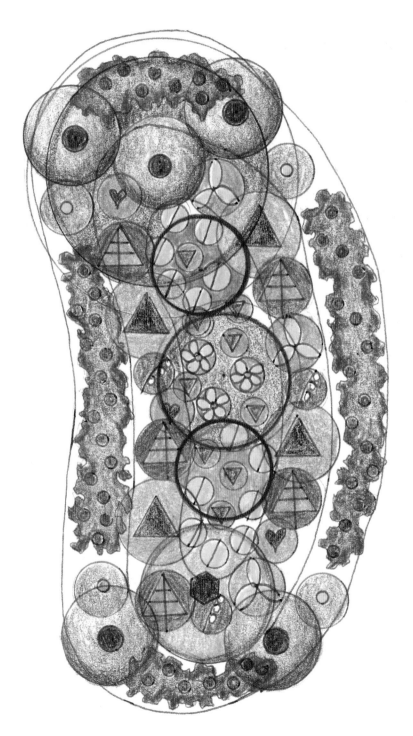

The plants for this location must be tough enough to withstand the extreme conditions of both hot, dry summers and cold, snowy winters. Spring bursts forth with the lovely white blossoms of the serviceberry. The succession of blooms continues with mock orange, oceanspray, Siberian iris, daylily, spirea, potentilla, and black-eyed-Susan. The wild roses will later produce large red rosehips. The Black Lace elderberry is the focal point; a great contrast plant, its pink flowers become edible berries for both humans and birds. Once again the twig dogwoods show off their colors, now against the winter snow.

Amelanchier alnifolia
Serviceberry

Arctostaphylos uva-ursi
Kinnikinnick

Camassia quamash
Camas

Cornus sanguinea 'Midwinter Fire'
Midwinter Fire Dogwood

Cornus sericea
Red Osier Dogwood

Echinacea purpurea
Purple Coneflower

Helictotrichon sempervirens
Blue Oat Grass

Hemerocallis 'Ruby Stella'
Ruby Stella Daylily

Holodiscus discolor
Oceanspray

Iris sibirica
Siberian Iris

Lobelia cardinalis
Cardinal Flower

Picea glauca 'Conica'
Dwarf Alberta Spruce

Physocarpus opulus 'Diablo'
Diablo Ninebark

Potentilla gracilis
Graceful Cinquefoil

Rhododendron groenlandicum
Labrador Tea

Rosa rugosa
Rugosa Rose

Rudbeckia fulgida
Black-Eyed Susan

Sambucus nigra 'Black Lace'
Black Lace Elderberry

Spiraea betulifolia
Birchleaf Spirea

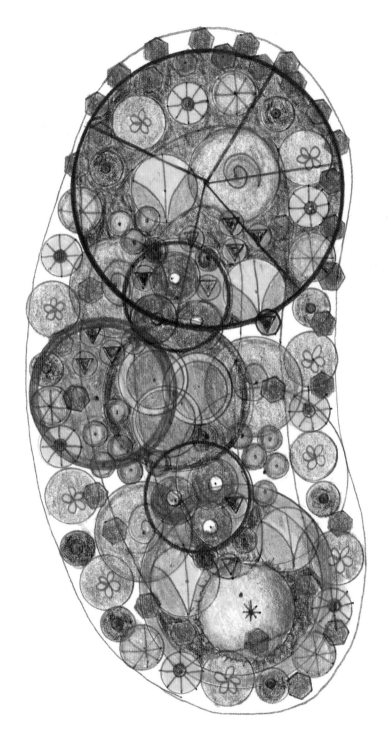

EAST OF THE CASCADES, FULL TO PARTIAL SHADE EXPOSURE

This plan includes plants that can not only withstand hot summers and harsh winters but also shade. What more can we ask of a plant?! With the arrival of spring the Indian plum will bloom, followed by bleeding heart, Siberian iris, ninebark, and hydrangea, and later by yellow waxbell. Once again, one of our most useful plants, the twig dogwood, takes center stage in winter. The wintergreen creates a nice evergreen groundcover with its minty red berries.

Betula pendula
European Birch

Cornus sanguinea 'Midwinter Fire'
Midwinter Fire Dogwood

Cornus sericea
Red Osier Dogwood

Dicentra spectabilis
Bleeding Heart

Gaultheria procumbens
Wintergreen

Heuchera 'Plum Pudding'
Plum Pudding Coral Bell

Hosta

Hydrangea macrophylla
Mophead Hydrangea

Iris sibirica
Siberian Iris

Kirengeshoma palmata
Yellow Waxbell

Oemleria cerasiformis
Indian Plum

Physocarpus opulus 'Diablo'
Diablo Ninebark

Polystichum munitum
Sword Fern

Scirpus microcarpus
Small-Fruited Bulrush

Typha minima
Dwarf Cattail

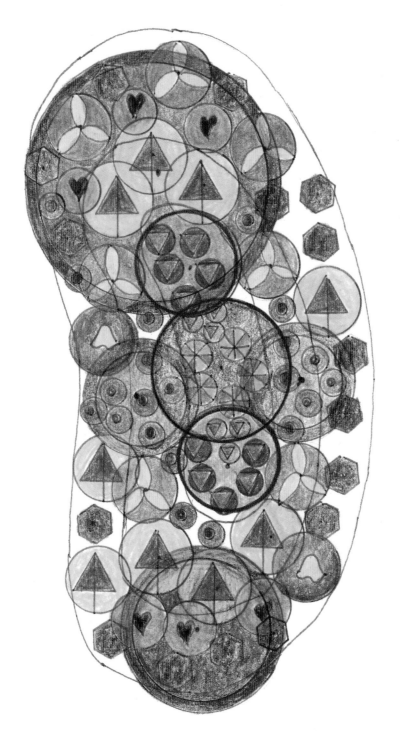

RAIN GARDEN

working green
for clean rivers

This residence
...rtner for clean rivers.

...ain garden soaks up
...runoff... ...roofs or pavement,
...pace and
...r... ...streams.

Resources

This list of resources is not comprehensive, but rather reflects some of our favorite books, websites, and retailers that can help you achieve your rain garden goals in the Northwest.

BOOKS AND MANUALS
Native Plants

Kruckeberg, Art. *The Natural History of Puget Sound*. Seattle: University of Washington Press, 1995.

Leigh, Michael. *Grow Your Own Native Landscape: A Guide to Identifying, Propagating, & Landscaping with Western Washington Native Plants*. Pullman, WA: Washington State University Extension, 1999. Order at www.pubs.wsu.edu.

Pojar, Jim, and Andy MacKinnon. *Plants of the Pacific Northwest Coast*. Rev. ed. Vancouver, BC: Lone Pine Publishing, 2004.

Stark, Eileen M. *Real Gardens Grow Natives: Design, Plant, and Enjoy a Healthy Northwest Garden*. Seattle: Skipstone, 2015.

Pruning

Gilman, Edward F. *An Illustrated Guide to Pruning*. 2nd ed. Albany, NY: Delmar Thomas Learning, 2002.

Turnbull, Cass. *Cass Turnbull's Guide to Pruning: What, When, Where & How to Prune for a More Beautiful Garden*. 2nd ed. Seattle: Sasquatch Books, 2006.

Rain Gardens

Carlson, Wayne, et al. *Eastern Washington Low Impact Development Guidance Manual*. Washington State Department of Ecology, 2013. Download at www.wastormwatercenter.org/ew-lid-guidance-manual.

Emanuel, Robert, et al. *The Oregon Rain Garden Guide: Landscaping for Clean Water and Healthy Streams*. Corvallis, OR: Oregon State University Extension, 2010. Purchase online at seagrant.oregonstate.edu/sgpubs/Oregon-rain-garden-guide.

Hinman, Curtis. *Rain Garden Handbook for Western Washington: A Guide for Design, Installation, and Maintenance*. Pullman, WA: Washington State University Extension, 2013. Download at http://ext100.wsu.edu/raingarden/homeowner-resources/.

Stormwater Management

Pazwash, Hormoz. *Urban Stormwater Management*. 2nd ed. New York: CRC Press, 2016.

Rossmiller, Ronald. *Stormwater Design for Sustainable Development*. New York: McGraw-Hill Education, 2013.

WEBSITES AND BLOGS
British Columbia

BC Landscape and Nursery Association: http://bclna.com/

City of North Vancouver Stormwater Management: www.cnv.org/your-government /living-city/environmental-protection /rain-drains-creeks

Rain garden installations in the North Delta area: www.vcn.bc.ca/cougarcr /raingardensvisit.html

Rain gardens in Vancouver: www.metrovancouver.org/media-room /video-gallery/metro-vancouver-close-up /3926329593001

Southern Vancouver Island and the Gulf Islands information: www.crd.bc.ca/education /low-impact-development/rain-gardens

University of British Columbia outreach programs: https://science.ubc.ca/community /outreach and https://support.ubc.ca /category/interests/outreach-programs/

Oregon

Oregon Nursery Association: www.oan.org/

Oregon State University Extension rain gardens program: http://extension.oregonstate.edu /stormwater/rain-gardens-0

Portland rain garden guide: www.portlandoregon.gov/bes/article/188636

Washington

12,000 Rain Gardens in Puget Sound Campaign: www.12000raingardens.org

City of Bellingham publication on rain gardens: www.cob.org/documents/pw/environment /rain-garden-cob.pdf

EarthCorps trains emerging environmental leaders from across the United States and around the world, engaging more than 10,000 volunteers each year to restore natural areas around the Puget Sound region: earthcorps.org

Rain Dog Designs, one of several registered contractors in the King County and City of Seattle RainWise program, contributed photos to this book and has worked with Zsofia on a variety of projects: http://raindogdesigns.com /wordpress/?page_id=43

Seattle Public Utilities RainWise program: www.seattle.gov/util/Environment Conservation/Projects/GreenStormwater Infrastructure/RainWise/index.htm

Snohomish Conservation District, a political subdivision of state government with no regulatory authority, provides advice and resources to farmers, city residents, and rural and suburban landowners. Zsofia has worked closely with the Snohomish Conservation District, but there are nearly 3,000 similar "conservation districts" across the United States: http://snohomishcd.org/

Stewardship Partners restores and stewards the watersheds of Washington and the Puget Sound through outreach and partnerships: stewardshippartners.org

Washington State Department of Ecology Low Impact Development (LID) guidelines www.ecy.wa.gov/programs/wq/stormwater /municipal/LID/Resources.html

Washington State University Extension rain gardens program: http://raingarden.wsu.edu/

Miscellaneous

Build Green Association guidelines for building rain gardens: http://buildgreen.ufl.edu/fact _sheet_bioretention_basins_rain_gardens.pdf

Deep Root blog about Curtis Hinman speaking on rain gardens and bioretention: www.deeproot.com/blog/blog-entries/at-the -forefront-of-bioretention-media-specifications -an-interview-with-curtis-hinman

Low Impact Development ideas for multiple states within the US: www.lowimpactdevelopment.org

Plant Amnesty offers general pruning advice and qualified gardener/arborist referrals: Plantamnesty.org

Plant guide: www.kitsapgov.com/sswm/pdf /RainGardenPlantGuide.pdf

RETAIL SOURCES
Compost, Mulch, and Bioretention Soil
BRITISH COLUMBIA
Carney's Waste Systems
Carneyswaste.com
Squamish, Whistler, Pemberton

City of Vancouver
http://vancouver.ca/home-property -development/compost-soil.aspx

Harvest Power (Harvest, Fraser Richmond Organics)
Harvestpower.com
Vancouver metro area

OREGON
Northwest Compost
Northwestcompostproducts.com
Portland metro area, including Vancouver, WA

Recology Organics
Thecompoststore.com
McMinnville and Aumsville

WASHINGTON
Barr-Tech
barr-tech.net
Eastern Washington and Northern Idaho

Cascade Compost/Corliss Products
Cascadecompost.com
Puyallup and Sumner areas

Cedar Grove
Cedar-grove.com
Six Western WA locations including Everett, Woodinville, and Seattle

Lenz Enterprises
Lenz-enterprises.com
Northwest Washington

Rich-Land Compost
www.ci.richland.wa.us/home
/showdocument?id=700
The City of Richland provides a list of authorized sellers.

Royal Organics
Roporganics.com
Central Washington

Washington State University
http://csanr.wsu.edu/compost/

OTHER
US Composting Council
http://compostingcouncil.org

Tools and Supplies
Filtrexx
www.filtrexx.com
DuraSoxx and other "compost soxx" solutions including EnviroBloxx, GardenSoxx, and the Living Wall Trinity system

Hori-hori
A hori-hori is the best gardening tool anyone can own. It can dig, cut, slice, saw (not very well), and lasts forever. Make sure to clean it and keep it in its case, especially because it is sharp. We like the Nisaku brand in stainless steel. Check with your local nursery or order online.

Rite in the Rain
www.riteintherain.com
Waterproof notebooks and pens

Index

Acknowledgments

Rain Gardens for the Pacific Northwest was created with the help of dedicated people who passionately believe in protecting our environment and sharing the knowledge and joy of rain gardens. The authors would like to thank those who contributed their time, energy, information, and photos, including: Aaron Clark at Stewardship Partners, David Hymel and Marilyn Jacobs at Rain Dog Designs, Philomena Kedziorski at Snohomish County WSU Extension, photographers Roseann Barnhill, Vicki Demetre, Sindea Kirk, Heidi Koonz, Cindy LaBlue, Holli Margell, and Stacey Sowers, and all the contributing rain garden owners.

We bestow our deepest admiration and appreciation upon our wise editors, Kate Rogers and Margaret Sullivan, at Skipstone. Thank you for believing in this book and making it real.

We would not be who we are without the exceptional landscape design and restoration programs offered by the Horticulture Department at Edmonds Community College developed in part by Walt Bubelis. Their classes provide students with the knowledge and tools not only to recognize and enhance the environment around us, but to understand the fragility and importance of the interconnected world and instill in us the conviction to be good stewards of the earth.

We would also like to thank our friends and family who support us while we nerd out working in, and writing about, rain gardens:

Zsofia: A very special thanks to Zsolt Pasztor who has always been there to build whatever design Jill and I dream up, smiling all the way.

Keri: Special thanks to Katherine Detore and Matthew Virkler.

Jill: My deepest gratitude to my twin sister, and forever best friend, Jan, who has been my biggest fan from the very beginning.

ABOUT THE AUTHORS

Zsofia Pasztor is the founder of the nonprofit organization, Farmer Frog, and the owner of Innovative Landscape Technologies. An award-winning landscape designer, certified professional horticulturist, permaculture designer, commercial urban agriculturist, tree risk assessor, and arborist, she teaches restoration horticulture, urban agriculture, and low impact development at Edmonds Community College and for other professional training programs. Zsofia has been involved with rain gardens in Western Washington from early on, being part of multiple teams who worked on different pilot and demonstration projects. Learn more about Zsofia at www.farmerfrog.org.

Seattle native **Keri DeTore** is experienced in fine art, graphic design, public relations, editing, landscaping projects, and horticultural restoration, and she incorporates native plants into all her landscape designs. With environmental groups such as People for Puget Sound, Pierce County WSU Extension, and Nature Consortium she has done outreach to communicate the importance of ecological stewardship. Keri is the owner of Lens Communications, a public relations business in Seattle, www.lenscomm.com.

Jill Nunemaker is an award-winning landscape designer who was born and raised in the Pacific Northwest. She has lived at times in the cold climate of Scandinavia and the tropical climate of Hawaii, which has given her a special appreciation of our unique Pacific Northwest climates and regions. She holds degrees in fine arts as well as landscape design, and is the owner of Verterra Landscape Design in Edmonds, Washington. Contact Jill at jill@verterradesign.com.

Real Gardens Grow Natives: Design, Plant & Enjoy a Healthy Northwest Garden
Eileen Stark
Find inspiration and instruction to create a lively, sustainable, and real garden of your own.

The Front Yard Forager: Identifying, Collecting, and Cooking the 30 Most Common Urban Weeds
Melany Vorass Herrera
A complete field guide with identification tips and recipes for 30 common urban weeds

Mason Bee Revolution: How the Hardest Working Bee Can Save the World—One Backyard at a Time
Dave Hunter and Jill Lightner
An easy-to-follow guide to keeping mason and leafcutter bees for pollination

From Tree to Table: Growing Backyard Fruit Trees in the Pacific Maritime Climate
Mary Olivella and Barbara Edwards
How to grow fruit trees successfully in coastal climates

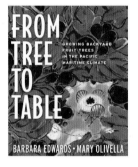

Backyard Roots: Lessons on Living Local from 35 Urban Farmers
Lori Eanes
City farmers share their secrets to growing food, raising animals, and building community.

Cool Season Gardening: Extend the Harvest, Plan Ahead, and Grow Vegetables Year Round
Bill Thorness; Illustrations by Susie Thorness
A comprehensive guide to growing winter crops in the Pacific Northwest

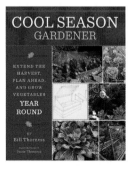

ABOUT SKIPSTONE

Skipstone is an imprint of Seattle-based nonprofit publisher Mountaineers Books. It features thematically related titles that promote a deeper connection to our natural world through sustainable practice and backyard activism. Our readers live smart, play well, and typically engage with the community around them. Skipstone guides explore healthy lifestyles and how an outdoor life relates to the well-being of our planet, as well as of our own neighborhoods. Sustainable foods and gardens; healthful living; realistic and doable conservation at home; modern aspirations for community—Skipstone tries to address such topics in ways that emphasize active living, local and grassroots practices, and a small footprint.

Our hope is that Skipstone books will inspire you to effect change without losing your sense of humor, to celebrate the freedom and generosity of a life outdoors, and to move forward with gentle leaps or breathtaking bounds.

All of our publications, as part of our 501(c)(3) nonprofit program, are made possible through the generosity of donors and through sales of more than 600 titles on outdoor recreation, sustainable lifestyle, and conservation. To donate, purchase books, or learn more, visit us online:

SKIPSTONE

LIVE LIFE

MAKE RIPPLES

www.skipstonebooks.org
www.mountaineersbooks.org